Fostering Family History Services

FOSTERING FAMILY HISTORY SERVICES

A Guide for Librarians, Archivists, and Volunteers

Rhonda L. Clark and Nicole Wedemeyer Miller

LIBRARIES
UNLIMITED™
An Imprint of ABC-CLIO, LLC
Santa Barbara, California • Denver, Colorado

Library of Congress Cataloging-in-Publication Data

Names: Clark, Rhonda L., author. | Miller, Nicole Wedemeyer, author.
Title: Fostering family history services : a guide for librarians, archivists, and volunteers / Rhonda L. Clark and Nicole Wedemeyer Miller.
Description: Santa Barbara, CA : Libraries Unlimited, [2016] | Includes bibliographical references and index.
Identifiers: LCCN 2015037572 | ISBN 9781610695411 (paperback) | ISBN 9781610695428 (ebook)
Subjects: LCSH: Libraries—Special collections—Genealogy. | Libraries—Special collections—Local history materials. | Family archives. | Local history—Archival resources. | BISAC: LANGUAGE ARTS & DISCIPLINES / Library & Information Science / General.
Classification: LCC Z688.G3 C58 2016 | DDC 020.72—dc23
LC record available at http://lccn.loc.gov/2015037572

ISBN: 978–1–61069–541–1
EISBN: 978–1–61069–542–8

20 19 18 17 16   2 3 4 5

This book is also available on the World Wide Web as an eBook.
Visit www.abc-clio.com for details.

Libraries Unlimited
An Imprint of ABC-CLIO, LLC

ABC-CLIO, LLC
130 Cremona Drive, P.O. Box 1911
Santa Barbara, California 93116-1911

This book is printed on acid-free paper ∞

Manufactured in the United States of America

CONTENTS

PREFACE

A wealth of "how-to" manuals is published each year aimed at the family historian. These works recognize the importance and popularity of genealogy as a pastime. They also reflect the increasing use of online research, DNA testing, and other technological applications for both finding and recording information. Yet very few volumes have been produced for the caretakers of family history collections, especially those located in public libraries and small, informal collections. Existing works are overview reference resources to familiarize librarians who will be working with local collections and include Jack Simpson's *Basics of Genealogy Reference* (2008) and David R. Dowell's *Crash Course in Genealogy* (2011). In addition, detailed guides to the resources of genealogy and local history collections exist, the most comprehensive of which are *Printed Sources: A Guide to Published Genealogical Records* (1998) and *The Source: A Guidebook to American Genealogy* (2006). Additionally several works offer information on the arrangement, description, and cataloging of family history resources in historical societies, and libraries such as Lois Hamill's *Archives for the Lay Person: A Guide to Managing Cultural Collections* (2013). Yet, while the resources of family history collections have maintained strong attention in the professional community, the use of these items as key components in institutional outreach, programming, and strategic planning has failed to capture significant attention from writers and researchers.

This work provides those information specialists working with family history collections some ideas and direction for offering their resources as an integrated part of their overall collections. The depth of materials and presentation style are chosen with the following assumptions:

- Many family history collections are staffed by volunteers, who may have experience in research for this area, but little knowledge of library and archival field standards and practices.
- The information professionals who provide reference and others services for family history collections may have little or no specialized education or training in this area.
- Those librarians, historians, curators, archivists, and volunteers who have had coursework or training sessions may be well-versed in one approach to such resources, but they may lack understanding in the approaches of other information settings.
- Few graduate-level courses available in library and information science programs focus on reference and outreach for family history.
- Local, state, and national classes that exist have often been viewed as specialized training, necessary for only those working on a daily basis with family history materials.

Based on these assumptions, this work is written to be accessible to a wide audience while still providing up-to-date information about resource curation and outreach. It provides numerous resource lists for further reading and checklists for suggested procedures and activities.

The topics of the nine chapters in this work demonstrate the growing need for integration of family history into general programming and outreach. They also acknowledge the need for community collaboration for digital portals and programs. In Chapter 1, for example, the conversation revolves around the definition of family history, and it emphasizes the fact that providing family history services are not necessarily tied to physical collections. Access to local history and genealogy resources are constantly improving as increasing numbers of digitized resources provide full-text searching and access from offsite. The role of the library is shifting to one that emphasizes services and search expertise, therefore, the importance of programming and outreach is presented as a key theme of the work regardless of whether or not the institution has a full family history collection. Multiple sample programming guides are provided throughout the work to emphasize the need for outreach and services using family history resources.

Chapters 2 and 3 address specific resources and reinterpret them in light of their potential for family history. Traditional local historical writing and oral history projects are discussed, along with programming ideas. Various formats for genealogical writing are presented, and the vast opportunities for vibrant family history narratives are demonstrated. The work addresses the importance of informal family history writing, such as blogging and the many options for online recording of family history information.

Chapters 4 and 5 focus on the need for libraries, historical societies, archives, and other institutions to provide information and programming on family collectibles, documents, and heirlooms. The archival community has taken the lead in such programming, but librarians and others should follow suit by posting relevant links on their home pages and by sponsoring programs on personal archiving. The way that families collect, preserve, and interpret their heirlooms will have a direct impact on the physical collections of future institutions. At the same time as staff members in institutions are encouraged to step up and provide programming on private and family collections, they also should consider the limits of their collecting abilities and the potential for user-added digital collections to solve potential space and staffing issues in the future. Good examples of such collaborations and efforts are showcased, particularly in archives and large historical societies.

Chapters 6 and 7 address the need to better train those working with physical and digital family collections. Chapter 6 discusses genealogy reference in a very different way than most published works have presented it, going beyond the reference interview and uses of specific resources. This chapter gives pertinent advice based on the authors' experiences with genealogical questions. The chapter also discusses how to organize volunteers and staff from an institutional perspective, and provides insights on reference service policies.

Chapter 7 provides an overview of the various cataloging and representation methods used by different cultural heritage institutions in providing access to common family history materials. It is increasingly important to understand how other institutions create metadata about items and how that metadata might be shared and utilized as access tools in other settings. The chapter offers guidelines for assessing the many different representations that might exist in one institution. Finally, suggestions are made on how to best manage the mixture of legacy and new approaches.

The last two chapters of the work address the types of sources typically sought in family history research, both in traditional and digital formats. Chapter 8 gives a brief overview of major resources found in family history collections. Though large works, such as *The Source*, provide an in-depth evaluation of resources, there is a need for an introductory overview suitable for beginning information professionals, volunteers, staff, and graduate students. The final chapter presents the "digital portal" as an important concept in providing access to collections. The emphasis is on collaborative portals as the new standard for providing information from local collections to the public. Basic checklists are provided to help very small institutions in evaluating their readiness for digital projects. Finally, a look at the many projects now being undertaken with the help of the general public will showcase the potential for re-imagining family history as a collaborative, dynamic, and integral part of library services.

Throughout this work, the notions of how to keep and preserve family heirlooms, versus how to use or enjoy them are explained. Hands-on programming experiences with artifacts and documents provide the patron knowledge and tools to take home and apply to personal, family collections. This work is intended to be used as a guide and a resource book for those in cultural heritage institutions who would like to expand their services and programming into broader family history topics. From grandma's quilts to dad's vintage tools, family garages are filled with meaningful artifacts, photographs, and documents that leave families wondering, "What should we do with. . .?" Libraries and other cultural heritage institutions should be a hub of information and programming to help families understand the value and uses of the family history items, and a continuing resource for researching family histories.

ACKNOWLEDGMENTS

I am indebted to the many who have supported and guided my work with local studies collections, especially my department chair Linda Lillard and my colleagues in the Department of Information and Library Science at Clarion University of Pennsylvania. I am grateful to the many, dedicated graduate students who took my courses on local studies collections and provided feedback on early chapter drafts for the book. Their enthusiasm and their amazing, widespread work in the field is inspiring. Also a heartfelt "thank you" to the wonderful members of the Titusville, PA Historical Society who welcomed a stranger with open arms many years ago and put her to work. I have learned much. And, finally, to my husband, James Henderson and our two daughters, Katherine and Elizabeth, whose patience and support were unwavering through the long writing and editing process. I certainly could not have finished this work without them beside me.

—Rhonda L. Clark

I would like to thank Beth Woodard and the late Rich Bopp at the Main Reference Room of the University of Illinois Library for their rigorous training of a clueless graduate assistant many years ago, and Cecelia K. Gaines, my friend and mentor, for her remarkable guidance at the Champaign Public Library. The outstanding staff at the Champaign County Historical Archives deserve thanks for their support of my teaching and research there. Also, thanks to Dean Linda Smith at the Graduate School of Library and Information Science at the University of Illinois for taking a chance on a brand new course, and to my student Matt Metcalf, who encouraged me to turn my course handouts into a book. In addition, the collective wisdom of the professionals on the Genealib listserv has been of tremendous help. Above all, thanks to Marc Miller and our descendants, Julia, Laura, and Richard, without whose patient forbearance this could not have been written.

—Nicole Wedemeyer Miller

INTRODUCTION: WHY PROVIDING FAMILY HISTORY SERVICES IS A GREAT IDEA

"When many of us cannot find meaning in the present places where we live and work, we look for it in the places we remember from our family past."

—David Glassberg[1]

For the past fifty years, a growth and democratization of the history field can be seen in everything from the people and activities deemed deserving of attention, the coverage of textbooks, and to the subjects represented in local historical museums. The social history movement among professional historians created vast scholarship from the 1960s forward that documented the lives of women, children, peasants, ethnic and religious minorities, and many others who had been consistently ignored in the bulk of historical writing prior to this movement.[2] The public history movement of the late twentieth century saw a rise in training for those who wanted to reach out to connect history to everyday people, developing and improving local historical sites, museums, and events.[3] Participatory history in the form of reenactments, history days in schools, and historic museum attendance are all flourishing. History is something people want not only to read about, but something they want to do.

Popular works on history line the shelves of bookstores, many attaining best seller status. Authors such as Doris Kearns Goodwin, Henry Louis Gates, Jr., and Erik Larson have captured the public's fascination with the past. U.S. history has been popularized on television, especially recently by shows such as "The History Detectives," "Antiques Roadshow," "Genealogy Roadshow," and documentaries, such as those produced by Ken Burns, "Who Do You Think You Are?" and similar programs on other networks feature celebrities' family histories which have spotlighted many library and archival collections. This television programming reflects the biggest renaissance of family history since the 1970s when the bestseller,

Roots: The Saga of an American Family, and the subsequent television miniseries based on it, made the general public aware of areas of U.S. history previously not well covered in school curricula, i.e., the social and family history of slaves, and touched off a flurry of genealogical research.[4]

The Social History movement paralleled and facilitated the rise of family history research as popular pastime which some claim is the second most popular hobby in the United States after gardening.[5] A 1994 survey of the U.S. public regarding their attitudes about history, funded by the Spencer Foundation and the National Endowment of the Humanities, concluded that family history is very important to everyone: "Almost every American deeply engages the past, and the past that engages them most deeply is that of their family."[6] This popularity persists despite the fact that most Americans' personal history is very challenging to discover for a number of reasons. Americans have always been on the move, which requires research in many locations within our own enormous country, and the majority of them have a mixed ethnic heritage, requiring research in many other countries of origin as well. In addition, the restlessness of Americans has contributed to a deterioration of their family knowledge, a shortening of generational memory. Many people do not even know basic facts about their own grandparents.[7] If family history is so challenging, why do researchers persist?

The answer is, for several reasons. First, as the pace of life appears to accelerate due to technological changes, many of us have turned back to the past as an anchor.[8] Ironically, the technology that keeps us moving forward so quickly is now helping in a significant way to track who has gone before us. The Internet has been a game-changer for family historians in several ways. First, researchers can now access some records online, many of them digitized images of originals that they used to have to travel long distances to exhume from courthouses, state and national archives, and libraries. Second, they can much more easily communicate with other researchers via message boards and email, so they can work collaboratively. They can trade large data files almost instantaneously by emailing GEDCOM files, the standard computer format for genealogical information. This allows much easier and freer research with data existing even in other countries. The websites of major archives in Europe and North America are providing increasing amounts of information online such as indexes or even digitized source material that just a few years ago would require travel or a paid researcher to retrieve.

Now families also can easily self-publish their findings. All they have to do is to post family trees on any one of several websites such as RootsWeb, or FamilySearch, for the world to see. Some of these sites are going interactive, so that others can add, and/or edit the information, which will increase the quantity of shared information, and ultimately could increase its quality as well. Finally, families can even make their own websites and, using a personal computer, compose a family history to post on it, or duplicate to distribute at a family reunion. In an era when families are physically scattered, this act of gathering and sharing family history brings them closer together.

To track down long-lost family members, researchers can check an online telephone directory, google their names, and perhaps the name of the town where they live, to find out all kinds of information about them before picking up the phone. Or maybe they do not need the phone, instead using Skype in order to interview a relative they have never even met. Some are finding that rapidly changing medical technology, DNA analysis in particular, is a way of reinforcing the research conducted via ancestors' paper trails. And pursuing a medical history of the family, along with their vital facts, may help prolong lives.

The growing popularity of family history may also, in part, be attributed to the graying of society.[9] An increasingly large segment of our population is made up of retirees who have the time and the resources to pursue this pastime. Many explain that they were always interested in their family history, but could not find the time to pursue it while they worked full-time. While genealogy classes are comprised of students of many ages, backgrounds, and both genders, a significant portion of them are mature in years, a fact which has implications for serving these students as they perform research.

Family history has also emerged in recent years to include a wide variety of activities that go well beyond genealogical research. The creation of family archives is increasingly seen by the archival community as a valid and important aspect of cultural heritage preservation.[10] From scrapbooking, to making family quilts, to developing digital family oral histories, the experiential aspects of family history are exploding. The evolution of community-based blogs and social media sites, such as those on Facebook, make the sharing of stories about relatives quick, easy, and instantly gratifying without the confines of the traditional oral history projects that require great amounts of planning and execution. Because activities such as blog-posting, scrapbooking, and writing down family stories are done by the family member, they build upon the heritage of previous generation storytelling culture and folk crafts.

Technology makes family history research and activities easier, but it certainly does not make them easy by any stretch of the imagination. Genealogical research is still a time-consuming activity, requiring years to accumulate the required documents, more time to organize and analyze them, and finally much more time to record the results. Experienced researchers realize that one is never truly finished with this process. And they run into the most frustrating impediments: destroyed and missing records, ancestors who move frequently, change their names, and others who seem to appear in hardly any records at all. Those researchers who descend from largely oral cultures, such as African Americans and Native Americans, face special challenges. Yet many persist because when a picture of their ancestors' lives begins to emerge from bits and pieces of the historic record, researchers gain an understanding of why they came here from far-flung areas of the globe to begin again. For help with this complex research process, where do researchers turn?

Enter a variety of institutions: libraries, archives, local history societies, genealogy groups, government agencies, and even museums. Many who work in cultural heritage institutions recognize that the popularization of history has prompted the need to better access historical information and to teach users how to access it in new and different ways. Some public historians and museum curators have taken the lead in addressing the need for interaction with the public, noting that Web 2.0 challenges traditional notions of curation and museum culture. The editors of *Letting Go? Sharing Historical Authority in a User-Generated World* argue that the notion of historical authority must be reconsidered, as the user becomes an active participant in the creation of historical content in museums and in less structured and formal family history sites.[11]

Librarians have long recognized the need for outreach to support community need, particularly in areas related to literacy, citizenship, and community integration. The work of the American Library Association (ALA) Programs office emphasizes the importance of cultural and social outreach, defining it as "essential" to the mission of libraries.[12] The Reference and User Services Association's (RUSA) values statement notes a priority on "the provision of innovative services and programs that meet the changing information needs of diverse populations."[13] In recent years, a focus on technological literacy or informatics has taken center stage, with a recent Institute of Museum and Library Studies (IMLS) study noting the importance of library services for technology in small or rural libraries which comprise 80.2 percent of all public libraries.[14] The Association for Rural & Small Libraries (ARSL) also emphasizes service and collaboration for service to patrons of small and rural libraries in its vision and objectives.[15] All of these mandates support the mission of institutions to collect information on communities, the families who inhabit them, and to help the public to access and understand that information.

In the digital age, librarians and information professionals are initiating many new outreach programs for the public in areas such as personal digital archiving and family history programming. Yet this level of initiative is not evident at all library and local cultural heritage facilities. This can be explained by the lack of available volunteers or staff members who have the knowledge to carry out such projects. Staff may feel untrained to work with local history or family resources. At some institutions, the mass of unprocessed collections that directly tie to aspects of family history may be intimidating. Some facilities simply do not have staff time allocated for family history programming. Yet the rewards of developing family history programming can be immense, raising the visibility of the institution and its perceived value in a community, while at the same time offering desirable tools and services to the public. In this age of falling foot traffic in public libraries due to e-books and magazines, an attempt to support family historians can be a service which will get patrons in the door.

The difficulty of instituting such services is lessened by consulting a host of online examples and resources from other libraries, archives, and historical societies. In addition, programming for family and community history can be planned with other institutions and organizations. Collaboration provides opportunities for outreach to all groups involved, and maximizes the knowledge and skill sets within those institutions. Even if an institution has never offered local history and genealogy services before, now is the time to begin. With a little knowledge and determination, anyone can provide local history and genealogical services regardless of current knowledge level, budget, and the physical content of collections.

NOTES

1. David Glassberg, *Sense of History: The Place of the Past in American Life* (Amherst, MA: University of Massachusetts Press, 2001), xiii.

2. Raphael Samuel, "What is Social History?" *History Today* (Online) 35, March 3, 1985.

3. Robert Weible, "Defining Public History: Is It Possible? Is it Necessary?" *Perspectives on History,* March 2008, http://www.historians.org/publications-and-directories/perspectives-on-history/march-2008/defining-public-history-is-it-possible-is-it-necessary, accessed September 3, 2014.

4. François Weil, *Family Trees: A History of Genealogy in America* (Cambridge, MA: Harvard University Press, 2013), 195. Two other authors claimed that Alex Haley, the author of *Roots,* had copied details from their novels. Nevertheless, Haley received a special Pulitzer prize, and the accusations did not diminish the impact his book had on the American public.

5. Suzanne McGee, "There's Gold in Family Roots," *Wall Street Journal* (Online) June 13, 2010, accessed April 7, 2015, http://www.wsj.com/articles/SB127637854515004969.

6. Roy Rosenzweig and David Thelen, *The Presence of the Past: Popular Uses of History in American Life* (New York, NY: Columbia University Press, 1998), 22.

7. Tamara Hareven, "The Search for Generational Memory" in *Oral History: An Interdisciplinary Anthology,* 2nd ed., ed. David K. Dunaway, and Willa K. Baum (Walnut Creek, CA: AltaMira Press, 1996), 242.

8. Weil, *Family Trees,* 5.

9. Findings from the *Fullerton Genealogy Study* by Pamela J. Drake, http://psych.fullerton.edu/genealogy/, reveal that genealogists are largely female and age 40 or older. In addition, observational evidence reveals that a majority are of retirement age. See "Is There a Perceived Age Demographic in Genealogy" a blog posting by Thomas MacEntee, http://hidefgen.com/perceived-age-demographic-genealogy/.

10. See, for example, the Library of Congress resources on Personal Digital Archiving, as well as funding support for capturing evidence of family archives seen in this recent NEH grant announcement: http://www.neh.gov/grants/preservation/common-heritage.

11. Bill Adair, Benjamin Filene, and Laura Koloski, eds., *Letting Go? Sharing Historical Authority in a User-Generated World* (Philadelphia, PA: The Pew Center for Arts & Heritage, 2011), 11–15.

12. American Library Association Public Programs Office, "Libraries Transforming Communities," accessed May 8, 2015, http://www.ala.org/transforminglibraries/libraries-transforming-communities.

13. "About RUSA," accessed April 7, 2015, http://www.ala.org/rusa/about.

14. The Institute of Museum and Library Services, "The State of Small and Rural Libraries in the United States," Research Brief No. 5, September 2013, http://www.imls.gov/assets/1/AssetManager/Brief2013_05.pdf.

15. "About ARSL," The Association for Rural & Small Libraries, accessed April 7, 2015, http://arsl.info/about/.

Chapter 1

THINKING OUTSIDE THE COLLECTION BOX

This chapter defines how genealogists and family historians approach their research in order to provide a knowledge base for those providing services in any cultural heritage setting. It further examines how family history services can be provided without a physical genealogy collection. Family history sources are examined, as are the many avenues for developing partnerships across institutions to provide outreach and services. Finally, programming ideas for family history topics are provided.

BEGINNING AT THE BEGINNING: DEFINING GENEALOGY AND FAMILY HISTORY

"In science, securities analysis, or the writing of history, we begin with curiosity, proceed into skepticism, and in the end must draw conclusions in the presence of much that remains unknown."

—Roger G. Kennedy[1]

Like practitioners of the subjects mentioned in the quote above, genealogists and family historians put together as many pieces of information that they can find, and then draw conclusions about their ancestors' lives. Often, some of the pieces are missing, due to lost records, or scant, in time periods that predate the existence of vital and census records. In order to serve family historians, one should have a grasp of what they are trying to discover, and how they analyze that information. This section will cover four questions relating to this process:

- What are genealogy and family history?
- Why have they become popular?
- What is a genealogical source?
- How is genealogical research organized?

What are genealogy and family history?

Genealogy is a part of family history. It is the study of the vital events in a family that establish that family's pedigree, or linkages between generations. This typically includes birth, death, and marriage events, but could also include divorce and adoption information. The information found in a family tree is the genealogy part. You may think of it as a research skeleton. See Figure 1.1.

The research has two basic approaches: **linear** and **cluster**. The linear method traces a single ancestral line backwards without covering collateral lines, i.e., the siblings of direct ancestors and the families the siblings created. Researchers mostly used a linear genealogy approach in the past, but now many of them realize the value of the cluster approach.[2]

Cluster genealogy traces and documents not just the line of direct ancestors, but all the collateral lines as well, which gives a broader picture of the family structure. Collateral ancestors are all the aunts, uncles, and cousins from whom a person is not directly descended, but to whom he or she is still related. Some researchers also advocate including friends and neighbors of ancestors in the research to give a truly complete idea of the complex web of kinship and social connections of which the ancestors were a part. This is also known as the FAN approach, which stands for friends, associates, and neighbors, and was coined by the family historian Elizabeth Shown Mills.[3]

Thus, **family history** is a more in-depth expression of genealogy. It interweaves information from a number of different fields into our ancestors' life stories.

A dedicated family historian will find it useful to consult information in areas such as: history, geography, biography, foreign languages, agriculture, political science, popular culture, onomatology, graphology, law, medicine . . . and the list goes on and on. It attempts to solve the questions of not just *who, where,* and *when,* but also *why.* Why did our ancestors live the way they did? If genealogy is the skeleton, then family history is the flesh on the bones.

Why have they become popular?

Genealogical and family history research are currently quite popular in many countries, including the United States. Genealogy's prevalence in U.S. life mirrors a long-term broadening of historical studies to address the lives of specific groups, such as ethnic minorities and women, and generally people in all levels of the social strata. U.S. history has been popularized in recent decades as never before, and a study of U.S. history is a large part of family history research. Also, the Internet has played a huge role. While it is *not* possible to complete online all of one's family history research, the Internet does offer a lot of information, much

Figure 1.1
Linear Approach

Linear Approach

Nicole Alaine Wedemeyer (1964–)

George Anthony Wedemeyer IV (1941–)

Dorothy Rita McAvin (1922–2004)

Pelagia Saitta (1896–1983)

Figure 1.2
Cluster Approach

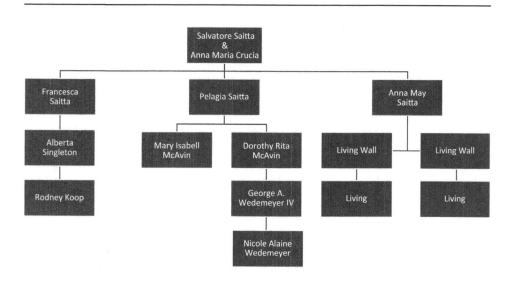

of it free, which greatly facilitates research. Websites such as Ancestry.com try to make the process fun and accessible. A popular "fact" floating around the Internet is that genealogy is the second most popular hobby in the United States. Is this really true?[4] Regardless of what ranking it actually holds among U.S. hobbies, without a doubt it is popular, the number of family historians is increasing, and, in an age when libraries are fighting for relevancy, libraries would do well to meet the needs of this group. Next, celebrities such as Oprah Winfrey, Henry Louis Gates, and others, have been featured on several television series in which their family histories have been researched and discussed (see www.pbs.org/wnet/aalives/). Hunt reports a similar rise in history-related television programming in the UK.[5] Finally, a growing segment of our population is made up of retirees who have the time and the resources to pursue this pastime.

The same sources used for family history are used for other research. These include:

- Tracing family descendants, the living heirs, in order to settle probate
- Uncovering medical health histories
- Tracing living people for a variety of reasons; they owe child support, they are estranged from their families, etc.
- Tracing birth parents
- Finding out about the people who built and inhabited old houses
- Assigning students a genealogical/local history component in their classes
- Providing information for microhistorians to research

THE BITS AND PIECES

What is a genealogical source?

Genealogists and family historians seek specific sources that will shed light on their families' pasts. A source contains evidence that establishes facts about an ancestor's life. Many sources are paper including documents, such as birth and death certificates, which are part of a paper trail that every individual generates during his or her life. Federal governments contribute hugely to this paper trail, as do state and local governments, and private institutions such as businesses, religious institutions, and social organizations. Some sources are not documents, but instead are artifacts. They could be a homemade hope chest, a rosary, or even a gun. Some sources are better and more reliable than others. For example, a marriage license is usually reliable because the two people getting married are the ones who supplied the information directly to the clerk who wrote it, although that still does not mean that it is always completely free from errors. In general, marriage records have a tendency to be a more reliable source than death certificates. Why? Because dead men tell no tales; a relative or friend is supplying at least part of the death record information, not the deceased.

Sources can be found in many places, such as courthouses, all types of libraries, archives, historical societies, churches, websites, and in relatives' attics and memories. Relatives may keep family papers, mementos, photographs, and ephemera, referred to as home sources, which can be a mix of many different types of records.

The quality and quantity of home sources that any given researcher has access to will vary greatly depending on the circumstances in his or her family.

Once found and analyzed for the information that they yield, sources should be cited during the recording process. Genealogists should support every detail on their family trees. The current standard method used is a genealogy style manual, *Evidence! Citation and Analysis for the Family Historian,* written by Elizabeth Shown Mills. A copy should be owned by every institution providing family history services. This reference guide provides comprehensive instructions and examples for citing a myriad of sources from vital and census records, and oral history interviews, to ephemera. Unfortunately for other researchers, many genealogists do not cite any sources at all, because of the extra effort involved.

Of particular importance to libraries are compiled sources which record information from original records either by transcribing them word for word, abstracting them, which means summarizing the important details, or extracting them, making word for word copies of selections from a document. Sometimes, compiled sources are the only version of the information that a researcher can access, either because the originals are not available to the public, or because they no longer exist. However, serious researchers make it their goal to access original records or facsimiles of them whenever possible.

In addition to sources and compiled sources, researchers also turn to reference tools, which, fortunately, many librarians and archivists are already well-versed with. Researchers use a combination of general and specialized reference tools, such as encyclopedias, dictionaries, maps, timelines, indexing of records, and websites which provide both genealogical evidence, and background and historical context. For example, *Southwest Louisiana Marriage Records* by Donald Hébert contains indexed names from Roman Catholic sacramental records from many parishes in a specific geographic area. Though more finding aids, especially indexing, are now found online, *it is crucial not to ignore print sources,* because the majority of genealogical information is still found there, and will likely remain so for quite some time. Fortunately, a huge number of print sources that can be used in family history research are described in *Printed Sources: A Guide to Published Genealogical Records,* edited by Kory Meyerink. It is a wonderful help for both researchers and the information professionals who guide them.

It is important to understand that many researchers want to access information by the names of the people they are searching for information about; however, many types of information do not have name access. Sometimes the information is organized by geographic area, or by subject, or type of record. Some organizations are trying to overcome this problem with homegrown access tools, which will be discussed in Chapter 7, "Maximizing Access to Local Studies Collections."

How is genealogical research organized?

Another concern for researchers is the proper recording of information. Once the patron locates relevant sources, he or she identifies **facts** from which he or she will build a basic framework, or skeleton, of information about individuals. The skeleton should include:

- A full name, or as much of the full name that is known: given or Christian name, middle name/s, surname. The maiden name of women is recorded. It is useful to put the surname all in capital letters, in order to make it stand out, for example: James Willis ROBINSON. This practice is particularly helpful when the various components of the name could be interchangeable.
- The dates and locations of the **birth, marriage, and death (BMD)**. A military style is used for recording dates (day, month, and year). Always spell out the month, so there is no confusion, e.g., 28 November 1964. When recording the place, always start from the most specific geographical location and work up to the broadest. The abbreviation of locations can lead to great confusion, so it is avoided. One writes for example: Oak Lawn, Cook County, Illinois, United States.
- The names of spouses, parents, children, and children's spouses should be recorded.
- The sources for each piece of this information should be cited.

Researchers typically document their own lives first. Then, like Ginger Rogers dancing with Fred Astaire, the researcher works backwards.

Many researchers begin to record facts on standard genealogical charts. The family group sheet is the basic format to record information for one nuclear family. Searching the Internet for the term "family group sheet" will bring up dozens of examples which can be printed for free, and the same can be done with the names of the other basic forms, such as pedigree charts, research checklists, and research logs. A nice summary of how to fill out basic genealogical forms can be found at About.com: http://genealogy.about.com/library/lessons/blintro1c.htm. Many institutions keep a supply of such forms to provide to researchers, either gratis or for a nominal fee.

PUTTING FLESH ON THE BONES

Next, the researcher will build on that skeleton by adding any of the following to the basic vital facts: occupations, physical descriptions, photographs, recipes, letters, and details about military service, religion, education, immigration and "the old country." In this way, the genealogical facts become fleshed out in order to become part of a rich family history. Information passed down orally is also used, but it has sometimes been distorted and needs to be checked for accuracy.

How is genealogical research organized?

While there are full-length books to answer this question, here are some basics to help organize genealogical research findings:

- Standard forms are used to record information, such as the family group sheet and the pedigree chart.
- Forms and other documents are stored in either file folders *or* binders. Each folder is labeled by surname, and then first names of the married couple within, for example: WEDEMEYER I, George and wife ALBANUS, Henrietta. Then separate folders are made for each of their two children: WEDEMEYER II, George, and his wife HARDY, Hazel; WEDEMEYER, Gertrude and her husband ZIBILICH, Joseph.

- Each file should contain: a research checklist, a printed form listing most of the possible records to locate about an individual; a family group sheet, a single page which lists information about one nuclear family; and a research log. All are available online in many different variations to download for free. Each file could also contain a timeline as well as assorted documents, notes, and articles pertaining to the family, the geographic locations in which they lived, their ethnic heritage, etc. It is helpful to arrange the documents in chronological order. And it is best not to include fragile, original documents in the working files. Instead, include a photocopy, or scan the documents and keep them in a file on a computer.

- A genealogy software program will be necessary after a large amount of information is accumulated. Such a program provides a template for inputting and sourcing information. The data is stored in a GEDCOM file, a standard format which makes it possible to share the files, even between two people who use different software programs, or with a website where researchers can post family trees. An online publication called GenSoftReviews gives ratings based upon user surveys: http://genealogy-software-review.toptenreviews.com/.

- Other aides include BMD cheat sheets, which provide a master list of vital events for all family members. They are helpful for researchers when going on research field trips so that they know what information to search for in what time periods. This could either be a printed list, perhaps generated by a genealogical software program or information accessible on a genealogical app for a portable electronic device. A "Favorites" list of bookmarked websites and some system such as Evernote for keeping track of miscellaneous information are also helpful.

- Relationship charts or kinship calculators are helpful to determine how various members of the family are related to each other. They can be accessed for free online.

Family history research is much more involved than this very brief overview; so if more information is desired, please refer to Appendix A, "Annotated List of How-to Family History Titles."

RESOURCES

Curran, Joan F., Madilyn Coen Crane, and John H. Wray. *Numbering Your Genealogy: Basic Systems, Complex Families, and International Kin*, rev. ed. Arlington, VA: National Genealogical Society, 2008.

"Introduction to Genealogy, Lesson 1c: 'Charting Your Course.'" *About.com*, n.d. http://genealogy.about.com/library/lessons/blintro1c.htm.

Meyerink, Kory, ed. *Printed Sources: A Guide to Published Genealogical Records*. Salt Lake City, UT: Ancestry Publishing, 1998.

Mills, Elizabeth Shown. *Evidence Explained: Citing History Sources from Artifacts to Cyberspace*. 2nd ed. Baltimore, MD: Genealogical Publishing Company, Inc., 2009.

Online Encyclopedia of Genealogy. http://www.eogen.com/. The many specialized terms and acronyms used in genealogical research are conveniently defined here.

Szucs, Loretto Dennis, and Sandra Hargreaves Luebking, eds. *The Source: A Guidebook to American Genealogy*. 3rd ed. Provo, UT: Ancestry Publishing, 2006.

THE MAIN ESSENTIAL IN FAMILY
HISTORY SERVICES

Today, family history services are less about providing sources, and more about providing how-to knowledge and guidance to researchers. They are *not* tied to having a substantial genealogical collection. More and more sources are online, digitized, and accessible for no or low cost, so libraries do not need to replicate them in their collections. In addition, the fact that genealogical sources are widely scattered at a variety of governmental and private institutions means that no single library or archival collection can possibly provide all sources for researchers. In plain terms, an individual collection is less important now, but showing researchers how to navigate the research process is more important than ever. The rallying cry of Curt Witcher, genealogy collection manager at the Allen County Public Library, one of the busiest such collections in the United States, is "Staff, not stuff." What he means is that a knowledgeable staff is far more important to provide good family history service than is the collection.[6] Whether researchers are turning to information providers for help is another matter.[7]

Another reason why the traditional collection is becoming less relied on is that patron-created content is proliferating, and will take a more central role in the search and research process. Already there are websites such as Family Tree on FamilySearch.org and WeRelate.org which allow people to record genealogical information collaboratively. Scans of original records and photographs can be attached to these trees, providing evidence of family connections, and are available for all researchers to consult. Information professionals should step forward to assist with the assembly and dissemination of genealogical information in this format, and also in a host of others. Professionals need to creatively approach the housing of the materials used to assist family history researchers, the materials that help them create their family records, and how to make it all accessible not only to them, but to others. More information on the creative recording of family history information will be covered in Chapter 2, "Record It: Preserving Family and Community History."

It is useful to re-imagine the resources, spaces, and goals of various cultural heritage institutions which work with family historians. At the resource crossroads of the historical society, library, and community archive sits the local studies collection, a term that has been used for decades in the UK to describe local history and genealogy resources. The broad sense of this term is useful and will be used throughout this text to denote a collection of resources, regardless of the specific institution housing them, which serves genealogists, family historians, and local historians, as well as a wide variety of information seekers with other needs, such as those wanting to know who built their Victorian houses, or schoolchildren seeking local history information for an assignment who also want to access local studies resources. The materials in local studies collections such as genealogical charts, locally-produced histories, yearbooks, and photographs, tie into the visible, widespread fascination with family and genealogical history in popular culture today.[8]

The keepers of such collections: archivists, librarians, curators, and volunteers acting in these capacities, have a huge responsibility to safeguard and preserve, and also to share the materials that are the tangible evidence of our collective past. The keepers must also decide what materials best represent this past, i.e., what out of the vast array of primary and secondary sources are "keepers." Add to this the fact that the divisions between formerly distinct types of repositories are blurring, though the public probably never had much of a handle on how they were different, and does not much care, as long as they get the information they want. An added challenge is that resources for funding these efforts are dwindling in some institutions. But a willingness to imagine new configurations for keeping our past, and to cooperate with other keepers, and with the public, will sustain these efforts.

PROVIDING SERVICES WITHOUT A FAMILY HISTORY COLLECTION

Several ideas will be discussed regarding organizing even quite small amounts of local studies materials. Some institutions not only lack a dedicated genealogy and local history area, but they do not have any materials of this kind at all. Is it still possible to assist with genealogical and other local studies research? Of course! First, there are certain general sources found in every reference collection that can be tapped. Next, it is highly likely that even the smallest of institutions has one computer with an Internet connection and a printer. This growing amount of online information is available for the information provider to help patrons access. Finally, the information provider can offer expertise in putting together a research strategy, analyzing information, and recording it. All it takes is some knowledge on the part of the information provider. Some specific ideas include:

- Help the patron print copies of basic family group sheets, pedigree charts, and resource checklists from the Internet. They are widely available for free on numerous websites. Either locate information about them or teach the patron how to fill them out. This is not an intuitive process; for example, find a sample research log and explain why and how it is used.

- Help the patron locate sources for the first geographic area in which they will be researching. This includes finding contact information for that county courthouse, local library, the genealogy/local history society, etc. *Red Book: American State, County, and Town Sources*, which has been digitized and is available online for free in the wiki at Ancestry.com will help with this task: http://www.ancestry.com/wiki/index.php?title=Red_Book:_American_State,_County,_and_Town_Sources.

- Locate a history of the area of research for the patron, either digitized online at a website like Google Books or the Internet Library, or identify the title of a print version on WorldCat.org, and offer to interlibrary loan it if possible. Use reference sources such as encyclopedias to supply background information, perhaps when a town or county was founded, who initially settled it, or basic information about occupations, ethnic groups, immigration, and other relevant topics. Even old editions of encyclopedias can be helpful with this.

- Teach patrons about the FamilySearch website, www.familysearch.org, and some basics of how to use it. Locate the nearest Family History Center (FHC) for them. Explain how the system of borrowing microfilmed records works.

- Explain to patrons that they and their relatives probably already have some information waiting to be discovered at home. Show patrons some information on what home sources are, either online or in a circulating book. These are sources containing genealogical information that are found at home, such as a Roman Catholic mass card, a baptismal certificate, a baby book, etc. Encourage them to start gathering and recording that family information.

- Help patrons figure out what type of records they need to locate in order to prove certain facts about an ancestor, such as the birth date. The online chart called "United States Record Selection Table" in the wiki at FamilySearch.org is helpful: https://familysearch.org/learn/wiki/en/United_States_Record_Selection_Table

- Introduce standard reference collection items that can be used for family history research. Examples include local telephone books and city directories which help pinpoint the dates when individuals were living in the community.

- Organize a monthly genealogy club if the area does not already have one. Research shows that genealogists like to work collaboratively to solve research problems.[9]

- Provide basic genealogical programming which instructs patrons on how to conduct research. If you cannot, find out who does.

- Keep track of anyone who is providing programming, both live and online types, and share that information with patrons. Genealogical calendar of events are on several websites including FamilySearch, Dick Eastman's Online Genealogy Newsletter, National Genealogical Society, and Adventures in Genealogy Education.

More information about negotiating genealogy reference questions and assessing family historians' information needs will be covered in Chapter 6, "The Negotiators: Asking and Answering Questions."

SELLING THE SERVICES

The introduction of this book suggests that local studies service is a great way to increase library usage in this era of a decline in foot traffic. The affluent are simply ordering what they want from Amazon.com and having it delivered to their doors rather than bothering with a trip to the library where they must be concerned with due dates and late fees. Many also are using e-materials, which, even if owned by the library, do not require a trip the library to use. Also, the use of Google has supplanted a large amount of reference business. If your institution is going to place a new emphasis on serving family history researchers, it is possible to attract patrons when the public knows about the new or improved family history services. Build it, and they will come, eventually, but a successful use of publicity can speed the process. Some suggestions for making this happen include:

- Highlight the new local studies reference specialty on the library website.
- Use social media like Facebook, Twitter, etc.
- Send press releases to the local newspaper, or on local radio or television.
- Make a sign or banner and an accompanying materials display in the library in a high-traffic area. Make sure that there are multiple copies of how-to genealogy books that can be checked out as part of the display.
- Display local historical photographs to attract attention. In addition, community members may be able to help identify unknown people and locations in the photographs.
- Try a "crowdsourcing" project that asks the public for input on the content and identities of people in the library's photographs.
- Mention those staff members by name who are going to provide family history services in the promotional materials.
- Highlight tricky/interesting questions that staff helped with in the library newsletter/blog.
- Post fliers in other public places like coffee shops, community centers, etc.
- Be a guest speaker at area clubs.
- Film an infomercial about the institution's family history services and post it on Youtube.com.
- Investigate whether any local teachers, especially social studies teachers, have a family history component to any of their assignments, and offer to appear as a guest speaker, and host a tour, highlighting the library's ability to help with that assignment. See the programming idea below about using/obtaining free use of Ancestry.com for students.
- Build genealogy programming around a celebration of Family History Month (October).
- Market to the institution's own administration and board. Prove the value of genealogy reference to the leadership by keeping track of genealogy reference questions separately from general reference questions, and also note by which method these questions arrived. Were they in-person, or by telephone, text, email, or snail mail? This data could help the department acquire a "bigger slice of the pie" when budgeting time rolls around.

RESOURCES

Allery, Linda. "Popularising Local History Services: New Century, New Ideas." *Aplis* 13, no. 3 (September 2000): 119–125. *Library & Information Science Source*, EBSCO*host*, accessed February 17, 2015.

"Marketing—Library Success: A Best Practices Wiki," http://www.libsuccess.org/Marketing, accessed May 13, 2015.

ORGANIZING AND NAMING THE RESOURCES

"It's difficult to imagine another area of study, research or enquiry where the source materials are so varied and so dispersed over a variety of resource providers at local level. The situation is further complicated by the potential relevance to the local studies enquirer of the material held in national, regional, academic and specialist institutions, both public and private."

—Michael Dewe[10]

A major concern often expressed by those who are considering whether or not to create or maintain a local studies room is that of space. Roberts reminds readers that there is a great deal of anxiety often attached to the local collection for those librarians who are untrained in local collection curation.[11] So many different types of materials make up these collections, and many, such as scrapbooks, have very complicated storage and access requirements.

Some institutions may have local history and genealogical material but have never before separated it from the general reference collection. With an influx of eager family history researchers, the time has come to do so. What are the options? The placement of local studies materials within institutions has always been varied. Here are some placements that have been tried:

- Local history and genealogical materials are paired in many types of libraries.
- Local history materials, together with manuscripts and archival materials, form "Special Collections" in academic libraries.
- Local history and genealogical materials plus government documents are grouped in some archives.
- Local history and genealogical materials plus the newspaper collection coexist in some public libraries.
- Local history and genealogical materials, plus artifacts organized into displays, are housed at the local history museum.

Conrad argues strongly that local history collections and genealogy collections are two separate animals,[12] which is true, but they have some overlap and frequently researchers need to use both. This is why it does make sense to house them in the same place. A newer organization employed in larger institutions such as public libraries in major cities is to roll all secondary historical materials together with local studies and archival materials. This produces one-stop shopping for information about the past. The St. Louis and San Francisco Public Libraries have already adapted this model.

Indeed, formerly sharp divisions between different types of institutions that provide information about history are starting to blur. For example, what was once known as the Chicago Historical Society is now called the Chicago History Museum. Researchers can still visit to use their archival materials, but the marketing emphasis is now on their exhibits. The slogan of the Massillon Museum in Ohio is

"Where art and history come together" and it houses art galleries, a local history museum, and a library/archives.[13] The truth is that what the distinctions are has probably never mattered to patrons as much as it has to information providers. The patron just wants easy access to information; whether that is from an archive, an historical society, a library, or a genealogy center, is completely beside the point. Thus, it behooves archivists to learn reference techniques, librarians to learn about preservation, and volunteers to learn it all! It is now a brave new world of sharing history, both in physical and virtual settings.

RESOURCES

Conrad, James H. *Developing Local History Programs in Community Libraries.* Chicago and London: American Library Association, 1989.

Dewe, Michael, ed. *Local Studies Collection Management.* Hants, UK: Ashgate Publishing Limited, 2002.

Filby, William P. *Directory of American Libraries with Genealogy or Local History Collections.* Wilmington, DE: Rowman & Littlefield Publishers, 1988.

Gordon, Tammy S. *Private History in Public: Exhibition and the Settings of Everyday Life.* Lanham, MD: AltaMira Press, 2010.

Phillips, Faye. *Local History Collections in Libraries.* Englewood, CO: Libraries Unlimited, 1995.

Salter, Anne A. "Historical Society Libraries," *Encyclopedia of Library and Information Sciences,* 2nd ed. Boca Raton, FL: Taylor and Francis, published September 23, 2011, http://www.informaworld.com/smpp/title~content=t917508581.

Smallwood, Carol, ed. *Librarians as Community Partners: An Outreach Handbook.* Chicago, IL: American Library Association, 2010.

ENHANCING THE LOCAL STUDIES COLLECTION

> **What Is Community Informatics?**
> Community informatics is making local historical information widely available, and it specifically speaks to the role of advocacy in this information access, allowing for disadvantaged populations to seek change through fair access to information.[14] Increasingly, judging by such recent initiatives as the ALA's "Libraries Transforming Communities" project, community and social informatics are seen as a part of a public librarian's goals.

Some institutions may not have a dedicated local studies center, but may wish to eventually establish one. This may not be quite as daunting as it seems, because there is some overlap between sources used to provide mainstream reference, and those used for local studies reference. Most libraries, even small- to medium-sized ones, already have the following:

- Internet access and a printer.
- Interlibrary loan service.
- Items in reference and circulation that give historical information, including almanacs, general encyclopedias, and W.P.A. guides to the states.
- Local history information such as monographs, pamphlets, and retrospective articles from the local newspaper.
- Sources of biographical information and the *Biographical and Genealogical Master Index* (this provides access to information in a variety of sources including professional directories, and general biographical sources like the *Dictionary of American Biography*).
- Books on ethnic groups in the United States.
- Collections of old telephone directories, either print or microfiche, and city directories.
- Back issues of newspapers on microfilm.
- Maps and gazetteers, both current and historical.
- Foreign language dictionaries.
- Encyclopedias of religious denominations.
- Travel books, which harbor lots of historical information.
- Copies of "how-to" genealogy books.

That foundation can be built on gradually as time and budget allows for a very low cost. The following steps can be taken:

- Distribute family group sheets, pedigree charts, relationship charts, and research checklists.
- Distribute lists of the in-house resources above.

- Distribute an annotated bibliography of circulating local studies books, with a separate section for reference titles.
- Establish a relationship with the folks at the local Family History Center (FHC)—send each other customers.

Here are several ideas, most of which involve a modest investment in staff time:

- Make available one-hour research consultations with a staff member.
- Make a foray into family history programming with something simple, such as a program on how to fill out basic genealogy forms.
- Take this show on the road: visit senior centers, retirement complexes, or Boy Scout troop meetings.
- Have a member of a genealogy or local history group, or a lineage society, present a talk.
- Write and distribute a locality guide for your area.
- Maintain surname files, either paper or digital, where people submit genealogical research they have done on local families. Encourage them to source the information.
- Add multiple copies of "how-to" genealogy books to your circulating collection. It is better to have three copies of one title, than one copy each of three different titles, because then one patron cannot check out everything you own on this topic.
- Add a few key reference titles, such as *The Source* and *Evidence Explained*.

The next ideas are feasible for a somewhat greater investment:

- Hire a genealogy expert to give a workshop or talk. They can be identified through the Association of Professional Genealogists website: https://www.apgen.org/.
- Use volunteers to start an in-house research aid, such as compiling an obituary index of the local newspaper, or conducting/updating a cemetery survey.
- Add subscriptions to one or two genealogical periodicals.
- Add a single online subscription genealogical database.
- Provide a scanner for public use.
- Become a Genealogical Society of Utah (GSU) affiliate library (again, some staff time is required to administer).
- Revamp the library website to advertise these genealogy services and resources.

For a major investment, you may:

- Subscribe to several online genealogical databases.
- Establish a genealogical reference collection as we still need some print resources.
- Purchase or lease a digital microfilm reader/printer.

Or, skip any major book, microfilm, or database purchases. Instead, place a trained information provider in a prominent location, along with a computer, and a sign that says "Ask Me about *Your* Family History."

WHERE TO PURCHASE FAMILY HISTORY MATERIALS

Because family history materials are produced by many groups that are outside of mainstream commercial publishing, such as clubs and even individuals, and because materials that are quite old can be useful, it is necessary to look at ways to acquire them outside of the book wholesalers that many libraries normally use. Some places to look are:

- Book dealers who specialize in used books.
- Genealogy booksellers like Origins Books and Park Books.
- Genealogy/Local Historical Societies who often publish their own materials which may not be sold anyplace else but through that organization.
- Amazon.com for self-published materials, especially e-books.
- Standalone websites for self-published materials.
- Local garage sales, estate sales, and charity resale shops for items like yearbooks, old maps, city directories.
- Niche publishers who sell their items directly such as Genealogical Publishing in Baltimore, Maryland.
- eBay.

If the item is old, be very careful of its condition. Dust can be vacuumed, but mold and mildew can easily spread very quickly from a single infected item to other items in your collection.

TO-DO CHECKLIST

- Check the publication lists on the websites of all the local historical and genealogical societies that fall within the geographical collection development boundaries of your collection.
- Contact area estate sale companies and put in "standing orders" for old yearbooks, maps, and any other local history/genealogical materials of interest.
- Read reviews of genealogical and local history books in major genealogical periodicals such as the *National Genealogical Society Quarterly*, and also in state genealogical/local history journals, not just in library journals.
- Use Cyndi's List, http://www.cyndislist.com/, in order to find specific publishers from your geographical area of interest. Look under the heading "Books—Family History Publishers."
- Create a wish list of desired titles that are found in the bibliographies and footnotes of other titles already owned, and then periodically search for them on the websites of used book dealers.

STRATEGIC PLANNING AND THE LOCAL COLLECTION

Perhaps you do not already have any planning documents? Or perhaps there are strategic plans, but they do not mention anything about the local studies collections?

Certainly many small public libraries do not have individual strategic plans and, those that do, may not include collection development, reference, or preservation planning for local special collections. Try inserting some basic goals into the next strategic plan. The ideas can be simple, such as adding a particular number of hours of dedicated family history programming or reference. They can deal with basic preservation and disaster planning for the collection, such as the following sample goals:

- Create a basic list of preservation tasks to be performed routinely, such as:
  - Vacuum and dust the stacks area regularly.
  - Check for evidence of insects along the floor, the backs of shelves, and in sections of the stacks that do not regularly circulate.
  - Check for mold.
  - Rent a humidistat to monitor humidity levels.
- Address disaster planning for the local collections:
  - Move items under or near water lines to a more safe area of the library.
  - Make a backup copy of any unique item that was developed by your staff or volunteers, such as indexes or guides. Have volunteers create an online database with information from card files, such as obituary files.
  - Make a list of who to call in your area for water damage, fire and smoke damage, and mold remediation.

COLLECTION DEVELOPMENT POLICIES

Serious consideration of the long-term commitment to housing, preservation, and access to local items should be undertaken before creating a collection development policy. It is wise to consider the best housing for any given materials and to decide what types of materials might exist in a community in duplicate form, such as local family genealogical charts. Other materials might best exist in archival housing or in a digital format. An examination of the typical uses of historical resources in the library or resource center could provide a basis for decisions on what to collect. Analyze the most common types of questions that the institution receives related to local studies, and make decisions based on that. Some institutions keep statistics based on items counted when they are reshelved; this helps identify high usage items that can then be prioritized in the materials budget.

It may be useful to consult some of the guidelines of the Reference & User Association (RUSA) pertaining to local studies services which can be found on their website. These include "Guidelines for a Unit or Course of Instruction in Genealogical Research at Schools of Library and Information Science" (2007), "Core Guidelines for Developing a Core Genealogy Collection" (2007), and "Guidelines for Establishing Local History Collections" (2012). As of this writing, the first of these guidelines is being revised, and the second is soon to be revised, but the following ideas found in them will likely survive the revision process:

- Collect items of local interest first.
- Collect materials covering all cultural and ethnic groups in the community.

- Collect research based on local families.
- Collect the following types of materials that may occur in various formats: vital records, censuses, probate records, land records, cemetery records, naturalization records, military records, newspapers and county histories.
- Collect materials on how to research and analyze genealogical sources.

Many institutions have placed their collection development policies online, so it is possible to view examples. They are easily located by searching with the phrases "genealogy collection development policy" and "collection development policy special collections."

THE USER-SUPPLIED COLLECTION: DONATIONS BY INDIVIDUALS

Donations can be a blessing and a curse. Sometimes, unique and well-preserved materials appear which are valuable additions to the collection. Sometimes, items in absolutely disgusting condition appear that can only be termed garbage by anyone's definition. Plan accordingly, and reserve space in the dumpster for such items! Some institutions have a special area reserved for examining and sorting donations that is apart from the regular collection, so that any problem items do not taint their holdings. Good ventilation, and disposable gloves and masks are a good health precaution. Removing odors from items in otherwise good condition may be possible through airing them outdoors, or sealing the item overnight in a bag with an odor-absorbing material, such as kitty litter or charcoal. Other suggestions include:

- Assign a staff member to regularly check donated materials for suitable candidates for the local studies collection.
- Make sure processing, cataloging, and storing the items is feasible.
- Make sure the items fall within the institution's collection development policy.

You may want to have a donations policy which states that individuals are free to leave materials, but that they will be assessed for suitability of adding to the collection as time permits. The library reserves the right to dispose of unsuitable items as it sees fit. The possibilities include selling the items at the Friends of the Library book sale, discarding them, or donating to a local charity. It may be hard to carry off this policy in a very small community, where people may demand to know on the spot what is decided about their donations. A decision should not be made while the donor is standing there; however, donors may certainly hear about what was decided through the grapevine.

TO CIRC OR NOT TO CIRC?

Many local studies collections do not circulate any materials at all, and this is understandable because many types of materials are either archival, or hard to find, and irreplaceable. The problem with this approach is that it is not very user-friendly. Researchers need to spend long hours poring over sources, and it is better for them to be able to do that in their homes, not just in the institution until fifteen minutes prior to its closing time. What can be done to fill both needs?

- Consider circulating how-to research materials.
- Purchase second/multiple copies of certain types of materials such as local histories that circulate, or acquire extra copies through donation.
- Compile a list of those materials relating to the geographical areas and topics in your collection that have already been digitized and their URLs.
- Suggest specific titles to researchers that they can borrow elsewhere when an item they need does not circulate in your institution.

RESOURCES

"A Guide to Deeds of Gift | Society of American Archivists," accessed October 10, 2014, http://www2.archivists.org/publications/brochures/deeds-of-gift.

Books & Publications: Genealogical Materials Online, www.academic-genealogy.com/bookspublicationsgenealogical.htm#Marketplace, accessed May 11, 2015.

Downs, Reginald. "List of Genealogy and Local History Acquisition Sources," accessed October 10, 2014, https://www.loc.gov/rr/genealogy/genealogy-acq.pdf.

Futas, Elizabeth, ed. *Collection Development Policies and Procedures*, 3rd ed. Phoenix, AZ: Oryx Press, 1995.

Hamill, Lois. *Archives for the Lay Person: A Guide to Managing Cultural Collections.* Lanham, MD: AltaMira Press, 2012.

Helling, William. "Creating Local History Collection Development Guidelines." *Preserving Local Writers, Genealogy, Photographs, Newspapers and Related Materials,* edited by Carol M. Smallwood and Elaine Williams, 105–115. Lanham, MD: Scarecrow Press, 2012.

IFLA. *Guidelines for a Collection Development Policy Using the Conspectus Model,* 2001, http://www.ifla.org/files/assets/acquisition-collection-development/publications/gcdp-en.pdf.

Roberts, Ann. *Crash Course in Library Gift Programs: The Reluctant Curator's Guide to Caring for Archives, Books, and Artifacts in a Library Setting.* Westport, CT: Libraries Unlimited, 2007.

DON'T GO IT ALONE—DEVELOPING
PARTNERSHIPS

"Cooperate with your local historical society, and take it upon yourself to fill in missing gaps; you could, for instance, photograph a main street over time, as it changes, and collect videos of annual holiday parades and high school basketball playoffs."
                                                                            —Bernard F. Vavrek[15]

CONNECTIONS TO OTHER COLLECTIONS

No cultural heritage institution stands alone, rather each is just one of many places that researchers will need to consult, even in small towns. It is important to analyze the community, to be aware of the other institutions that exist within the same city, township, borough, county, region, and state that also have information that patrons seek. If a directory of organizations related to historical collections within a geographical area, and a summary of the types of materials they hold does not already exist, then create one. Professional genealogists call such a finding aid a **locality guide**.[16] It should list contact information, hours, and a general description of holdings (print, archival, and digital) for local institutions housing collections of local heritage materials. It should state whether there is overlap between collections; that is, do two different organizations hold city directories, and in which format? More detailed information on how to create a locality guide is found in Appendix B.

A locality guide is not only a useful tool for staff members to consult in order to make good referrals, but it is also wonderful to share with researchers who will then have a much better grasp of where they should be directing their questions. Finally, a locality guide could be shared with other institutions with the hope that it will promote cooperation, so that all may provide the maximum access to the maximum amount of information. In a library setting, one might put the contents of a locality guide into a format consistent with other help guides, such as the LibGuides for the library.

ORGANIZATIONS WITH A PRIMARY GOAL OF HOUSING RESEARCH COLLECTIONS

This is a listing of institutions that researchers should generally turn to first because they have a primary goal of housing local studies collections:

- The local special collection holdings of local public, academic, or other libraries
- Historical societies
- Heritage groups
- Genealogical groups
- Archives, private and governmental, presidential libraries
- Museums

OTHER ORGANIZATIONS WITH INTERESTING COLLECTIONS

Other organizations hold items of interest that researchers may not think to consult. Sometimes, these organizations will donate old records, or copies of them, to a cultural heritage repository. These include:

- Academic libraries and archives often hold much of value to researchers, usually in areas labeled "Special Collections." Researchers sometimes mistakenly think that they will not be allowed to research here if they are not students or faculty members, or they are too intimidated to do so because of the size and complexity of the resources. However, information professionals in other institutions may make the initial inquiry to help patrons access these materials.

- Municipal archives often hold decades or even centuries of records from official documents like ordinances, to correspondence and memorabilia. Retention schedules and de-acquisitioning guidelines exist by state although some municipalities may ignore or even are unaware of them, so one should always check to see what years and types of materials exist where. Some documents may have gone to local archives, but others may still be in existence at the local municipality.

- Churches and religious institutions have records. Some religious denominations have national archives where copies of locally generated records are sent. Other denominations do not have such archives at all, and so the records generated by a local religious institution may be the sole copy. Sometimes church archives are affiliated with a college or university. Some of these institutions do not have very complete collections or are poorly funded and run, while others safeguard a substantial collection well. Also, some religious institutions are not affiliated with a national or international denomination at all.

- Businesses maintain records that could be of interest to family historians. For defunct businesses, it is always worth a try to look at local archival holdings, in the event some of the records were donated. For active businesses, there may be the possibility of getting information from the owners, though there will likely be no formal method to do so. A polite letter of inquiry might be a good way to start. For historic or long-lived businesses, look also for published histories, or check the corporate website.

- Charities and nonprofits such as the YMCA and YWCA, Catholic Charities USA, and many other nonprofits provide services to the community, such as shelter and programming. Some of their records are useful for broadening a family history in such organizations.

- Service organizations may retain a few records that are housed with the officers, or at a fixed location. Many service groups, such as Rotary International, Lions Clubs International, and Kiwanis International, were founded approximately 100 years ago, so local chapters may have centennial celebrations with documentation of membership, useful for family history research. Some national groups have both state and local archives.

- High school and college alumni associations can be wonderful sources of information, particularly for published sources, such as yearbooks and photographs.

- Historic sites and museums often have research facilities, including both published and archival and manuscript repositories. Vertical files may contain photographs of the region, as well as local publications naming businesses and individuals.

- Cemetery offices may have an office with a staff who keep records. Those in more populous areas that are owned by a business or a religious institution tend to keep records. Some cemeteries never had written burial records of any kind while others have records held by volunteer caretakers, such as a cemetery board; these are difficult to access because they might be located in a board member's home.

- Mortuaries and funeral homes keep good records because they are required to by law. It is not unusual to find a local funeral home that has been owned by several generations of the same family making it easy to track even if it has changed its name over time. Now there are companies that own chains of such establishments, which could also account for a name change when they buy out the local funeral home. Records from defunct funeral homes may have been donated to an archive, if they have not already disappeared.

Cultural heritage institutions should solicit copies of records from local organizations for two compelling reasons, to preserve them and to make them accessible. First, though some organizations are now putting record indexing or scans of records on their websites, many of them retain a single copy of their records in their offices. In rare instances, a copy of the records from these organizations may be housed in a different location to guard against disaster. Second, it can be difficult for patrons to track and access these records, and the staffs of such organizations are often not well-equipped to handle researchers' queries.

A POSSIBLE ALLIANCE

Even in some small towns, researchers seeking information about the past may have to do so in multiple locations: the public library, the local history society, at a college or university, government offices, and in the basements and attics of people holding onto organizational and church records. The duplication of effort, not to mention the precarious storage conditions, of some of these arrangements is evident. Making these local studies materials available in one location, or at least in less than a half dozen locations, has both practical and fiscal benefits. But how to accomplish this? Of the few different possibilities, probably the most common one is when the local history and/or genealogy society and the public library team up. Litzer reminds us that information providers should not just consider individual patrons, but also strive to build relationships with genealogical groups.[17]

A common scenario is that the society has a collection, but cannot house it in an independent location any longer due to declining membership, increasing rents and utility bills, and numerous other factors. The library has a building where some extra space could be found to house local studies materials. It sounds like a "marriage made in heaven," but questions arise that will need to be answered before the offer is extended by the library to the local history or genealogy society:

- Who now owns the society's materials, the society or the library?
- Who will decide if they are kept separately from the library's own local studies information or integrated into the collection?
- Who will fund additions to the local studies material?

- Who will provide assistance to researchers using the materials?
- Who will pay the bill for processing the collection?
- Will library card holders be allowed to check out some of the materials, or only society members?

All of these questions need to be negotiated before the partnership goes forward. Here are some ideas for decision-making and implementation:

- Have a written agreement drawn up laying out legal ownership of the collection.
- Have an agreement about future additions to the collection. Will they be made by society members without question or must they be approved by library staff? Staff members are the ones who must properly store, catalog, and provide access to the collection.
- Have an agreement about the funding of new materials. Should they come from the society, the library, or both? That decision will occur after a dialogue, and will depend on the financial circumstances of both parties.
- Have an agreement about organization of the materials from both the society and the library. The collection should be organized in a manner most beneficial to researchers. This would probably mean that like materials will be shelved together, regardless of who provided them, but stamped information inside the item could identify its provenance, if desired. (This may contradict the agreement in the second bullet.)
- Have an agreement about who will help with processing materials, creating finding aids, and even with providing reference assistance. Volunteers from the society may wish to do this, but they should do so in cooperation with library staff.

Sometimes, the two institutions have difficulties making the partnership work. One, or sometimes both, parties are very territorial, concerned with what is theirs, and determined to keep what they have staked out, forgetting that they need to forgo a certain portion of their former individuality in order for the "marriage" to succeed, and to function as one information-providing entity. In addition, challenges in communication are common when each continue to act fairly autonomously. The two groups can often have unmatched goals, which also feeds into the above problems. But even if the two entities do not join collections or share space, they may still be able to jointly sponsor programming.

In some instances, partnerships can be elevated to the sharing of resources for digital collaboration. Such arrangements are increasingly common and bring great visibility to the groups involved. Here, again, some issues may arise, which can pose significant problems if not worked out ahead of time. These issues demonstrate the need to negotiate clear, written partnership agreements in a timely manner:

- Digital divide: Two institutions that are operating at very different levels of digital ability may find it difficult to navigate a partnership, but the difference could be viewed as a potential positive arrangement. If one institution could provide the scanning/cataloging resources for a digital collection or exhibit, while the other institution supplied primary documents, photos, and staff or volunteers to research cataloging information, the relationship could work very nicely. The main issue to negotiate, outside of the workflow, is that of acknowledgment for the partnership in a visible way throughout the final product.

• Copyright and privacy issues: Many institutions have very different views of risk when it comes to copyright, which translate into differing policies upon acquisition of items. For a successful partnership, each partner must be comfortable with the level of risk assumed for each context of collaborative activity. For example, if hosting a digital collection together, the use of any gray-area materials should be discussed and the most restrictive interpretation of the two copyright policies utilized.

For more information on digital projects and collaborations, see Chapter 9, Pooling Our Resources—The Digital Portal.

OTHER KINDRED INSTITUTIONS

Because local studies collections deal with local history as well as genealogy, it is a good idea to consider those groups/institutions/government bodies nearby that deal with historic preservation, which can be defined as the effort to preserve, interpret, and promote historic buildings, districts, and sites. Local planning commissions, economic development organizations, historical societies, municipalities, and other entities may need to engage in planning and grant-writing for the preservation of local structures. Such organizations share general goals to preserve places and sites of significance to the past. One of the most common results of historic preservation planning is the naming of particular buildings or districts to be placed on the National Register of Historic Places. This one register includes both individually-listed places, such as buildings or archaeological sites, and groups of buildings, such as historic districts. Within historic districts, individual buildings may be designated as "contributing" to the district or "significant" within the district. Since some federal-level government preservation grants are specifically intended for individually-listed structures or those identified as contributing or significant in a district, these designations are important to the planning process.

In addition, some townships adopt ordinances that are attached to the historic districts in their communities which allow for protections of the structures. The state of Pennsylvania, for example, allows for the creation of Historic Architecture Review Boards (HARBS), which are created by ordinance to allow for review of proposed exterior renovations or demolitions of structures within the historic district. Such boards provide recommendations to the local city councils in the applications process for these exterior changes. In addition, in Pennsylvania, preservation is allowed through zoning, most commonly through the use of a historic overlay. Local planning commissions are responsible for edits to zoning ordinances, while local governments approve the changes, after public review. This process insures that there are a good number of constituents involved in the development of protection measures for historic properties.

Local revitalization groups also may hold information of use to family historians. These groups may write grants to preserve the historic character of the downtown or residential districts. There may be some resources or even professionals who work in the area of historic preservation for a region. Their websites can provide many resources for research of an area, including house styles and historic plaque programs documentation, and bibliography of note for the region. In addition, such groups may fund conferences that bring together specialists and speakers who are well-versed in the history of a region.

Many of these groups draw heavily on local, state, and federal offices that oversee preservation. The National Park Service website is a great place to start for information on historic preservation at the federal level. States all have a historic preservation officer and staff who administer preservation grants and programs at the state and regional levels. In addition, many other preservation and planning organizations exist that might be good partners for local cultural heritage events, collection preservation, and digitization projects. Here are the websites for such organizations:

Advisory Council on Historic Preservation, http://www.achp.gov/index.html

American Planning Association, https://www.planning.org/

National Association of Tribal Historic Preservation Officers, http://www.nathpo.org/

National Park Service, http://www.nps.gov/

National Register of Historic Places, (rated at local, regional, or national level of significance) http://www.nps.gov/nr/

The National Trust for Historic Preservation, http://www.preservationnation.org/ Preservation Action, http://www.preservationaction.org

Preservation Historic District on National Register (rated at local, regional, or national level of significance), http://www.nps.gov/history/nr/faq.htm, http://www.preservationnation.org/

A list with additional organizations related to many aspects of cultural heritage is provided in Appendix C.

BECOMING A GENEALOGICAL SOCIETY OF UTAH (GSU) AFFILIATE LIBRARY

If there is not a nearby Family History Center (FHC) or it is open only very limited hours, it is logical to consider taking on the role of receiving Family History Library (FHL) microfilms at your institution. The FHL has a collection of two and a half million rolls of microfilm containing information from all over the world for the use of family historians. Their eventual goal will be to digitize and index all of those records, but that is going to take many years, possibly even decades, to accomplish. In the meantime, much of the information will still need to be accessed via their microfilm interlibrary loan program. For a modest fee, microfilms can be ordered online and sent to a designated microfilm center. Many are in the church-run Family History Centers (FHC), but many are also in participating libraries. The requirements needed to participate include: a secure place to store the microfilm that have been received, the microfilm on permanent loan to researchers, and enough microfilm reader printers to handle the increased traffic that this program will generate. Information on the program is available online:

http://broadcast2.lds.org/elearning/fhd/help-center/family-history-centers/
quick-start-guide/english/quick-start-family-history-centers-aug-2014.pdf

---

The LDS Church and Genealogy

The Church of Jesus Christ of Latter-Day Saints (LDS), sponsors the largest genealogical organization in the world, the Genealogical Society of Utah (GSU), which has amassed a huge amount of information in Salt Lake City. The organization has sent teams of volunteers all over the world to microfilm a variety of civil, religious, and historical records. It has been captured on two and a half million rolls of microfilm, which are stored in a granite mountain vault, but which can be borrowed from a network of Family History Centers (FHC) and participating libraries. These microfilms are beginning to be digitized, and placed on their website, www.familysearch.org, to be viewed by anyone for free. The website also offers a digitized collection of books and periodical articles.

The GSU sponsors a worldwide network of Family History Centers, or FHC, that are usually located at or near a church, and are free and open to the public. Generally, they are run by volunteers who are church members, though some of the volunteers are not. There researchers can use a variety of online subscription databases, can get guidance on the research process, and help with ordering and using the microfilmed records. Eventually, the entire microfilm collection will be digitized, but until then, many records in their collection still need to be accessed through the microfilm ordering program. These are ordered online at https://familysearch.org/films/. For a modest fee ($7.50 per reel as of this writing), a copy of the needed microfilm is generated and sent to the designated FHC of choice, or to a library which participates in the microfilm program. It usually takes two to six weeks for a microfilm to arrive, and it will be kept at the facility for six weeks, or until the researcher is finished. It is possible to renew the microfilm for an extra fee, or even to get it on permanent loan. The researcher cannot take the microfilm home, but will have access to it in the permanent collection of the FHC or library forever.

In addition, the GSU operates a library in Salt Lake City, the largest genealogical collection in the world. Again, anyone can use this facility for free, assisted by numerous paid and volunteer staff members, but none of the items in this collection circulate. The Church of Jesus Christ of Latterday Saints (LDS Church) is interested in genealogy because they encourage their members to trace their families as far back as possible in order to posthumously baptize some of those family members into their church. However, they make it a policy not to proselytize nonchurch members who use their research facilities.

THE SKY'S THE LIMIT: PARTNERING WITH FOR-PROFITS AND OTHER GOVERNMENTAL AGENCIES

Perhaps because most family history facilitators work in a nonprofit institution, businesses, both local and national, may not be on their radar. However, it may be possible to collaborate with one in order to achieve a goal that will benefit researchers. This is now being seen on a very large scale, with giant repositories such as the National Archives and Records Administration (NARA) and the Family History

Library entering into agreements with companies such as Fold3.com, or Ancestry.com in order to complete large scale digitization projects.[18] Without these agreements, the records would remain hidden in the depths of archives or vaults for years or even decades. Instead, they are put online, sometimes for free, sometimes behind a paywall, but accessible more readily and cheaply nonetheless than when they could only be accessed by sending for a copy, or by a visit to retrieve it. But such partnerships do not need to be on such a grand scale.

Some of the subscription-based genealogical websites also partner with small libraries and archives in order to acquire content that they can digitize and put online. This can be anything from old microfilmed newspapers, to local history books, to unique archival material. The institution gets free digitization, and a backup of some of its collection. The company gets to improve its offerings and attract more users to its website. Companies that make such arrangements include, any of the Ancestry.com websites including Fold3.com and Newspapers.com, as well as Findmypast.com, MyHeritage.com, and ProQuest.com.

Another type of partnership could be between a local business and a cultural heritage facility. For example, perhaps a facility could use help financing a digital reader-printer, or a high-end scanner. A local business may be willing to underwrite the cost, particularly if there was a plaque attached to the equipment identifying the donor, as well as an article about the donation in the library newsletter and in the local newspaper. Or perhaps a business would like to adopt a reference book or database subscription, with identification like a bookplate or an acknowledgment of the gift on the website.

In the same way, partnerships could be forged with area government agencies, or organizations that deal with businesses, such as the local Economic Development Council (EDC), the Better Business Bureau (BBB), or the Chamber of Commerce. The evidence that there is a link between bringing visitors to an area, and providing and highlighting local history and genealogical resources is growing.[19] For example, the state of Oklahoma has successfully built a website (http://www.travelok.com/genealogy) loaded with information to entice researchers: free genealogy starter kits are available, as well as a beautiful booklet outlining sources in all 77 counties. Even entire countries such as Ireland and Scotland have started to market their history to potential family history researchers.[20]

STRATEGIC PLANNING

Finally, it is important to note that most collaboration will involve both formal and informal planning steps. Many grant applications ask for references to formal planning documents, called strategic plans or action plans, therefore one should become familiar with the strategic plans of relevant organizations. Also it is important to understand the goals of institutions one may want to partner with for programming or projects. Start by examining existing planning documents, local library, organization, or district strategic plans and preservation plans, vision statements, mission statements, and municipal planning documents. This last category generally deals with historic preservation, but not always.

Once the goals of various organizations have been examined, take time to brainstorm the institutions' informal goals. Analyze what are their effective goals by creating a list of their actions with regard to local collections over the past five years. If considering a partnership, it would be useful to create some very basic goals together. Perhaps by starting with the goal of the partnership, a statement or two put into writing could become the beginning of an agreement.

The first step in being able to partner with another organization is to understand how that partnership would help the organization reach its own goals with respect to the local collection. Not every institution will be able to provide preservation, organization, cataloging, and reference support for a local collection. However, once a rudimentary scan of local resources, reference, and access is created, it is useful to understand the extent to which each organization has undergone a planning process that includes historical documents, reference, and outreach. For example, if one goal of the collection is to extend the number of hours of genealogy online reference, but there simply are no funds for this reference, it might make sense to provide reference in collaboration with another institution, either by referring patrons to the correct online chat room or email, depending on the days/times, or by providing a single digital portal that can parse inquiries. Clearly, issues of concern immediately arise, such as consistency in approach, depth, and expertise in the reference interview. These concerns should be viewed as a natural part of the collaboration opportunity, not a reason to forego the attempt.

RESOURCES

Bastian, Jeannette Allis, and Ben F. Alexander. *Community Archives: The Shaping of Memory.* London: Facet, 2009.

"Federal Financial Assistance for Historic Preservation Projects: Cultural and Arts Programs," http://www.achp.gov/funding-cultural.html, accessed May 6, 2015.

Gillibrand, U.S. Senator Kirsten E. *A Guide to Historic Preservation, Arts & Cultural Institutions, & Tourism Funding Opportunities and Incentives: How to Navigate the Funding Process.* Washington, DC: Senator Gillibrand's Office, 2015, http://www.gillibrand.senate.gov/imo/media/doc/Gillibrand%20Historic%20Preservation,%20Arts%20&%20Cultural%20Institutions,%20&%20Tourism%20Funding%20Opportunities%20and%20Incentives%202015.pdf.

Litzer, Donald S. "Library and Genealogical Society Cooperation in Developing Local Genealogical Services and Collections." *Reference & User Services Quarterly* 37 (Fall 1997): 46. *Academic OneFile.* Web, accessed February 13, 2015.

Mannon, Melissa. *Cultural Heritage Collaborators: A Manual for Community Documentation* Bedford, NH: ArchivesInfo Press, 2010.

"Mentoring a Genealogy Society Librarian," https://genealogyeducation.wordpress.com/2006/09/22/mentoring-a-local-genealogy-society-librarian/, accessed May 11, 2015.

Meringolo, Denise D. *Museums, Monuments, and National Parks: Toward a New Genealogy of Public History.* Amherst: University of Massachusetts Press, 2012.

Waterton, Emma, and Steve Watson. *Heritage and Community Engagement: Collaboration or Contestation?* London, UK: Routledge, 2010.

PROGRAMMING FOR GENEALOGISTS AND FAMILY HISTORIANS

"The numerical strength of genealogists can, when given proper direction, provide a powerful rationale for the development of new programs."

— Roy Turnbaugh[21]

A question arises as to the impact of programming involving local studies materials on staffing. Libraries and other cultural heritage institutions today face many budget challenges. If basic activities such as collection development, cataloging, and reference are so time-consuming, then how can something over and above basic services like programming also be achieved? However, investing some staff time in planning programming can have several positive outcomes.

Certain types of programming can be seen as reference service on a grand scale. Programs built on the use of local studies resources in the library can very efficiently instruct multiple patrons simultaneously as to how to use a specific online database or print reference sources focusing on a subject or a geographical area. Demonstrating on-site resource use falls in line with expected reference duties in local history rooms, as does providing support for patrons who wish to use online genealogy information provided through sites such as Ancestry.com and FamilySearch.com.

Programming acts as an excuse to send researchers a specific invitation to visit the institution, an invitation that will likely garner free publicity and increased foot traffic. Free programming also garners good will. If you have room for a limited number of researchers, ask for them to reserve a ticket.

Programming goals should build not only on the traditional local history items found in the collection, but also aim to project beyond these items to encompass a whole new suite of family writing that may or may not have a place in the collections of the history room. By providing forums that provide a place to discuss family documents, stories, keepsakes, etc., the library can be a reliable place for patrons to turn when posing the question, "Where do I begin?" Even libraries that have no local history holdings can benefit from developing outreach and programming for family and local history activities, building on the work of the patrons themselves. Librarians should be looking at the possibility of collaborating with other local institutions, such as historical societies, archives, and museums in providing opportunities for family history programming.

Becoming familiar with popular family history activities is useful in planning family history programming. The recording of family stories in web blogs, Facebook, and written histories showcases family events, people, and shared values. Scrapbooking allows family members to document individuals, events, and moments in personal, artistic ways. Like quilting bees of the past, today's scrapbooking nights provide opportunities to carve out small amounts of time for networking and socializing in busy lives, while still producing physical artifacts that hold personal meaning to family groups. The appeal of using and digitally manipulating family photographs also can be seen in the wide range of sharing venues in Web 2.0. This "doing" culture of the family history movement ties neatly into potential outreach opportunities for libraries and into related concepts, such as "maker spaces."

Library programming for family history can be viewed not so much as a series of "lessons" that patrons master, but more like book club or children's story-time programming. These are ongoing events where individuals document, discover, research, share, and interpret their family's past, which can be repeated and enjoyed numerous times. The library can serve as an amplifier for a movement that is already strong in popular culture. By providing a central location for activities, vetted speakers, reliable books and magazines, sample videos, etc., the library can raise opportunities for those who want to participate in family history events. In this way, the family history movement ties in well with clarion calls to shift public library and other information institutions to a "doing" and "teaching" environment for both hands-on and technology-related skills.

In addition, while many online resources exist that can be utilized for programming, there are still patrons interested in family history who are not highly literate in computer culture, and who would appreciate programming focusing on physical artifacts without expensive and complicated software. Because programming is such an important aspect of family history services, ideas will be given for sample programs at the end of many of the chapters in this book. The fully described programs will be followed by a list of additional ideas.

CONCLUSION

This chapter provides a basis for understanding that a physical local studies collection is not needed to provide family history services, and that a variety of cultural heritage institutions can work with each other, and with other nonprofits and businesses to provide them. Partnerships provide an excellent vehicle for raising awareness of local studies documents held from private families to major institutions. Libraries, historical societies, and archives staff should recognize the current fascination with local studies by offering a variety of programming to the public. In the next chapter, the focus will shift to a specific type of local studies writing, historical narratives, and how local studies collections can be improved and programmed using some nontraditional forms of family history writing.

PROGRAMMING IDEAS

1. How to Grow Your Family Tree

This is a brief introduction about how to start the research process that is aimed at the absolute beginner who has no idea how or where to start. It should be a 1–1.5 hour event.

This type of program is very commonly put on by many types of institutions, and is usually well attended. Some large institutions regularly schedule this program, even on a monthly basis. The idea is to cover the following basic ideas:

- Define genealogy.
- Start with yourself, and work backwards.
- Linear versus cluster research.
- How to record information on standard forms.
- Define what a source is.
- Explain how to gather home sources.
- Recommend basic books about the subject that contain examples. (See Appendix B for ideas.)
- Tell them what their local resources are such as libraries, the Family History Center (FHC), the historical society, etc.

Distribute a basic handout. A PowerPoint presentation is nice with a few pictures of what you are talking about, although it is also possible simply to hold up sample forms with a small group. If only one staff member presents, then end after the talk. If there are several pairs of hands available, then extra time could be added in order to consult with the participants individually, and to answer their questions. This could be easily accomplished if the program were jointly sponsored with a local genealogical/local history group, a DAR chapter, etc.

2. The "Spotlight on. . ." Program

This overview shows how to best access and use a specific resource in the collection. It is aimed at all levels of researchers and should last about one hour for the presentation and questions. This is an opportunity to highlight something your institution owns which researchers do not often think to ask for. Examples may include city council records, court cases, tax lists, and less well-known finding aids.

3. The Story of Your Life

This a program aimed at getting children interested in family history. There is a book by Dr. Seuss called *My Book About Me,* which is basically a colorful template which allows children to record all kinds of facts about themselves. Think about a program acting as a similar fun and colorful template which encourages them to record information about their families, starting with themselves. Depending on the ages of the children involved, it is best to limit this program from 45 to 60 minutes.

- For specific ideas on how to format the "template," refer to an award-winning website called "Family Tree Project for School or Home" at http://www .hiddengenealogynuggets.com/familytreefun/familytreeschoolproject.php.
- Ancestry.com has a program for teachers whereby they supply free use of their website to schools for a period of time in order for them to augment their curricula with research projects. More details can be found on their website at: http:// ancestryk12.com/. They also supply lesson plans and a free downloadable book called *Family History Research Study.*

4. Reaching Out to Ethnic Groups

This program aids members of a specific ethnic group within your community to document their heritage. A good way to advertise and attract attendees is to hold this program in conjunction with a local church, or a social/heritage group. Schedule the program for two hours to allow plenty of social interaction. Outline the resources available, both locally, nationally, and internationally to carry out this type of ethnic research. Highlight help from both cultural heritage organization and government offices, such as consulates. It may be helpful to bring in an outside speaker, such as a subject specialist from a college or university. At the conclusion of the program, refreshments might be served, such as desserts from an ethnic bakery. Canadian librarian May P. Chan provides this type of programming to the Chinese community at the Regina Public Library in Saskatchewan, Canada.

Additional Ideas

- Lock-In Night: a library or archive that generally is only open during the day will open during the evening for as late as researchers want to stay.

- Scavenger Hunt: teach researchers the resources in your local studies center by giving them clues which lead to a resource and another clue.

- Senior Outreach: some retirement homes and senior clubs have vans that they can use to transport their residents/members for activities. Suggest that these groups bring residents to the local studies center on a regular basis.

- Items could be utilized in programming for experiential history: tutorials on how to collect information, brainstorm, and write and best practices for the verification of information and citation can be provided.

NOTES

1. Roger G. Kennedy, *Rediscovering America* (Boston, MA: Houghton Mifflin, 1990), xi.
2. See Chapter 4, "Considering the Collateral Kin: Genealogical Research in the Full Family Context" in Marsha Hoffman Rising, *The FamilyTree Problem Solver: Proven Methods for Scaling the Inevitable Brick Wall* (Cincinnati: FamilyTree Books, 2005), 67–89.
3. Elizabeth Shown Mills, *QuickSheet: The Historical Biographer's Guide to Cluster Research (the FAN Principle)* (Baltimore, MD: Genealogical Publishing Company, 2012).
4. Dick Eastman, Eastman's Online Genealogy Newsletter, "How Genealogy Became Almost as Popular as Porn," May 31, 2014, http://blog.eogn.com/2014/05/31/how-genealogy -became-almost-as-popular-as-porn/.
5. Tristram Hunt, "Reality, Identity and Empathy: The Changing Face of Social History Television," *Journal of Social History* 39, no. 3 (Spring 2006): 843. *Historical Abstracts*, EBSCO*host*, accessed February 16, 2015.
6. Curt Witcher, "Making the Financial Case for Genealogical Librarianship," (speech given at the Genealogy Preconference, ALA Midwinter, Philadelphia, Pennsylvania, January 24, 2014).
7. Elizabeth Yakel and Deborah A. Torres, "Genealogists as a Community of Records," *American Archivist* 70 (Spring/Summer 2007): 111, doi/pdf/10.17723/aarc.70.1.ll5414u7 36440636.
8. For information on how family historians participate in activities related to their research, one can consult a variety of genealogical blogs, such as Eastman's Online Genealogy Newsletter, DearMYRTLE, The Armchair Genealogist, and Genea-Musings, to name a few.
9. Yakel and Torres, "Genealogists as a Community of Records."
10. Michael Dewe, ed., *Local Studies Collection Management* (Hants, UK: Ashgate Publishing Limited, 2002), 25.
11. Ann Roberts, *Crash Course in Library Gift Programs* (Westport, CT: Libraries Unlimited, 2007), ix–x.
12. James H. Conrad, *Developing Local History Programs in Community Libraries* (Chicago, IL: American Library Association, 1989): 87.
13. "MassMu™," accessed May 4, 2015, http://www.massillonmuseum.org/.
14. Kate Williams and Joan C. Durrance, "Community Informatics," in *Encyclopedia of Library and Information Science*, 3rd. ed., 2010, doi: 10.1081/E-ELIS3-120043669.
15. Bernard F. Vavrek, "Wanted! Entertainment Director," *American Libraries* 32, no. 6 (June 2001): 71, *Library & Information Science Source*, EBSCO*host*, accessed February 13, 2015.

16. Elizabeth Shown Mills, ed., *Professional Genealogy: A Manual for Researchers, Writers, Editors, Lecturers and Librarians* (Baltimore, MD: Genealogical Publishing Company, 2001), 276–277.

17. Donald S. Litzer, "Library and Genealogical Society Cooperation in Developing Local Genealogical Services and Collections." *Reference & User Services Quarterly* 37 (Fall 1997): 46. *Academic OneFile*. Web, accessed February 13, 2015.

18. David E. Rencher, "Partnerships in the 21st Century: Libraries, Societies, and Commercial Companies Can Create an Amazing Partnership." (Genealogy for Librarians Day preconference, ALA Midwinter, Chicago, Illinois, January 30, 2015).

19. Bharath M. Josiam and Richard Frazier, "Who am I? Where did I Come from? Where do I go to Find out? Genealogy, the Internet and Tourism," *Tourismos: An International Multidisciplinary Journal of Tourism* 3 (2008): 48, accessed May 4, 2015, http://mpra.ub.uni-muenchen.de/25361/.

20. J. Timothy Dallen and Jeanne Kay Guelke, eds., *Geography and Genealogy: Locating Personal Pasts* (Aldershot, UK: Ashgate Publishing Limited, 2008), 126.

21. Roy Turnbaugh, "Impact of Genealogical Users on State Archives Programs." *Library Trends* 32, no. 1 (07, 1983) 49, http://search.proquest.com/docview/57145946?account id=14553. (Authors: This URL does not link to this article.)

Chapter 2

RECORD IT: PRESERVING FAMILY AND COMMUNITY HISTORY

This chapter is a discussion of family and local history materials produced by historians, enthusiasts, and families for a variety of purposes. "Histories" are broadly grouped here as works presenting either a narrative or vignettes about the past, including books, pamphlets, family notebooks; family genealogy charts and materials; family and organizations' cookbooks; histories on websites; and blogs. The traditional local history has much to offer family historians, as do newer, less structured formats of historical writing, which are explored in the chapter. Additionally, many innovative formats for writing family histories have emerged recently, including the use of web and social media formats. The chapter concludes with programming ideas for the writing of family and related local histories.

LOCAL HISTORICAL WRITING
AND TRADITIONAL FORMATS

"Local history has great affinity with genealogy as an amateur pastime or hobby, as both are similarly enfranchising to the participant and relatively straightforward to undertake. Both bring the local—that which is close and familiar—to life. . ."
—Jerome de Groot[1]

Works written for the purpose of recording specific family or organizational history may appear in many varied formats. Often topics that can be understood as "local" have captured the interest of professional historians and writers. Certainly in many larger metropolitan areas and in some smaller locales as well, one may find highly detailed written histories on particular families, cities, and businesses within those cities. These works generally have been produced in a formal publishing environment including a review and editorial process. The outcome traditionally takes the form of a published book that is marketed by the company to libraries, organizations, and interested individuals. For example, university presses sometimes have local history specializations such as Fall Creek Books, an imprint of Cornell University Press, publishing titles on the history of New York state including biographies and works on general regional history, architecture, business and industry, and urban development.[2] Histories may cover urbanization, industry, and professions, such as publishing firms, family businesses, etc. They further provide useful citations and indexes of names to those discussed in the works.

It is critical for cultural heritage professionals to understand the various methods of documenting published histories, as the reliability and usefulness of these works may depend upon their level of citation and documentation. Some of these works are written by trained historians, with advanced degrees in history. These historians seek to articulate an explanation of the larger societal forces and conditions that created change. They evaluate the trajectory of the past. They may bring a theoretical model to the work and use this model, such as feminism, as a lens through which events and motives are understood. These works tend to be heavily cited and rely upon original source materials.

Sometimes the writing style and documentation within academic works can be intimidating. Despite this, local studies collections should include any of these works that are applicable to the region, especially because the academic work may be the only source of reliable historical information for the area. Well-documented histories can provide wonderful clues and interpretations of the history of a region. In many libraries, these works already fall into the collecting policy for the institution, but they may not be housed with the other local studies materials. Some thought should be given to placing a copy in with the local studies materials, since these academic press works may otherwise be overlooked as excellent starting points for family historians who need to understand a context or time period. Formal, cited histories of regions and businesses can provide:

- Indexes that include names of persons and places.
- Citations that reference original source materials, including letters, diaries, business and government documents, which may be extremely useful to the family historian.
- Photographs and other visuals of relevant people and places.
- Narratives with contextual information about the formation of places and the evolution of families, discussions of interactions among various family members, information on the growth of family businesses, etc.
- Well-crafted biographical works with the levels of detail regarding family, marriages, illegitimate relations, etc.

Popular history writing also plays an important role in bolstering interest in local studies. Biographical writings in particular are common for major trade publishers to produce. These works often provide valuable clues for further investigation of historical contexts and relationships among people who could factor into family historical writing. While the voluminous tales of war and political interactions may not resemble "local" history to the degree other writings do, they nonetheless contain context and narrative that can be useful to those establishing a basis for understanding immigration, migration, the role of religion in society, and a host of other themes. There is much to be said for the excitement that surrounds works of noted popular historical writers like David McCullough, Allison Weir, and Doris Kearns Goodwin.

Academic and more popular, trade press historical publications are considered "secondary sources" by historians and are not appropriate as genealogical documentation. These works, however, can still provide valuable background information for family history research. Their footnotes and bibliographic essays may give clues for locating additional family documents or materials. They also provide an excellent basis for the types of programming libraries and other cultural heritage institutions may want to expand upon.

IS IT TRUE? EVALUATING THE ACCURACY OF NONDOCUMENTED LOCAL STUDIES MATERIALS

Local history works often follow a publishing model which lists few or no sources, or provides only a brief bibliographic essay. The editors of an important work on writing local history, *Nearby History: Exploring the Past Around You*, express the general sense that in the past trained historians produced metaworks to explain large changes in society, while amateur historians produced narratives focused on the daily events and lives of the local setting.[3] They also noted that these lines were beginning to blur. Local historians can and do produce meticulously researched local works that can offer context, interpretation, and evidence. Yet, in some cases, local history writing may violate professional standards, such as basing a work too heavily on newspaper sources, or reporting family lore as fact. Newspapers are often considered somewhat unreliable resources by trained historians since the reporter is usually interviewing others about an event, and is often not an eyewitness to the event. The urgent nature of newspaper deadlines further plays into the question of reliability. The newspaper, however, is often the only source available to answer certain questions for local historians and genealogists; therefore its use for local history and genealogy reference is extremely important. Additionally, a reading of the local newspaper from a specific locale can provide invaluable contextual information for family history.

Family and community histories take many formats outside of traditional publishing venues. Many family researchers are familiar with county histories or city directories, but many other types of local history works have been produced since the late nineteenth century, including full-length works on cities, industries, and biographies of key political and cultural figures. Works appearing about a locale from the late nineteenth and early twentieth centuries are likely well-known friends to the family researcher. But what of more recent acquisitions? Family histories that are self-published, for example, are increasingly common.

Histories written about local events and people often are very important in their ability to capture the values and proud moments of the community. Though some local histories may not be concerned with any sort of grand synthesis, earthshaking conclusions, or even overarching narrative, their value lies in the sense of importance that simply telling the story of the local community brings. Such works can be highly valuable in the local history room, but most local materials do not go through a publication vetting process unless they are the tiny minority that are published by university presses in the area or by other publishers with a review process.

How then are the issues of truth and reliability to be considered by those building local studies collections and utilizing them for family history reference? Local history writing falls into a unique category of materials from the perspective of collection development. Though many of the books about local history may be used as reference materials, a large percentage of these local histories do not go through a normal publication review process. Therefore the materials lack verification of reliability as standard reference resources. Do professional organizations provide any guidance on this topic? Reference and User Services Association (RUSA) guidelines for establishing a local history collection list the need to develop an acquisitions policy, but do not elaborate on how to identify appropriate works.[4] Yet it is in the world of librarianship that the call to evaluation of these resources should be most clear. Librarians, volunteers, historians, and even archivists who may find themselves providing local studies reference services may all need to consider how local historical works should be collected and utilized for family historians. Without clear guidelines, it is up to the individual staffs to develop acquisition and reference approaches. Generally, libraries should collect anything related to the local area, particularly if it is presented as nonfiction local history. Perhaps choosing a select group of locally-produced materials for standard reference use is a good idea, while allowing patrons to read and evaluate the rest on their own. In the end, even "vetted" works by professional historians may suffer inaccuracies and present interpretations that are subject to debate.

It is up to those working in individual institutions to understand the strengths and weaknesses of their area's histories. It may be at first glance that some works appear to be thinly cited, but, some local history works lacking citation are based on a wide variety of great sources. Conversely, one encounters historical works written entirely upon one resource, such as newspaper accounts, ignoring the fact that other sources are available. In addition, there are family histories where the relating of documented events are intermixed with unsubstantiated interpretations of those events. But it is important to realize that almost every work can prove valuable in some way, and some works that might not pass a routine "screening" based on citations could turn out to be highly useful.

Here are some suggestions about how local histories can be evaluated and used more effectively. Work with local historical groups to understand who the authors are and/or persons who could answer queries about the information in these books. Get to know your local authors. Talk with them and ask them about their work and research. Most are very happy to talk about it. If there is no bibliographic essay in their book or article, ask them if they might produce one for a programming session to help out researchers in locating the information in their works. Find out if the author is willing to be on a list of local historians who could be contacted if patrons have questions, or work with the local historical society or others to compile such a list.

Get to know your resources. Assess the local histories on hand. Are they self-published? Vanity presses? Reputable historical presses? Primarily image-based publications? It will be possible to recognize, in many cases, the origin of the material in them. Much of the source material will be in your collection already, such as county histories, newspaper accounts, and photographs. Make notes about each work, and create a guide as to their suitability for reference use for other staff members. Information about the author is also good to include in some notes about these works. Integrate knowledge about local histories into reader's advisory.

Understand when a memoir is just a memoir. Let works stand on their own if the author's personal knowledge is the source of the information. Generally we accept firsthand accounts with little or no documentation as valid primary sources, but let the reader/researcher take responsibility for fact-checking if he or she wants to quote or use the material in another way.

Build community by sponsoring programming with local historians in tandem with other organizations. The enthusiasm that local historians fuel in the community is priceless. Provide resources to anyone who wants to write local history in whatever way is possible. Perhaps sponsor writing groups in the library or discussion nights in coordination with the local historical society.

SUPPORT FOR WRITING LOCAL HISTORY

Cultural heritage organizations should also be in the business of supporting new local history writers. Fortunately, printed and organizational resources already exist to assist in programming or in answering queries. The American Association for State and Local History (AASLH) has played a pivotal role in providing resource materials and support for those who would like to develop local history narratives. The aforementioned *Nearby History: Exploring the Past Around You*, discusses how to research a wide variety of resources that touch on family history, such as published documents, photographs, documents, oral histories, and archival materials. The perspective is one that validates the importance of the local. Previous incarnations of the AASLH "nearby history" works included separate booklets on how to approach the history of school, business, churches, and other organizations. The AASLH also publishes *Writing Local History Today: A Guide to Researching, Publishing, and Marketing Your Book,* and the professional publication *History News,* which includes the regular column "On Doing Local History" by noted scholar and specialist in local history, Carole Kammen.[5]

Additionally, the public history movement of the last several decades supports the efforts of public historians to record, interpret, and preserve historical resources in a given locale. The "doing" of history in museums, historical sites, and historical societies can be realized in re-enactments, in seminars aimed towards family authors, and in a variety of programming events.[6] This "doing" culture, particularly in the digital age, sees some scholars interested in local history applying their knowledge to the distribution of the historical narrative in a variety of ways that extend well beyond the written narrative.

Major events and personalities can also inspire writers for a regional or national audience in the popular press. In the Oil Heritage Region of Pennsylvania, for example, multiple histories depict the origins of the oil industry in its earliest commercial phase. Famed "muckraker" and journalist Ida Tarbell has attracted the attention of numerous biographers. Even if a library does not have the main collection of local materials, it may be useful to keep duplicate copies of such items at branch locations, since they can be high demand items and can be used for programming purposes. Similarly, one may look to state, county, and local historical societies for reliable works on local history. Items relevant to local history in a wide variety of locales may be produced by such organizations, including materials that can help with reenacting and the understanding of social history, such as the series of printed patterns for women's nineteenth-century garments produced by the Wisconsin Historical Society.

ADDITIONAL SOURCES OF LOCAL HISTORICAL WRITING

A number of recognized formats for local history writing, such as the county history, appeared in the nineteenth century, yet a great deal of writing aimed at preserving the history of communities, families, and organizations exists on a much more informal level. Pamphlets, brochures, and fliers commonly seen at the local level are created by organizations for celebration of their centennials and other anniversaries. Institutional or company histories likewise may be created as a part of a landmark celebration and printed in bound volumes in small numbers. These brochures can date back to numerous celebrations, centennials, etc. in the community. Though they often lack any documentation such as footnotes or bibliographies, they also may be the only written narratives and analyses of historical events in an organization's past, and are well worth retaining in the community; typically such items do not circulate. Libraries without archival holdings may want to defer these items to other institutions in the region, retaining facsimiles copies if copyright law allows, because a coordinated effort to ensure all such materials are preserved is advisable.

The publications of local organizations, such as churches, businesses, social clubs, and municipalities should be collected by local studies curators. Churches seldom have full, written histories of the life and events in the congregation, but often there exist shorter, less formal variants. Church jubilee brochures, for example, may provide the only narrative-format history of the local institution. While these documents may suffer from an overabundance of "lineages" (pastors, buildings, etc.), they nonetheless provide a chronological framework that is useful context for family historians and others. The works often provide valuable detail with regard to names of those active in the congregation, as well as pivotal points of transition in the church's congregation.

The Centennial History of the Trinity Methodist Church, published in 1961, provides a good example of the materials that may be found in such writings. This particular work is more substantial in length than many other centennials and was written by a Professor Emeritus of Duke University, Benjamin Guy Childs, but the contents mirror that of many other, shorter jubilee publications. There are chronologies and discussions of church pastors, leaders, and committees. The stories of local beginnings and endings are intertwined with references to national-level wars and religious schisms. Childs spends a good deal of time praising the contributions of church supporters, naming a number of men notable for their work in backing various church building projects.[7] Such connections are commonly seen in nineteenth-century church histories, since that era was one of church building and the establishment of educational facilities with the financial support of wealthy individuals in the community. The detailed listing of names of those who served as pastors, committee chairs, and other leaders, including some women who served in the Women's Auxiliary, and as teachers and leaders in the educational programs, provide excellent clues to those seeking verification of an ancestor's presence in the church and town. Similar resources that define the history of a congregation from the perspective of an anniversary moment are common. The publication may be a brochure of a few pages, or a full-length book, as in the case of the Trinity Methodist Church. But, increasingly, with the Internet, social media, and a wealth of images available, the art of documenting local religious groups is evolving.

Church members who are seeking information on writing the history of their congregation would be well advised to check the national-level resources of their denomination or religion first, as there often are quite useful guidelines to writing, as well as retention schedules for the church's primary documents. The Presbyterian Church of the USA, for example, provides a wealth of information for local congregation history committees on their national historical society and archives website, including instructions on the writing of a congregational history.[8]

There are also many examples of specialized writings by specific organizations or businesses in the local area. Business materials that may provide only small snippets of narrative about the history of the sales, leaders, markets, and products are useful in piecing together the past, so it is useful to keep brochures, advertisements, and other business memorabilia in the local history vertical files. Photographs of family business products and inventions can be useful in documenting the past as well. Family historians can come upon extremely useful information in business histories, which may name those family members working in the company, as well as define relationships. Patrons who bring in information about a family business, such as the name of the company found on a radiator, can lead to valuable information in printed county and other histories. This is especially true as public domain local histories may be full-text searchable in a Google search.

Other types of informal local histories may be produced by families or individuals. Local organizational, community, or house histories may exist as printouts or even handwritten narratives in notebooks, provided by the author to a select few persons. Such items may be collected in local historical collections in the vertical files or the local history section, but their value and role in documenting the history of a region should be discussed in more depth in library instructional literature for both collection development and programming. This is particularly true for "unsynthesized" types of history, lacking a chronological or overarching thesis such as blogs, diaries, and even cookbooks, though in individual social media postings, synthesis of particular ideas and topics are often clearly and eloquently articulated.

NONTRADITIONAL LOCAL HISTORY: THE FAMILY OR ORGANIZATIONAL COOKBOOK

Family and organizational cookbooks provide glimpses into the past lives of family members in a way that ties family traditions and culture into a montage of memories, foodways, and stories. Whether done on a home computer and printed, or using professional companies that compile and print the book with photographs, these works create wonderful insights into family history and tradition. The compiler of the cookbook in some ways functions as historian, creating a system of reporting recipes that is generally divided by food type, but that also connects individuals to specific foods. Through the acknowledgment of others as authors, notes on modifications and memories, by detailing the intersections of family traditions through recipes, these family-developed works stand as minihistories of family foodways. In the case of the Scheer family cookbook, each of the children of one ancestor, Adam Scheer, had a section divider in the book filled with the photographs of his or her own family. The introduction to the work included a multipage reflection and general history, which provides a brief, but personal overview of the family, discussing the family store, general health history, and personalities of the relatives. Layers of documentation can be found in the recipes themselves. Those who contribute describe not only the process of making each item, but how particular persons made variations on the recipe. Foods strongly associated with a particular person in the family are given their name, "Dora's Buttery Lemon Bars," though the recipe might be contributed by someone else.[9] Special memories are captured in recipe notes, such as the naming of a sandwich after Grandfather Adam.[10]

In addition to self-published family cookbooks, professionally published ones are appearing as well. They often feature known chefs and/or food writers, and they offer family history intertwined with old photos and recipes. A well-known example in Louisiana is called *Who's Your Mama, Are You Catholic, and Can You Make a Roux?* by Marcelle Bienvenu, a food journalist and cookbook author. See Figure 2.1.

Bienvenu's book chronicles many rituals that her family and many others in the region participated in, such as crawfish boils, preparing the fishing camp in spring, and *boucheries* or hog butcherings. A family cookbook, whether self-published or professionally published, can be an important source of local history.

COLLECTION DEVELOPMENT FOR LOCAL HISTORIES

Because of the related nature of local history materials to family history, any collection development policy to assist in family history services should include published materials that are relevant to the region. The following items should be a part of a regular scan for materials to be acquired and posted on the local studies' website as possible for inclusion:

Figure 2.1

Book cover: "Who's Your Mama, Are You Catholic, and Can You Make a Roux?" Reproduced with permission of Acadian House Publishing. Lafayette, LA, www.acadian-house.com.

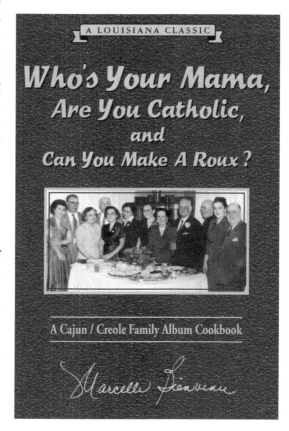

- Books published by reputable presses.
- Writings by local historians found in newspapers, as reports for clients, etc.
- Local histories in a self-published format—establish a vetting process or policy and include as needed.
- Jubilee pamphlets, organizational histories, and short historical pieces in newspapers, which are commonly filed in a vertical file, but now should have digital access. Please see Chapter 7 for ideas.
- History blogs that are written both on past events and on the historical process such as source evaluations that pertain to the region.
- Short historical writings that appear on web pages are digital resources that should be cataloged and linked to cultural heritage websites. Examples are the introduction on a cemetery website, or a description of an alumni society for a local high school.

RESOURCES

Amato, Joseph A. *Rethinking Home: A Case for Writing Local History.* Berkeley, CA: UCLA Press, 2002.

Cox, Richard J. *Documenting Localities: A Practical Model for American Archivists and Manuscript Curators.* Lanham, MD: Scarecrow Press, 1996.

de Groot, Jerome. *Consuming History: Historians and Heritage in Contemporary Popular Culture.* New York, NY: 2009.

Hyvig, David E. and Marty A. Myron. *Nearby History: Exploring the Past Around You*, 3rd ed. New York, NY: Rowman & Littlefield, 2010.

Kammen, Carol. *On Doing Local History*, 3rd ed. Lanham, MD: Rowman & Littlefield, 2014.

Kammen, Carol, and Bob Beatty, eds. *Zen and the Art of Local History.* Lanham, MD: Rowman & Littlefield, 2014.

Mason, Thomas A., and Calder, J. Kent. *Writing Local History Today: A Guide to Researching, Publishing, and Marketing Your Book.* Lanham, MD: Rowman & Littlefield, 2013.

Weiskopf-Ball, Emily. "Experiencing Reality through Cookbooks: How Cookbooks Shape and Reveal Our Identities." *M/C Journal* 16, no. 3 (2013): 13. *Communication & Mass Media Complete*, EBSCO*host*.

FORMS OF FAMILY HISTORIES

"Until the late 1970s, few genealogies told the story of a family. Most consisted of traditional lineage and ancestor, or descendant charts. During the last ten or twelve years, more and more books use genealogies as a framework upon which to stretch the fabric of individual and family lives or family history."

—Raymond S. Wright III[11]

Wright published this statement in 1995, but even he could not have foreseen then how family history writing has taken off in recent years, largely due to social media and the Internet. But well before this growth, the long-established field of genealogy existed, with research protocols and formatted documents to show research results. When properly executed, genealogical records document a family lineage based on information from reliable sources. However, it is common to encounter renditions of family trees on user-input sites with significant errors and no documentation. Family history, however, is not necessarily restricted to the establishment of lineages, but is a much broader work, encompassing detailed background information about history, social history, and more. For some, jotting a few ideas about particular family members on a family website might be the extent of the documentation desired, while others may dedicate years to the creation of a full-fledged written history that may eventually appear in bound format. But it is clear that the definition of family history writing is no longer relegated to traditional channels of historical writing. Those working in local studies collections will be called upon to assist family historians with their work. In order to provide assistance, it is useful to understand some of the variations of family history writing that exist. The following section will outline and explain methods and formats for such work beginning with traditional methods, and working to more recent informal and web-based methods.

GENEALOGIES

Family historians start by recording information on family group sheets, pedigree charts, and, even timelines, but this can be just a starting point, because, ultimately, many want to record the information in a way in which it will reach a lot of other people, and in a way in which it is interesting to read. There are many motivations for writing a family history. One is a desire to capture the information for future generations, a process which has psychological benefits. Research by psychologist Dr. Marshall Duke shows that communicating family history to children gives them a strong sense of security and grounds them, which helps them to deal with crises.[12] But, of course, there are countless other motivations for doing so as well.

Before embarking on family history writing, patrons need to be aware that there are some boundaries. The information being recorded is personal information, not just of the author, but also of many others who are related to that author, which means that there are ethics involved. The National Genealogical Society has set some guidelines for publishing genealogical information. They include the following ideas:

- not including information on living people without permission
- not including others' writing without acknowledgment
- acknowledging who owns the home sources you are citing, as well as who provided oral history information

For more details, please see "Standards for Sharing Information with Others," at http://www.ngsgenealogy.org/cs/standards_for_sharing_information.

WRITING A FAMILY HISTORY NARRATIVE

If patrons decide that they will make the time and effort to create a **family history narrative,** they may ask for information on how to go about this. In the past, mostly genealogies were written, and these were often quite Spartan affairs, with little more than names and a few dates. Sometimes just names were provided, as in the New Testament genealogy found in Luke 3:34–38. However, family histories, as opposed to genealogies, contain background information on the family, in addition to vital information like birth, marriage, and death dates, which places the family in social, historical, and cultural contexts.

Many examples of traditional genealogies have been digitized at family search.org, googlebooks.com, and the internetarchive.org. These were written long ago, in the nineteenth and early twentieth centuries, in a very stiff, formal style. They often lack any sort of documentation which may indicate that the information was gathered from the memories of various family members rather than by researching sources. Fortunately, many newer family histories are better in many ways. They are written as if they were telling fascinating stories of the past, which they are, and they include the sources of where the information came from, whether that be from census records and other government documents, or from an interview with a relative.

The most important things family historians need to decide before embarking on a writing project are the scope and format. Are they trying to answer a single question that relatives asked them to figure out, e.g., "Who was the wife of Henry Miller?", or are they trying to trace one line back to the Civil War, or are they trying to tell the story of their father's family as far back as they can go?

As to the format, will they photocopy and staple a print version? Will they submit it to a local history periodical? Will they post it on a website? Will they write a book and seek a vanity press, or a commercial publisher? Will they choose an electronic format? Regardless of which decisions researchers make from the above list of questions, here are the goals they should have for their writing project:

- Information should result from a solid background research. No family is an island, untouched by local, national, and world events.

- The history will be thoroughly sourced and documented. The citations can either be given in the form of footnotes, located on the bottom of every page, or endnotes, one long list located at the end of each chapter.
- The word "history" contains the word "story," meaning that the approach should be to make it interesting as well as informative. Encourage a creative nonfiction approach. The narrative should NOT begin, "Henry Miller was born on May 11, 1811. . . ."
- Not every minute detail that was uncovered during the research process needs to be in the narrative. Judgment should be exercised, and the writer needs to be aware that too many details can bog down the story.
- Extra information can be provided in the footnotes and/or in appendices. Genealogical charts can be included in the back, or printed on the endpapers if it is a book. Providing them is a kindness to the reader, who can find it hard to keep track of a large cast of "characters."
- An index is a must and a table of contents is also helpful. Both relatives and other researchers are going to want to look up their own branch of the family first. A list of helpful software for indexing is provided on the webpage of the American Society of Indexing, http://www.asindexing.org/reference-shelf/software/.

MORE ADVICE FOR FAMILY HISTORY WRITERS

When the above has been mastered, the next list will be of further help:

- Researchers who already have made timelines of family events can use these as outlines for narratives.
- Those writers who struggle to find their format and voice can search the Internet under the heading "writing family history templates" for tools which can help them structure their family histories.
- Researchers can write collaboratively with other family members by using a box account or Google Docs to share information and drafts of the narrative.
- Writers can use the website, www.genwriters.com that offers information and tips.
- Researchers will find that almost as many books have been published on how to write family histories as on how to do computer genealogy. A recommended book is *You Can Write Family History* by Sharon DeBartolo Carmack. This book contains helpful charts which specifically detail the many formats of family history writing.
- Writers may want to enter one of the many writing contests existing in the family history field. A sampling can be viewed at: http://genealogy.about.com/od/education/tp/competitions.htm.
- Software exists that helps manage the sources of researched writing projects. Two popular choices are Scrivener Writing Software, which must be purchased after a free 30-day trial, and Zotero, which is free. Caution: Many genealogy software programs have a feature called a report writer that converts the inputted genealogical information into a prose report. The resulting writing is mechanical, soulless, and repetitive. Past editors of the *National Genealogical Society Quarterly,* Gary B. and Elizabeth Shown Mills, relate how friends spent a small fortune to publish their

family history, but because they used software to generate the text, the result was hardly a pleasure to read.[13]

DONATING THE FINISHED PRODUCT

When researchers have a finished product that has been published, they may be looking for ideas as to where they can place copies to maximize exposure to their work. The best approach is to examine the work for the geographical locations covered, and then find institutions related to those locations with appropriate collections, such as libraries, both public and academic, heritage societies, etc. Also, genealogical collections that are national in scope will most likely be interested in such a donation. These include, The Family History Library in Salt Lake City,[14] The Library of Congress,[15] Mid-Continent Public Library,[16] and the Allen County Public Library.[17] The Library of Congress prefers a print format over a digital one.[18] The care with which the family history has been put together could impact whether institutions will accept it or not. A family history that is full of spelling errors and which is not sourced may be rejected.

SUBMITTING ARTICLES TO PERIODICALS

Many genealogy and local history publications are always looking for article submissions, and they run the gamut from small local history and genealogy newsletters to nationally known and distributed journals. Writers will need to pick an appropriate venue for their own subject matter and writing style. Staff members can help them check to see which periodicals cover their area of interest, usually geographical, by using the *PERSI* index and/or a subject search limited to periodicals on WorldCat. Publications put out by surname associations can be found by searching a surname + family + association.

Those interested in writing for the national genealogical journals such as the *National Genealogical Society Quarterly* (NSGQ) and *The New England Historical and Genealogical Register* (NEHGR) should be aware that the articles need to be in a fairly specific format. The place to turn for information is the Board for Certification of Genealogists (BCG). Their website, http://www.bcgcertification .org/, provides examples of three distinct types of writing required of those aiming to become a certified genealogist, and they are also the standards for scholarly genealogical journals:

- The Proof Summary
- The Kinship Determination Project
- Compiled Lineages, Pedigrees, and Genealogies

For further information consult *Genealogy Standards: 50th Anniversary Edition*, Board for Certification of Genealogists, Nashville, TN: Ancestry.com, 2014. In addition, samples of writing in these formats may be found at the BCG website, and at the following two websites:

http://www.archives.com/experts/jackman-susan/where-is-your-proof.html and
http://www.ngsgenealogy.org/galleries/awards_files/FHWC_sample.pdf.

TYPES OF BOOKS THAT CONTAIN FAMILY HISTORY THEMES

Ambitious researchers may decide to eventually publish a full-length book. It is a
good idea to understand the various types of books published with family history
themes in order to perform reader's advisory with our family history patrons.
Researchers/writers are always looking for good examples of others' work, but also
simply may like reading about families.

* **A personal history, aka autobiography,** is an individual's own story. Family history
  researchers are supposed to start with themselves and then work backwards. Your
  own story may not feel like history now, but it will be in a few years, and writers
  do not have to be at the end of their lives to attempt this, although sometimes
  grandparents embark on this type of writing with their grandchildren in mind as
  the audience. If some researchers do not like writing, but like to talk, they can record
  their story, and then someone can transcribe it. A popular example of autobiography
  is *A Heartbreaking Work of Staggering Genius* by Dave Eggers. One writer, the former president of Smith College, Jill Ker Conway, completed four volumes of
  acclaimed autobiography while still in her middle years.

* **Family memoirs** are not sourced, are based entirely on recollections, usually just of
  the author, and do not always include a family tree to help the reader keep track of
  the cast of characters. A memoir is much easier to write than a fully documented
  family history, and may be an appropriate type of writing project for some people.
  Examples include *Cheerful Money* by Tad Friend, *Angela's Ashes: A Memoir* by
  Frank McCourt, and the elegiac and lyrical *Five Thousand Days Like This One* by
  Jane Brox are all wonderful reading, but it is not clear where any of the information
  came from. *Family* by Ian Frazier was researched, because the research process is
  referred to in the narrative, and some sources are discussed, but none of them are
  listed in the form of footnotes. However, a bibliography of background history sources is included.

* **Readable family history** are documented family stories that read like compelling
  fiction. It is possible to take the best elements of memoirs, and merge them with
  sourcing, in order to produce great writing. However, there have not been many
  examples that have been published so far. *Slaves in the Family* by Edward Ball is
  often mentioned as a good read in this genre. Wright recommends *Kindred Saints*
  by William G. Hartley as another example.[19]

* **Family histories written as fiction** allow the author some latitude, but an effort is
  made to incorporate accurate historical research. They are based on family stories,
  and sometimes also on research, but the events can be greatly dramatized and
  embellished. Examples include *The Emigrants,* a series of four meticulously
  researched books by Swedish author Vilhelm Moberg. He used many personal diaries, oral histories, and Swedish, and U.S. newspapers as sources. These novels are
  considered classics of Swedish literature, and have been translated into English.

Another example is *Cane River* by Lalita Tademy, a novel set in Natchitoches Parish, Louisiana about a free family of color. This book, a pick by Oprah Winfrey for her book club, was based on professional research provided by the genealogist Elizabeth Shown Mills.

- **New hybrids** are beginning to appear which combine historical and genealogical research techniques with other subject areas. An example is *The Jeffersons at Shadwell* by Susan Kern, in which the author tells the story of Thomas Jefferson's parents' household through a combination of uncovering archaeological evidence sifted from around their home's foundation, and evidence found in deeds, tax lists, and probate documents that the couple left behind. The author puts to rest the theory that Peter Jefferson, Thomas' father, was from a lower socioeconomic class than his wife and the other members of their community. In this book, archaeology, family history, and social history collide.

RESOURCES

Bair, Chris. "Using DropBox to Backup and Share your Important Files – or Why I Don't Bother Carrying a Flash Drive Anymore," December 28, 2012, https://familysearch.org/blog/en/share-backup-dropbox/.

Carmack, Sharon DeBartolo. *You Can Write Your Family History*. Cincinnati, OH: Betterway Books, 2003.

MacEntee, Thomas. "Google Docs for Genealogists," August 29, 2011, https://www.youtube.com/watch?v=xAAQ2cMjuZM.

Wright, Raymond S. III. "Writing Family History," in *The Genealogist's Handbook: Modern Methods for Researching Family History*. Chicago and London: American Library Association, 1995.

ONLINE AND DIGITAL RECORDING
OF FAMILY HISTORY

Personal Reflection: Marketing Our Pasts

Many genealogists have had the experience of trying to show information to another family member, and then either the family member's eyes glaze over, or he or she informs them that he or she is suddenly needed elsewhere and disappears. If the information is displayed in the form of a family group sheet or a pedigree chart, is it any wonder? It is very difficult for the average person to see beyond a set of names and dates in order to understand the lives they represent. Or perhaps it is a report generated by Family Tree Maker software, which is a boring and mechanical repetition of the same sentence structures. New and more interesting methods of disseminating our family history research are needed so that the next generation, which wants visual and instantaneous information, will preserve the research, and add to it. Family historians need to market their family histories to their own family members. Fortunately, technology has enabled them to do better than the old formats. They can link photographs, documents, and audio and video footage to text to tell our stories using many free online tools and websites. They can use smartphones to record information from cemeteries. They can record grandparents reminiscing, and then share the footage on YouTube. They can literally show their family histories to their family members, and to the world. —NWM.

ONLINE FAMILY TREES

It is also important to know that there are also many websites where researchers can build a family tree, either by inputting information manually, or, as mentioned earlier, by downloading a GEDCOM file, which is a standard computer file format for genealogical information. Many of these websites are interactive, meaning that others can also add information to them; some are on free websites, and others on subscription websites. A summary of the most popular websites of this type is given in Chapter 5, "The Negotiators: Asking and Answering Questions." However, already new formats for presenting genealogical information will appear that go beyond traditional formats like trees. Computer programmers are working on new ideas such as GeneaQuilts, a Java program which creates a visualization of genealogies of up to 10,000 individuals.[20]

PUBLISHING A FAMILY WEBSITE

Many family historians publish their family histories on a stand-alone website, completely separate from the numerous places to publish family tree information online on both free and subscription-based websites. Here are some examples of well-done family history websites, which can give researchers ideas about the possibilities:

"Family Genealogy: Geary, Jewel, Tucker & Little Families" has virtual photo albums pertaining to the various family lines, scanned and transcribed documents such as Bible records and pension files, and explanations of the research process: http://www.family-genealogy-online.com/.

"A Family Tree: Acree/Sachse/Hoover/Ogden/Skipworth/Nelson/TenEyck/
Williamson & Associated Families" has many unique features such as lists of
ancestors sorted by occupations, dual timelines which juxtapose the families'
migrations with historical events, and a section listing ancestors' burial sites with
photos: http://acreetree.net/default.html.

"Jacob and Anna Maria Schneider's Descendants" presents simple but effective
chronologies of sources for individual family members: http://freepages.genealogy
.rootsweb.ancestry.com/~leshipman/schneider_descendants.html

The "Matacia Family History Site" uses a combination of photographs, scanned
documents, and narrative: http://mataciahistory.wordpress.com/.

Online sources of information are readily available to supply guidance to those
families wishing to launch a family history website. There are two types of software
which can help. Some software programs for recording family history now also allow
one to generate a website, such as RootsMagic 7. Another type of software simply
generates a template for a family history website, such as The Next Generation of
Genealogy Sitebuilding (TNG). Make sure that patrons understand that registering
their website with genealogy directories and popular search engines will increase
their potential audience.

SURNAME PROJECTS

If a researcher does not want to generate and maintain an entire website, then
adding information to another already established website is a possibility. One type
is a website devoted to a surname project, a compilation of information RE a single
surname. Generally, these are devoted to either unique surnames, or a single branch
of a family with a more common surname. For example, see the Miner/Minor
Family website: http://alum.wpi.edu/~p_miner/Miner.html. Some surname
websites are now in a wiki format. For example, see "The Whitney Research
Group," http://wiki.whitneygen.org/wrg/index.php/Main_Page.

FAMILY AND LOCAL HISTORY IN SOCIAL MEDIA

Social media is playing a vital role in the popularization of family and local history. Not only are family websites and blogs important for the writing of family narratives, but also for local history that may contain references to families and persons.
Bernadette Lear's blog on Pennsylvania library history shows the potential of using
an informal forum to record thoughts on primary sources and materials uncovered
in her work. The resulting blog is an interesting combination of personal narrative,
day-to-day incidents during the research process, and reflections on the ideas in the
materials she read during the course of the day:

Friday, January 17, 2014

Are you related to Phoebe Albert, Harriet Bowers, Dorothy Boyer, or Beatrice
Saylor?

I was sorting through miscellaneous documents and photographs at the Dauphin County Library System's McCormick Riverfront location when I found a small blue and yellow scrapbook with the words "County 1936" hand-drawn on the cover. It only measures about 9 inches tall and 6 inches wide and consists of about a dozen leaves. Several pages in, there is a small photograph of a stone building, perhaps a garage or workshop. Above it, penned by a feminine hand, is a brief verse:

> "We were a part of the County
> For eight short weeks or so,
> And we want to leave this record,
> That our achievements you may know."

Subsequent pages consist mainly of statistical tables. They apparently track the daily work of 4 people: Harriet J. Bowers, Beatrice A. Saylor, Phoebe J. Albert, and Dorothy J. Boyer (in order of their appearance). There is a numerical table for each woman, tallying the number of items she "washed" and "mended" for each weekday from June 22nd through August 14th. Over the course of 8 weeks, the team repaired 5331 items.

Bernadette A. Lear, In Search of Pennsylvania Library History, "Are You Related to Phoebe Albert, Harriet Bowers, Dorothy Boyer, or Beatrice Saylor?" (January 17, 2014), http://palibhist.blogspot.com. Reprinted with permission.

This blog entry demonstrates the power of a simple posting in helping family historians make connections to specific places. The entry contained two photos of the women that had been placed in the diary. The blog's author, library historian Bernadette Lear, spent considerable time attempting to find out more about the women's whereabouts and background, using library records and typical resources like the U.S. Census, but the information itself indicated the women may have been in the area only a very short time. Nevertheless, this blog posting could give important clues to family historians.

A wealth of other genealogical blogs is also available, from advice on how to use resources, to detailed narratives of genealogical pursuits, to how to write family history. *Family Tree Magazine* publishes an annual listing of the forty best genealogy blogs. However, accessing blogs for family and contextual community history may prove difficult, as there is no systematic indexing of them. Locating genealogical blogs can be done simply by including "blog" as a search term, but the website called Genealogy Blog Finder indexes over 1700 of them under subheadings, and is found at http://blogfinder.genealogue.com/. Hopefully, the local studies community will begin to link such resources to catalogs and databases in order to provide better retrieval.

In addition to blogs, researchers have discovered ways to post queries, photos, and information via social media. Many researchers have already written blog posts and articles about how this can be done effectively, and this topic is regularly featured at genealogical conferences.

A VISUAL APPROACH

In the past, family history writing was mostly prose only out of necessity. It was simply too expensive to reproduce many pictures, maps, and other illustrations. Digital technology allows researchers to pursue many new highly visual options for recording family history. Many researchers now prefer to reverse that ratio, and express their history mostly in images accompanied by small amounts of explanatory text. Here are some options:

- Post captioned photos on photosharing websites such as deadfred.com, ancientfaces.com, Instagram, and Shutterfly.
- Create a collage of photos, maps, and old documents with captions on Pinterest.
- Document points of interest with descriptive captions on a digital map using Historypin.
- Write a family history digital magazine using Flipboard e-magazine.
- Compile a digital scrapbook. Conventional scrapbooking has been popular for several years, but now family and community historians can create digital scrapbooks.
- Link multiple images to tell a story at storylava.com.
- Make a playlist, meaning a multimedia list of links on one topic, which can include blogs, videos, music, pdf files, podcasts, etc. They can be compiled on the following websites: MentorMob, Learnist, and Edcanvas.
- Produce a family history video using a combination of old photographs, home movie footage, scanned documents, and music. Editing software is available for under $100.00. Some popular ones include CyberLink, PowerDirector 14, Corel Videostudio Pro X6, and Adobe Premiere Elements 14.
- Family history videos that are posted on YouTube can be made public or private, and are starting to proliferate. An example of one that uses the above-mentioned elements plus humor can be found here: http://www.youtube.com/watch?v=maiUJsRtzPU&feature=youtube.

RESOURCES

"Create Your Own Family History Site," http://personalweb.about.com/od/memorials andtributes/a/1familyhistory.htm.

"Digital Scrapbooking 101: Use Your Computer to Create Beautiful Heritage Albums," http://genealogy.about.com/od/heritage_scrapbooking/a/digital.htm, accessed May 21, 2015.

Genealogy Home Page Construction Kit, www.cyndislist.com/constructionkit.pdf.

"Genealogy Web Site Creation," www.cyndislist.com.

"How to Find Genealogy Pages and Groups on Facebook," https://www.youtube.com/watch?v=4VpfnMD7w8w.

Murphy, Nathan W. "Family Tree Magazine's Forty Best Genealogy Blogs in 2013," https://familysearch.org/blog/en/family-tree-magazines-40-genealogy-blogs-2013/.

NGS. "Guidelines for Publishing Web Pages on the Internet," http://www.ngsgenealogy .org/cs/guidelines_for_publishing_web_pages.

OurStory is a website that allows families to record their stories, http://www.ourstory.com/.

Partners In Rhyme Royalty Free Sound Effects and Royalty Free Sound Effects, http://www.partnersinrhyme.com/pir/PIRsfx.shtml, accessed May 21, 2015.

"Sharing Your Family History Using Multimedia," presented at Rootstech 2014 by Michael LeClerc, http://lanyrd.com/2014/rootstech/scwpch/, accessed May 21, 2015.

Smith, Drew. *Social Networking for Genealogists*. Baltimore, MD: Genealogical Publishing Co., 2009.

"Success: Using Facebook Groups for Genealogy," http://youngandsavvygenealogists.blogspot.com/2014/04/success-using-facebook-groups-for.html.

"10 Ways to Use Twitter for Genealogy," http://blog.familytreemagazine.com/insider/2009/06/10/10WaysToUseTwitterForGenealogy.aspx.

"Uses for Facebook in Genealogy," http://cyndislist.blogspot.com/2010/04/uses-for-facebook-in-genealogy.html.

CONCLUSION

From published formal histories of families and towns, to the informal writings and ephemera produced by townspeople and organizations, the value of the information in these works for local and family historians cannot be overlooked. Information providers can make researchers aware of the great variety of print and digital formats that they can use to record their own histories. In the following chapter, another type of traditional history format is examined—the oral history.

PROGRAMMING IDEAS

1. Blogging the Past: Easy Ways to Connect to Family through the Web

This program demonstrates how easy it can be to set up a family history blog. It should be a 1.5 to 2 hour event.

Showing patrons how easy it is to use the blogging and website tools on the Internet is a great way to interact with the public and encourage family and local history work. If any of your local historical societies or libraries use Facebook or other social media sites, then demonstrating those sites is a great way to connect the patron to the web as well.

Be sure to emphasize the importance of writing down family stories, personalities, important service to the military, community, or family that is notable. But also talk about the routine of life such as a "typical" day on the family farm, as a schoolteacher, as a parent of young children at home, etc. This session is intended to provide families a way to easily put down their ideas and to share them. By the end of the evening, they should:

- Understand the term "social media."
- Understand the difference between blogging and making a website.
- Have seen at least one example of a family history blog and one of a website.
- Have a list of sites they could choose from when creating a blog or website.
- Have a list of companies they could contact if they wanted help to create a site.
- Have done some brainstorming about what stories they might want to put in a blog.
- Have some hands-on experience with creating a blog.

To conduct the session, you might start with some examples of blogs and family websites. Small group work with computers to learn how to set up a blog can be useful. Focus on one family story in the group and have the group help one person blog a short entry. Share the stories and blogs postings in a large group.

2. So You Want to Write a History of Your Church? Of a Centennial? Of a Celebration?

This program is designed to help those interested in various local histories to conquer the hurdles to starting a writing project. It would be useful to demonstrate

Figure 2.2
Pinning Down Your Family History

PINNING DOWN YOUR FAMILY HISTORY:

How Pinterest can help you display, organize, and share your family and community history

December 14, 2013
Champaign County Historical Archives

some different types of local historical writing. Have some brainstorming sessions to find out what the participants want to write. Provide additional resources to them to support their goals.

3. Pinning Down Your Family History[21]

This session introduces patrons to the world of Pinterest. See Figure 2.2. There should be some introduction to the basics of Pinterest, such as how to create an account, how to create a pin, and how to annotate it. Show how pins can be both copied from other boards, how they can be created from Internet content, and from digital files stored on a computer. Show examples of other boards that present family history and community history information. This could be especially effective to commemorate a local event, like a sesquicentennial, highlight a local institution, or simply be a compilation of memories and/or reminiscences. An example of a library that did this is the board called "Home Sweet Home—Around Arlington Heights" which is found at https://www.pinterest.com/ahlibrary/home-sweet-home-around-arlington-heights/.

Additional Ideas

- Getting Started with Genealogy: Base a program on how to use a genealogy software program.

- Family History Writing: Host a collaborative family history writing workshop in which participants bring sections of writing projects to share in order to get and give feedback.
- The Grandparent Book: Base a program using a free resource such as this one: "Programming Idea—Creating a Grandparent Book" *The Smithsonian Folklife and Oral History Interviewing Guide,* 35–39, http://www.folklife.si.edu/resources/pdf/interviewingguide.pdf.

NOTES

1. Jerome de Groot, *Consuming History: Historians and Heritage in Contemporary Popular Culture* (New York, NY: Routledge, 2009), 64.

2. See Fall Creek Books, 2015, http://www.cornellpress.cornell.edu/presses/?fa=publisher &NameP=Fall%20Creek%20Books.

3. David E. Kyvig and Myron A. Marty, *Nearby History: Exploring the Past around You,* 3rd ed. (New York, NY: Rowman & Littlefield, 2010), ix–x.

4. RUSA Guidelines for Establishing Local History Collections, 2012, http://www.ala .org/rusa/resources/guidelines/guidelinesestablishing.

5. Other relevant historical professional associations include the American Historical Society (AHA) and the Social Science History Association (SSHA), producing journals and books that demonstrate, instruct, and support the writing and recording of history. These, along with several more organizations related to local history, are listed in Appendix C.

6. Valuable information on the evolution of public history as a field can be found on the website of the National Council on Public History: http://ncph.org/cms/what-is-public -history/.

7. Benjamin Guy Childs, *Centennial History of Trinity Methodist Church* (Durham, NH: Trinity Methodist Church, 1961), 14–17.

8. Presbyterian Historical Society. "How to Write a Congregational History," http:// www.history.pcusa.org/services/resources-opportunities/writing-congregation-histories.

9. *Scheer Kids Cookbook: A Collection of Recipes by the Scheer Kids* (Kearney, NE: Morris Press Cookbooks, 2003): 273.

10. *Scheer Kids Cookbook,* 313.

11. Raymond S. Wright III, *The Genealogist's Handbook: Modern Methods for Researching Family History* (Chicago, IL: American Library Association, 1995), 3.

12. Dr. Duke and colleagues devised a set of twenty questions called the "Do You Know. . .?" scale. Children who had communicated enough about their families and were able to answer the majority of the questions tended to be stable adults. See "Of Ketchup and Kin: Dinnertime Conversations as a Major Source of Family Knowledge, Family Adjustment, and Family Resilience," The Emory Center for Myth and Ritual in American Life Working Paper No. 26, May 2003, http://www.researchgate.net/publication/ 267720308_Of_Ketchup_and_Kin_Dinnertime_Conversations_as_a_Major_Source_of _Family_Knowledge_Family_Adjustment_and_Family_Resilience/links/546efbe50cf2b 5fc17609310.pdf.

13. Gary B. and Elizabeth Shown Mills, "Wizardry with Words," Editors' Corner, *NSGQ* 88, No. 1 (March 2000), 3.

14. "Gifts, Donations and Loans to FamilySearch," https://familysearch.org/sites/default/uploads/Donations-Guidelines-REVISION-12-July-2012.pdf, accessed May 21, 2015.

15. James Sweany, "Write your Family History – and Send it to the Library of Congress!" Library of Congress Blog, January 13, 2014, http://blogs.loc.gov/loc/2014/01/write-your-family-history-and-send-it-to-the-library-of-congress/, accessed May 5, 2015.

16. "Donations," http://www.mymcpl.org/genealogy/donations, accessed May 21, 2015.

17. "Share Your Research," http://www.genealogycenter.org/Donate.aspx, accessed May 21, 2015.

18. Email response from James Sweany to Nicole Wedemeyer Miller, May 21, 2015.

19. Wright, "The Genelogist's Handbook," 130.

20. It is difficult to understand how this works from a written description. It is best to view the demonstration video on YouTube, at https://www.youtube.com/watch?v=gncBzqI7R-Q.

21. A program with this title was sponsored by the Champaign County Historical Archives and presented by practicum student Gina Tangora on December 13, 2013.

Chapter 3

TELL IT: ORAL HISTORY FOR THE TWENTY-FIRST CENTURY

Family historians usually learn quickly that some information cannot be obtained from any other source other than by talking with family members. Family history interviews can be conducted informally or formally, but they are more successful when questions are thought out in advance, and the results are recorded. Likewise, historians have recognized oral history interviews to be a valid method to capture information. Information providers can help both individuals and their institutions to collect, record, and store such information. This chapter explores the evolution of oral history projects in cultural heritage settings, including recent variations in the digital age. It provides programming ideas for oral history projects in a library or other local studies setting.

A BRIEF HISTORY OF ORAL HISTORY

"The planners [of early oral history projects] had a connection with journalism, and saw in the daily obituary columns proof that knowledge valuable to the historian, novelist, sociologist, and economist was daily perishing; memories perishing forever without yielding any part of their riches."

—Allan Nevins[1]

Oral history is a process that has allowed historians and others to collect information from eyewitnesses to history, many of whom would never have recorded it in writing on their own. Oral histories can be valuable sources for family historians because the information can contain many details about daily life, ordinary life. The first significant oral history project in the United States occurred in the 1930s when the Works Progress Administration (WPA) interviewed former slaves, and then transcribed the interviews. Interestingly, the information was not much used by scholars until several decades later, but was eventually recognized to be a treasure trove collected just before it was too late, for many participants in the project were quite old.[2] This valuable information has been digitized, and can be viewed for free on the American Memory website of the Library of Congress. The equipment used to record in that time period was both expensive and cumbersome, which may explain why many oral history projects were not conducted at that time.[3]

About a decade later a former journalist, now professor, named Allan Nevins realized the historical value of spoken interviews, and was able to convince his institution to fund them. In 1948, he founded the Columbia University Oral History Research Office. The initial subjects of these interviews were prominent people in business and government. Nevins was given some funding by the university, but was always scrambling for more funding from private sources. Eventually, as the reputation of the project grew, other universities began to found their own oral history programs.

The oral history movement really gained momentum in the 1960s. By that point, enough people were engaged in recording oral history that the Oral History Association was founded in 1966. And it was not just academics who were recording oral history, because this time period also saw the rise of the Social History movement. History was now being recorded "from the bottom up," i.e., from the point of view of ordinary people, and oral history was seen as an ideal method with which to capture it. Suddenly, everyone's story mattered.

RELATED MOVEMENTS

After the oral history movement was in full swing, the storytelling revival was revving up. Storytelling, the passing on of local information, which is a type of folklore, is also an ancient tradition. A more formally organized revival of that tradition began in the United States in 1973, when the National Storytelling Festival was held in Jonesborough, Tennessee. Soon after that event, the National Association for the Preservation and Perpetuation of Storytelling was founded. After some reorganization and name changes, it has morphed into the National Storytelling Network and the International Storytelling Center. At the same time that storytelling was being validated as an accepted way to record folkways and the oral traditions of individuals and communities, the Social History, Public History, and Microhistory movements were taking hold and all sprung from the idea of history by and for the common person. Organized storytelling events are now common, and they are not just for children. They occur at community festivals, and are sponsored by many types of cultural heritage institutions.

As storytelling and oral history began to be seen as a legitimate source of historical information about communities, a high school English teacher in Georgia had his students interview community members, write up the information, and then publish those stories in a magazine. In the fall of 1966 this magazine, *Foxfire*, which was named after the natural phenomenon of bioluminescent fungi in the Georgia woods, became an instant success, and teachers all across the United States at many different levels of the educational system emulated the model. The issues of the magazine were also published in book form and distributed nationally.

The Connection to Collective Memory

Collective memory is a term often used by historians in conjunction with oral history, i.e., one of the purposes of oral history is to capture collective memory. In simple terms, collective memory is defined as memories shared by a group of people, and then passed from generation to generation. The origin of the term is credited to the French philosopher and sociologist Maurice Halbwachs. He differentiates collective memory from individual memory. Everyone possesses both types of memory[4] and oral interviews can capture both of them.

RESOURCES

Dunaway, David K., and Willa K. Baum, eds. *Oral History: An Interdisciplinary Anthology*, 2nd ed. Walnut Creek, CA: AltaMira Press, 1996.

Mendonca, Adrienn, "Foxfire," last edited by NGE staff August 19, 2013, http://www .georgiaencyclopedia.org/articles/education/foxfire.

Olick, Jeffrey K., et al. *The Collective Memory Reader*. New York, NY: Oxford University Press, 2011.

Radner, Jo. "On the Threshold of Power: The Storytelling Movement Today," *Storytelling, Self, Society* 4, Issue 1, Article 3 (2008). http://digitalcommons.wayne.edu/storytelling/vol4/iss1/3.

Ritchie, Donald A., 3rd ed. *The Oxford Handbook of Oral History*. London and New York: Oxford University Press, 2014.

Shopes, Linda. "Making Sense of Oral History," *History Matters: The U.S. Survey Course on the Web*, http://historymatters.gmu.edu/mse/oral/, February 2002.

ORAL HISTORY AND LOCAL STUDIES COLLECTIONS

"Of course, more oral history doesn't automatically translate to better oral history."
—Clifford Kuhn[5]

Oral History is thriving in the twenty-first century, bolstered by changes in technology. Interviews are now recorded digitally, and can be accessed free via the Internet. They are sponsored by government agencies, colleges and universities, libraries and other cultural heritage institutions, and private foundations. Information providers have claimed a role in oral history field, by not simply cataloging, storing, and preserving it, but also by creating it. Many oral history projects have been shepherded by librarians and archivists, particularly projects on the local level.[6] Also, many teachers of all educational levels have used oral history projects since the late 1960s as a way to engage students in a way that simply having them read a textbook could not. No single profession or group owns local history.

Happily, the demise of the analog era and its endless rows of underutilized oral history tapes has been replaced with a digital renaissance of oral history recording technology. Not only are new projects recorded in such a way as to provide instant, online access, but these technologies are being used to recapture legacy tape collections and can provide new access and uses for them. Oral history recordings created in a digital format are referred to as **born digital,** which distinguishes them from analog ones later converted to a digital format. Many oral history interviews are now also visual, because they are captured on video. Much online information provides guidance on how to go about capturing and storing digital audio files as well as free tools for doing so. Of particular note is a resource "Ask Doug," at the Oral History in the Digital Age website which rates and explains the various recorders and microphones one can use for digital projects, as well as a search feature by price and by the level of quality needed for the project.[7]

The digital format allows institutions to provide free access to oral history interviews directly from their websites, a big improvement in their access. The Sound & Story Project of the Hudson Valley, a nonprofit organization committed to capturing the stories of this New York region, provides a wonderful example of the kind of reformatting and reuse that can occur by applying digital technology to analog oral history collections.[8] Funded in part by a grant from the Institute of Museum and Library, this nonprofit organization undertook the reformatting of hundreds of archival oral history tapes into a new digital format.

The website of this nonprofit organization provides a rich testament to the potential for projects focused in a specific region. See Figure 3.1. Not only have old tapes been reformatted into accessible, digital surrogates, but new recordings are being done on a constant basis by the organization. Innovative projects include a mobile recording "cube" which can be moved to various locations on a temporary basis to collect stories. One can also download an app to geolocate a position and record a story to be submitted to the project. Partners include historical societies, libraries, and museums. An awareness of the potential for oral history can be seen in the innovations of this site. The use of "shorts," excerpts from longer interviews that are available for listening independent of the original recording, makes digital recordings more relevant and useful. A casual browser of the site can locate short recordings on a variety of topics, as well as long digital recordings and transcripts.

Here are more examples of other major current oral history projects:

- The Veterans History Project, at the American Folklife Center, Library of Congress, collects oral history interviews from military and support personnel from all U.S. military conflicts, along with documentation.
- University programs, such as the Southern Oral History Program at the University of North Carolina and the Center for the Study of History and Memory at Indiana University, participate in a variety of projects which strive to interview individuals from all walks of life.
- The Ellis Island Oral History Project, conducted by National Park Service staff, has done over 1700 interviews with immigrants who came through Ellis Island since 1973.
- StoryCorps is a non-profit organization that has collected over 50,000 interviews since 2003.

A few very focused projects include:

- The 9/11 Oral History Project at Columbia University conducts interviews with survivors of and witnesses to the terrorist attack on New York City: http://library.columbia.edu/locations/ccoh.html.
- New York City Taxi Driver Oral History Project conducts interviews with one single occupational worker in one single geographic location: http://taxiscab.com/pages/2760900-new-york-city-taxi-driver-oral-history-project
- The Southern Foodways Alliance is an academic organization that studies "the diverse food cultures of the changing American South." They collect oral histories related to this mission: http://www.southernfoodways.org/our-work/.

Many other oral histories done on a smaller scale can still provide wonderful resources for family and local historians. In order to develop a project, it is good to research what is being done in the area, what resources are available, and potential partners. Below is a list of places to check for educational materials, such as webinars, publications, grant information, and partnerships:

- Federal level:
  - Oral History Association
  - Institute of Museum and Library Services
  - National Endowment for the Humanities
  - Grants.gov

Figure 3.1
Sound & Story Project of the Hudson Valley. Used with Permission from Sound & Story.org.

Home   About   Hire Us   The Cube   Listen to Stories   Get Involved   DIY Audio

Search

Book a 2015 Visit Now

The Cube will be hibernating over the winter,
but will awaken in the spring ready to collect
some more stories. It is not too early to begin
planning and booking a visit.

Last year our dream of collecting stories on location throughout the Hudson Valley became a
reality. The Cube, our mobile recording booth assembles in a couple of hours allowing us to
travel from town to town collecting stories. For more information read our FAQ.

The 2014 Cube season runs from May through October. Our schedule is limited, so be sure to
book early by emailing us at info@soundandstory.org

Click here for more photos.

Click here for the Press Release.

Read our FAQ.

The Cube was custom designed and built by Hugo Martinez at MAT-TER Design + Build Studio.

Initial funding for The Cube was provided by a National
Leadership Grant from the Institute of Museum and Library
Services and administered by the Southeastern NY Library
Resources Council.

- State level:
  - State library (look especially at Library Services and Technology Act, LSTA funding)
  - State archival and museum institutions
  - State-level genealogical societies
- Local level:
  - Library districts
  - Schools
  - Historical societies
  - Archives
  - Museums
  - Civic organizations
  - Churches

- Regional level:
  - ◦ Economic development organizations
  - ◦ Planning organizations
  - ◦ Historic preservation sites

CURRENT BEST PRACTICES

Because of the labor intensive nature of oral history projects, they are usually organized by a committee, not an individual, and are often cosponsored and run by more than one institution. Willa Baum, a long-time oral historian wrote an article called "The Expanding Role of the Librarian in Oral History," which was based on a lecture she had delivered two years before to library school students at Louisiana State University. It was published in 1978, but the advice it contains is timeless. Here is a summary of what Baum says is how a librarian can support such projects:

- provide how-to oral history materials
- provide background information on localities, persons, and subjects to be covered in the interviews
- provide a release form which donates the interviews to the library
- devise procedures to describe the recordings
- build a showcase program around the project, whereby participants are honored, and a small selection of the interviews are shared[9]

Lathrop suggests that an abstract be created consisting of a short paragraph which describes the *who, what, where,* and *when* of the interview. This information can be used as the basis for any cataloging of the interview. In addition, an index can be created of all the interviews in the project. Finally, an invaluable aid to researchers is to transcribe them, which is fairly labor intensive. However, research indicates that if given a choice between listening to the interview itself, or reading the transcript, most researchers choose the latter.[10]

Increasingly, it is useful to create indexing terms throughout the interview. Such technology is available in digital software for oral histories. In this way a researcher may go directly to the mention of a relative, since that person's name is entered and correlated to a specific point in the recording. At the Louie B. Nunn Center for Oral History at the University of Kentucky, several major innovations are being developed to create indexes for oral histories that are faster than transcribing and provide subject access. Doug Boyd, lead in a team to develop oral history technologies, notes, "The Oral History Metadata Synchronizer (OHMS), a web-based system, provides users with word-level search capability and a time-correlated transcript or index, connecting the textual search term to the corresponding moment in the recorded interview online."[11] The cost of indexing an interview is far less than that of transcribing (Boyd estimated $30 for a one-hour interview index, versus $200 per hour for a transcript).[12] OHMS is an open-source program, free to download and modify, though, for smaller institutions without tech support teams, it likely would be best to look for an integrated setting, such as OHMS with CONTENTdm. As developers continue work on the program, it is intended to become a user-friendly, low-cost program available to small institutions, as well as large institutions, for their oral history projects.[13]

Traditionally, oral history projects operated with a couple of legal forms. One form would give permission to tape an interview, while the other donated the interview to the institutions. Here are examples of those types of forms:

> Consent Forms, http://www.indiana.edu/~cshm/informed_consent.pdf
>
> Deed of Gift Form, http://www.indiana.edu/~cshm/deed_of_gift.pdf

More recently, particularly considering the digital implications of gifting an interview, the argument for using a Creative Commons license to retain copyright for the interviewee is advocated. In a Creative Commons license, specific uses of the interview, including free redistribution of the material, is named, while copyright is retained by the interviewee.[14] It would be wise to consult a variety of potential guides for oral history projects to select a model agreement that best reflects the needs of the institutions involved in the project. Certainly some form of documentation with the signature of the narrator should be obtained, even in very small and informal settings. Without such a release, the institution is very limited in how it can use the information in the interview. The recent guide by John A. Neuenschwander, *A Guide to Oral History and the Law,* provides detailed information such as copyright release models and Creative Commons licenses.

DEALING WITH OLDER FORMATS

Maybe your institution will not create oral history, but already houses it. There is additional information to understand about the storage and curation requirements of the older formats. The original format of oral history recordings was reel to reel tapes, and then cassette tapes. Because decades have elapsed since oral history interviews were first recorded, and this format has a life expectancy of about ten to thirty years, many of them have deteriorated significantly, some beyond the point of salvage. It is very important to plan for the long-term storage of oral history recordings, whether they are being stored by an institution, or by an individual. A planned transfer of the information from an aging format to a new one is a logistical and budgetary necessity. This process, called "migration," should be a part of the organization's workflow.

First, decide if the collection still falls within the current collection directives of the institution. Like any resource, if it is determined that an oral history collection falls completely outside the collection purview, then an appropriate home should be identified and the item deacquisitioned. If the collection will be retained, then the next step is to assess it. What is the physical condition of the tapes? Is there any visible deterioration or damage? Has there been a partial migration of the information or on-demand digitization of individual items?

Then examine the documentation of the collection. Early oral history projects may or may not have had good documentation such as a description of the project's background, release forms that specified permitted uses of the recordings, and transcriptions. If this information is sparse or lacking, is it possible to augment it retrospectively?

The final concern is access. Oral history projects often could contain hundreds of hours of tape, with individual interviews lasting a wide span of time. From the perspective of an archivist or historian, the goal of preserving memory was perhaps achieved by such a project; however, the separate goal of access was less successful. An entire collection might have a MARC record in a library or a single entry in a historical society database. Even if a researcher was interested in a time period or theme, the prospect of listening to dozens, perhaps hundreds or hours of tape significantly lowered the potential for use over sources that could be quickly scanned or that had more full description.

TO-DO CHECKLIST

- Take an inventory of all oral and audiovisual history recordings held by the institution.
- Do a preservation audit of the collections.
- For future workflow, create a schedule by which the oral history collections will be checked for condition.
- Include in the workflow a schedule for how often and when the items will be migrated.
- Create a strategic plan for the collection, including assessment of needed transcripts, indexing, or cataloging (see Chapter 6 for more on access).
- Investigate the possibility of grant funding to undertake these projects.

Personal Reflection: Information Lost

While doing genealogical research on my family several years ago, I plugged several of my surnames into the search engine of the public library website, which has prepared finding aids to several of its archival collections, and these names are included in the website search. I got a hit which indicated that one of my family members, a first cousin thrice removed, had recorded an oral history interview many years before, and a copy was available at the library. Excitement seized me. I had never even met anyone from this branch of the family, and yet some of its stories had been preserved!

This interview is one of dozens that is part of a project that had been initiated by a local history group. The program began in 1972, but tapes have been added to it sporadically since that time. Although other interviews in the collection had been dated and/or transcribed, the interview in which I was interested had not been.. Because the project began in 1972, and the interviewee died in 1985, that was the range of years in which it must have been recorded. That meant that the tape was 25 or more years old. It turned out to be easier to obtain a copy from the state museum than from the public library. I called the archivist who explained that they had just recently copied the tapes in a digital format, and for a fee, she could burn a copy onto a disc and mail it.

When it arrived, the interview was almost unintelligible. The degradation of the tape caused there to be lots of hissing sounds in the background. The conditions under which the interview was recorded also contributed problems. The interviewer was the daughter of the interviewee.

She conducted the interview in her mother's apartment on a busy thoroughfare, and apparently the windows were open, because traffic sounds intruded several times, including the sounds of a passing ambulance. Another hindrance was the tendency of the mother and daughter to talk at the same time. I could only make out short phrases from time to time—tantalizing hints of the stories that were just out of my grasp!

I am lucky enough to be friends with a professor of electro-acoustic music. I brought my "sad" CD over to him, and asked if he could help clean up the background noise. He tried, but could only remove a small portion of it. My friend explained that the degradation of the original tape was simply too far advanced to be able to remove all the problems from the digital copy.

Needless to say, I did not give up! With repeated listening, and comparing the phrases I was able to glean with those from a written reminiscence produced by an older sibling of the interviewee, I was able to produce a partial transcription. But the lesson is very clear for the guardians of oral history collections: this is not the type of item that you can shelve and forget about indefinitely. Both analog and digital media have definite lifespans. The cassette tape that my cousin used could have lasted anywhere from ten to thirty years, depending on storage conditions and the quality of the tape. It did, which meant that waiting twenty years or more to migrate to a different format was too long, and precious information was lost. NWM

RESOURCES

Boyd, Douglas A. "Designing an Oral History Project: Initial Questions to Ask Yourself," in *Oral History in the Digital Age*, edited by Doug Boyd, Steve Cohen, Brad Rakerd, and Dean Rehberger, Washington, DC: Institute of Museum and Library Services, 2012, http://ohda.matrix.msu.edu/2012/06/designing-an-oral-history-project/. This article links to a multitude of others on various aspects of this topic.

Digital Imaging. "General Resources," http://cool.conservation-us.org/bytopic/imaging/.

Institute for Oral History, Baylor University, *Report: Archiving Digital Oral History*, AASLH, 2011, http://download.aaslh.org/AASLH-Website-Resources/Archiving _Digital_Oral_History.pdf.

MacKay, Nancy, et al. *Community Oral History Toolkit*. Walnut Creek, CA: Left Coast Press, 2013.

Neuenschwander, John A. *A Guide to Oral History and the Law*, 2nd ed. Oxford, UK: Oxford University Press, 2014.

Oral History Metadata Sychronizer (OHMS), http://nunncenter.org/ohms-enhancing -oral-history-online/.

"Principles and Best Practices | Oral History Association." http://www.oralhistory.org/ about/principles-and-practices/, accessed October 10, 2014.

Ritchie, Donald A. *Doing Oral History*, 3rd ed. Oxford, UK: Oxford University Press, 2014.

Sommer, Barbara W., and Mary Kay Quinlan. *The Oral History Manual*. Lanham, MD: Rowman & Littlefield, 2009.

StoryCenter, http://storycenter.org/. This organization offers workshops and webinars to educators, cultural heritage collaborators, and others.

"Suggestions for Digital Equipment Suitable for Oral Historians," Giving Voice to the Past, accessed May 26, 2015, http://www.oralhistorynsw.org.au/some-suggestions-for -digital-equipment-suitable-for-use-by-oral-historians.html.

Vitale, Tim, and Paul Messier. Video Preservation Website, updated April 19, 2013, http:// videopreservation.conservation-us.org/.

HELPING FAMILIES TO CREATE ORAL HISTORIES

Like institutions, individuals can conduct and record their own oral history interviews in order to capture information about their families that will not be available from any other sources. They work particularly well in the following circumstances:

- the subject does not have much education, or is unwilling to write down information
- the subject is elderly, and/or enjoys reminiscing about the past
- a pair or small group of family members would be willing to talk about specific topics while being recorded—sometimes they are able to jog each others' memories

There are many sources of information on how to conduct oral history interviews. A very brief summary of this process is presented below.

CHOOSING THE SUBJECT

Personality plays a role here. The subject must be willing to talk. Naturally taciturn individuals may not produce very good interviews. It is worth tracking down distant relatives because they often have a different perspective on family members or events from other relatives who may be more closely related. Another useful approach is to record several family members individually discussing the same event. The results will reveal a sort of consensus on the details of that event, but also may reveal intriguingly different perspectives.

PLANNING

Schedule the interview well in advance if possible, in a location that is private, quiet, and convenient for the interviewee. If someone can assist the interviewer by managing the recording device, that is helpful. It is preferable to schedule a few short sessions, rather than one marathon session, that way the subject is not too taxed. Also, the time between sessions often helps jog the subject's memory. Get the written consent of the interviewee if the information is to be shared with others.

RESEARCH

It takes information to get information so it is important to find out basic facts of the subject's life ahead of time, and to have them written down for quick reference. An overview of the subject's important life events, such as birth, marriage, education, and at least some of the places he or she lived, is very helpful to know, and will help the interviewer to structure questions in advance. Knowing the context of the person's life, some historical background of the times and places in which they lived is important to help the subject overcome memory lapses during the course of the interview.

THE INTERVIEW PROCESS

The list of questions should be worked out ahead of time, however good followup questions to comments that the interviewee makes that are not necessarily on the preplanned questions list. Part of the interview must unfold organically. It can be effective to ask the same question more than once, especially if the answer the first time was "I don't remember." Many such lists of family history sample questions are available online, such as the one at: http://oralhistory.library.ucla.edu/familyHistory.html.

EQUIPMENT

Handheld digital recorders range greatly in price, but the most expensive ones are not necessary. The most important features include a removable memory card, the ability to connect to a computer to transfer audio files, the ability to record in multiple audio file formats, and built-in noise filtering software. It is important to test the equipment and practice with it before the actual interview. Other helpful items to have on hand are extra memory cards, paper and pen or electronic device for taking notes, water, and tissues.

POSTINTERVIEW PROCEDURES

- Make sure that a written statement that lists the basic facts about the interview such as who was involved, when and where it was recorded, etc. is stored with the recording.
- Try to check the "facts" reported by a subject in an interview; people's memories can be unreliable.
- Transcribe the interview soon afterwards, if one is desired. There is now software that helps with this task, and it is free. Please see the resources list.

SHARING THE INFORMATION

Researchers may simply want to use the information gained from interviews to help them understand where to start their research, or to augment what they have already found. But some may want to share the interviews with others, and there are many options for doing so:

- Upload on FamilyTree at www.familysearch.org, a website that allows one to link audio files to family tree information.
- Email the digital file of the interview to others in the family using a Dropbox account.
- Attach the recording to a family website—if the subject of the interview is still alive, either make this closed access, or get permission to post in a public site.
- Create a playlist of several interviews that can be shared.

THE ROLE OF FAMILY LORE

Certainly oral history interviews can be a wonderful way to capture information that families pass aurally, i.e., family lore. Most families have a core of information that is rarely written down but instead is told and retold through several generations. Because the information has been transferred many times, each teller often adds embellishments and details can be misunderstood, misremembered, and misplaced, just as in the childhood game of telephone. A statement is whispered into another's ear, who then whispers it into his or her neighbor's ear, and so on, all around a circle. After the last person in the circle hears the sentence, he or she repeats it. It usually sounds nonsensical. Then the first person is asked what the original statement was, usually bearing little resemblance to the end statement, and the whole group bursts out laughing. Such are the dangers of transmitting family lore aurally within families. Usually there is some kernel of truth left in these stories, but they must be carefully evaluated, and the details cross-compared with written documentation, if possible, to try to evaluate their accuracy.

Although an oral history interview is an effective way to capture families' oral traditions, researchers should be reminded that these stories should not automatically be accepted at face value. Here are a few examples of distortions that occur. Many families pass along lore that states that three brothers came over from the old country to settle in the United States, not one, not five, but three. Why three? Maybe because of all the threes which are found in literature from the three musketeers to the three bears. And there are usually no sisters included in this statement. Why? Sisters are much harder to track as they marry and change their names. But in reality, the actual number of family members who came over often turns out to be different from the three that were reported in the family lore.

Another example is the Indian Princess legend. Many families are convinced that they have Native American ancestry, and not just run-of-the-mill Native American ancestry, but royal descent. Somehow it is never from a Native American male. In a similar vein, author Herbert Asbury wryly comments that many in New Orleans claim descent from the casket girls, girls of good family who were sent to provide wives for the French soldiers and bureaucrats in the city, but that no one appears to be descended from the female prostitutes and pickpockets who were swept off the streets of Paris and sent there.[15] Apparently, both family lore and collective memory can be selective!

THE INFORMAL OR IMPROMPTU INTERVIEW

The proliferation of technology in our everyday lives means that there is a greater array of tools with which stories can be recorded. If patrons find the idea of planning a formal taping of a sit-down interview daunting, they could try something much quicker and impromptu. Simply have them use their smartphone in order to capture a quick reminiscence at the dinner table. Or have them Skype an interview with a long distance relative, the results of which can be digitally preserved. There are also apps that can help. One example is called StoryPress, and it can be used on an iPad to capture family stories on the go, http://www.fastcoexist.com/1682277/an-app -to-capture-your-grandma-s-life-story. Think how precious even those brief attempts to get a relative talking, and capturing what they have to say, will be when they are not around anymore. Some online trees such as Family Tree at FamilySearch allow genealogists to attach audio and photographs, and there are a number of websites that allow the sharing of such material with varying levels of privacy.

USING AN ESTABLISHED ORAL HISTORY PROGRAM

Some researchers may find the challenge of organizing equipment, research, and travelling to their family members to be difficult. They might want to use an established program to record individuals in their families. One example is StoryCorps, http://storycorps.org/, a nonprofit organization founded in 2003 with the goal of recording as many stories of ordinary people as possible. The organization owns special trailers that it sends around the country in order to record interviews. Two copies of each interview are burned on a CD; one goes to the Library of Congress while the other goes home with the interviewee. The interviews can be scheduled through their 800 telephone number, or through their online reservations page. Another possibility is to download their free app in order to record a "Do-it-yourself" interview, which is available from the Apple App Store, or from Google Play.

Another example is Memoro: The Bank of Memories, also a nonprofit organization that aims to collect the memories of individuals, schools, companies, and other organizations by archiving recorded interviews and photographs. It focuses on individuals born before 1950. The archived recordings can all be accessed through their website, http://www.memoro.org/us-en/servizi.php.

The Social Voice Project is another nonprofit that collects recorded stories, and they use The Internet Archive to store the files. They collect the recordings as part of several initiatives that they conduct including the Veterans Voices Initiative, the Public Safety Initiative, the Senior Citizens Initiative, the Family Initiative, and the Grassroots Activism Initiative. Information is found at http://thesocialvoice project.blogspot.com/p/whats-your-story.html.

Personal Reflection: Capturing Immigrant Stories

Twenty years ago in my early days of teaching history, I saw first-hand the power of oral tradition in new immigrant populations. I was at a small college teaching an Asian history course. One of the participants in the class was a Hmong woman, the first female in her family to attend college. Hmong immigrants to the United States at that time often had a difficult transition from a tumultuous past, sometimes from years of living in internment camps in Laos, to a highly industrialized, literate culture. In addition, they often were relocated in groups to very urban areas away from the east and west coasts. For this young woman, the first woman in her family allowed to attend college, life was full of a variety of cultural realities. During the class, she very graciously invited me to a family funeral, where I sat with another history professor for over an hour listening to traditional gongs and drums, watching the comings and goings at an elaborate altar, lined with gift offerings of food and other items around large photographs of the deceased.

We became increasingly perplexed, as we did not see any bodies for the three persons the ceremony honored. It turned out this was a ritual to send the spirits to the afterlife and that the physical burials had already occurred. The difficulties of conducting a traditional three or more day ceremony had forced a transition away from what would have the norm in Laos. Unlike most funerals I have attended, there was no scripted aspect of the ceremony: no reading, no hymns, and no sermon. Hmong culture relied instead upon oral traditions, with the rituals in the ceremony clearly symbolizing cultural beliefs, such as filial piety (familial respect), seen particularly of the women in the family to these deceased older women.

I knew that my student was trying to communicate something to me as she patiently answered our questions and pointed out that one of her relatives must spend twenty-four hours at the altar to demonstrate her respect. Perhaps, it was just helping me to understand the depth of her culture and its transitions into an immigrant environment. Perhaps, she wanted me to know how much was demanded of her by the traditional family norms, while she was struggling to become a very different Asian woman in the United States. Perhaps, she just wanted to share.

I was incredibly honored and humbled by that experience. There is no substitute for the pageantry of cultural rituals and seeing such a personal Hmong ritual for the first time made a deep impression on me. I hope that this young woman made a successful entry into her new culture, while still holding on to her native past. On that day, her culture was displayed in the music and symbolism of the ritual and altar more clearly than any written description could have conveyed. —RLC.

RESOURCES

The American Folklife Center, Library of Congress. "Oral History Interviews," http://www
.loc.gov/folklife/familyfolklife/oralhistory.html#planning.

Audacity is free, open source, cross-platform software for recording and editing sounds,
http://web.audacityteam.org/.

"Online Resources for Learning About Creating Oral Histories," October 16, 2012, https://
familysearch.org/blog/en/online-resources-learning-creating-oral-histories/.

Powers, Willow Roberts. *Transcription Techniques for the Spoken Word*. Lanham, MD:
AltaMira Press, 2005.

Smithsonian Center for Folklife and Cultural Heritage. "The Smithsonian Folklife and
Oral History Interviewing Guide-Introduction," accessed October 10, 2014, http://
www.folklife.si.edu/education_exhibits/resources/guide/introduction.aspx.

Tanner, James. "Understanding and Buying Digital Voice Recorders," June 28, 2013,
https://familysearch.org/blog/en/understanding-buying-digital-voice-recorders/.

"Top 10 Free Transcription Software That Are Essential To Your VA or Transcription
Business," January 31, 2013, http://www.vagueware.com/top-10-free-transcription
-software-that-are-essential-to-your-va-or-transcription-business/.

Williams, Michael M. *Researching Local History: The Human Journey*. New York, NY:
Routledge, 2014.

CONCLUSION

The value of oral history information for families and communities should not be underestimated, and digital technology is improving the ease of collection of and access to oral history interviews. Information providers can assist both individual researchers and community groups to record and collect them. This can be accomplished in a variety of ways, from impromptu stories captured on a mobile device, using the facilities of an organization like StoryCorps, or planned, formal interviews that are videotaped. In the next chapter, ideas will be presented for helping patrons with sorting, organizing, and storing their personal documents.

PROGRAMMING IDEAS

1. Engaging Teens: "The Ingredients of Me"

This is an introduction to genealogy aimed at a teen audience. It should be a 45 minutes to a 1 hour event.

Teens are an almost untapped group when it comes to family history services, yet if presented to them in a correct way, they can be drawn into the fascinating task of documenting their family histories. The term "genealogy" should not be used to describe this process. Explain to teens that they are recording their life stories, but that they need to put them in the context of the people who contributed to making them who they are. Their ancestors are the ingredients of their lives.

How will teens be most excited to record their stories? Certainly not by filling out family group sheets! Instead encourage them to record videos that they could post on YouTube, accessible to a private group of their family members. The program leaders will show them how to use home sources, including photos, and more documents found online, along with other visuals such as maps, pictures of geographic locations, ships, etc. with which they could put it together.

They can use PowerPoint or another presentation software, and then add narration and even music. This occurs in two sessions: one to teach them how to find the sources. Then they work on it independently at home, and then a second session in which they share the results with the group at a wrap-up party.

2. LC's Veterans Project: Men and Women in Blue, Green, and Camouflage

The Library of Congress has a division called the American Folklife Center which started an ongoing oral history project in 2000 that attempts to capture the reminiscences of Americans who served in the armed forces, and it is called the Veterans History Project (VHP). Individuals or organized groups can submit taped interviews, either in audio or video formats. Supporting documentation is also accepted, such as old letters, maps, and photographs. There are guidelines which can be accessed at the project's website at http://www.loc.gov/search? new=true&q=Veterans+History+Project. Some of the finished interviews are able to be viewed from the website, but others must be accessed in person from the Library of Congress.

A variety of different groups have participated, such as high school students, grades 10–12, organized by their teachers, community groups under leadership from the local library, Boy Scout troops, and more. Sometimes more than one group in a community is working on recording interviews independently. For example, in Champaign, Illinois, one group was headed by teacher Marian Kuethe Wyatt at Centennial High School, but additional interviews were submitted by the local PBS station. Comparing notes with any other local groups who participate would help to prevent any overlap.

The scope of a project aimed at submitting material to the Veterans History Project can vary in size from a single interview to dozens. Decisions like this, and many others will need to be thought through in advance. Here is a suggested planning list:

- How many individuals will be involved in producing the interviews?
- How many veterans will be interviewed?
- Where/by what means will veterans be approached?
- In what quiet, private space, possibly needing to be handicapped accessible, will the interviews be conducted?
- Who will complete the paperwork that needs to accompany the taped interviews?
- Who will schedule the interviews?
- Who will investigate what equipment needs to be borrowed/purchased?
- Who will edit the tapes, and create copies? (One set for the Library of Congress and another to give a copy of the interview to the veteran.)
- Who will handle the publicity needed to attract veterans, and the publicity to announce that the project has been completed?
- Will participating organizations absorb the costs, or will grant funding be sought?
- Where to send the interviews?

Additional Ideas

- Interviews which capture information about a significant event in the community, such as a weather-related disaster, the winning of a championship by a local team, or a special milestone anniversary such as a bicentennial.
- Interviews which capture information about a group within the community, whether that is an ethnic, neighborhood, religious, or social group.
- Interviews that can be put in a time capsule inside a new building to capture what the community is like now.

NOTES

1. Allan Nevins, "Oral History: How and Why It Was Born," *Oral History an Interdisciplinary Anthology*, 2nd ed. David K. Dunaway and Willa K. Baum, eds. (Lanham, MD: AltaMira Press, 1996), 31.

2. Linda Shopes, "Making Sense of Oral History," *History Matters: The U.S. Survey Course on the Web*, http://historymatters.gmu.edu/mse/oral/, February 2002, accessed March 3, 2015.

3. "Celebrating New Deal Arts and Culture, 80 Years since the Crash!" http://www.indiana.edu/~libsalc/newdeal/FMP.html, accessed February 18, 2015.

4. Maurice Halbwachs, *On Collective Memory* (Chicago, IL: University of Chicago Press, 1992).

5. Clifford Kuhn, "The Digitization and Democratization of Oral History," *Perspectives on History: the Newsmagazine of the American Historical Association*, November 2013, https://historians.org/publications-and-directories/perspectives-on-history/november -2013/the-digitization-and-democratization-of-oral-history, accessed May 25, 2015.

6. Willa K. Baum, "The Expanding Role of the Librarian in Oral History," *Oral History: An Interdisciplinary Anthology*, 2nd ed., David K. Dunaway and Willa K. Baum, eds. (Lanham, MD: AltaMira Press, 1996), 322.

7. http://ohda.matrix.msu.edu/2013/06/the-oral-history-review/.

8. http://www.soundandstory.org/.

9. Baum, "Expanding Role," 332–334.

10. Suellyn Lathrop, "Steps in Preserving Oral Histories," *Preserving Local Writers, Genealogy, Photographs, Newspapers, and Related Materials*, Carol Smallwood and Elaine Williams, eds. (Lanham, MD: Scarecrow Press, Inc., 2012), 278.

11. Doug Boyd, "OHMS: Enhancing Access to Oral History for Free," *Oral History Review* 40, 1 (2013): 95, doi: 10.1093/ohr/oht031.

12. Boyd, "OHMS," 99.

13. University of Kentucky Libraries, Louie B. Nunn Center for Oral History, http://www.oralhistoryonline.org/.

14. See the Creative Commons website for more details: https://creativecommons.org/.

15. Herbert Asbury, *The French Quarter: An Informal History of the New Orleans Underworld* (New York, NY: Thunder's Mouth Press, 2003), 13.

Chapter 4

SORT IT: ASSESSING AND STORING HOME SOURCES

Home sources, personal documents, photographs, and other heirlooms are an important source of information for family history research. A rapidly graying population has meant that many, family historians and nonfamily historians alike, are faced with the task of either downsizing their home sources and other possessions drastically, or dealing with a household filled with such items after a relative dies. Either scenario can be difficult, particularly if an individual retained significant amounts of documentation and possessions from prior generations. Librarians and others can assist with the process of sorting through home sources by providing crucial information, such as a system for evaluating the paper trail, information on the identification and valuation of heirlooms, places to donate items, and information on scanning which helps families to store, share, and disseminate their information.

THE SORTING SYSTEM

In earlier days, people did not generate many documents in a lifetime. However, that has not been the case in the twentieth and twenty-first centuries! Even an average person may have generated several cubic feet of documents, not including his or her collection of personal photographs. Therefore, the task of sorting through the accumulation of a lifetime can be overwhelming. But even large tasks are more manageable when broken down into chunks. The basic plan is to:

- Sort documents by type, and separate out all photographs. Information on sorting and analyzing photographs will be given in Chapter 5, "Picture It: Gathering, Analyzing and Storing Family Photographs."
- Evaluate nonpaper objects and separate the heirloom artifacts from the other more ordinary household ones.
- Decide which items will be retained and by whom, which will be discarded, and which will be donated.

What documents to keep from a financial and legal point of view is going to depend on individual circumstances, and more information on that topic will be found in the resources section. One ironclad rule is not to discard any documents that contain a social security number or other private information of a living person without first shredding them. What to keep from a genealogical standpoint is a different issue. Documents fall into several major categories, and more examples of document types that fall within these categories will be found on the "Family and Home Information Sources Checklist" at http://www.byub.org/ancestors/charts/oldpdf/checklist1.pdf. It could be argued that virtually any scrap of paper related to an individual has genealogical value. However, the list below is arranged in three groups. The first group lists items that unquestionably have genealogical value. The second group are items that are not quite as valuable genealogically. The third group are items that do not need to be retained for genealogical purposes.

Tier 1: Greatest Importance Genealogically
vital records such as birth, marriage, and death certificates, divorce decrees and adoption papers

citizenship papers

passports

military papers

religious documents and publications such as the Bible, Torah, and Koran

estate planning papers such as wills and trust documents

deeds and other important contracts

educational information

employment records

health records

household inventory/documentation of possessions for insurance purposes

personal correspondence, address books, and diaries

documents of prior generations

genealogical research

Tier 2: Less Important Genealogically

financial papers, such as tax returns, mortgage papers, and bank records

insurance policies

bonds and stock certificates

titles to automobiles

bills and receipts

Tier 3: Genealogically Insignificant

credit card information

appliance manuals and warranties

papers relating to home maintenance

As the documents are sorted, they should be culled for condition. See figure 4.1. Unfortunately, storage conditions are often less than ideal, and old papers may have been wet or infested with insects. If that is the case, wear a mask and nitrile gloves, and work in a well ventilated area. Protect your work surface with an old sheet if it is not washable. Separate moldy/mildewed items from the rest of the items. Discard any materials that are in such poor condition that they are not readable and cannot be salvaged. Some items may have been only damaged, but restoration is possible. A conservation specialist could be consulted, and is located by contacting the American Institute for Conservation of Historic and Artistic Works (AIC).

Most of the above categories will be comprised of loose documents, but other types of documentation found in the household will also need to be dealt with. Framed documents should be examined to see if they are archivally sound. That means that they have been matted and backed with archival quality and acid-free materials, and that the glass is coated to guard against ultraviolet damage. Most framing will not be of this sort, and so the document should be removed from the frame if possible. Published works such as yearbooks and company directories should be checked for information on family members. Some of these may have been digitized and are available online. Others are not, so patrons should consider selective scanning and then donation, because many institutions have trouble replacing mutilated or stolen copies of yearbooks. Also the pages of all books in the household should be checked for old letters, photos, and documents that may have been stored inside. Check the hard drives of computers for digitized photos, documents, and other information to be preserved. Even more documents might be stored in a safety deposit box at a bank.

Assistance with sorting household items is available from a variety of professionals. There are professional organizers, some specializing in photographs, estate liquidators, auction services, and packers/movers. Professional genealogists might help with extracting family information from documents and recording it in various formats, as well as placing documents and photographs in appropriate institutions. Information on seeking valuations and appraisals will be given below. After all documents and personal information has been gathered and sorted, decisions with other family members must be made regarding what will be preserved, and how it will be preserved.

KEEP OR TOSS? FAMILY OBJECT VALUE AND USES

Whether or not a family object holds monetary value, its worth to the individual or to the family may be significant. Library and archival advice on family objects also focuses on how to preserve them. The Library of Congress provides a web page on "Family Treasures" that draws on basic principles from the preservation field. It discusses optimal storage conditions for family items, emergency preparedness, and also what materials to use to make a family time capsule in order to ensure longevity of the materials the family desires to preserve for future generations.[1] Recommended long-term formats for a variety of physical and digital items, such as prints, still photographs, books, web pages, text files, and databases also are provided. Please refer to the resources lists in this chapter for more information on preservation of objects, documents, and photographs.

Figure 4.1
This Collection of Documents, Photographs, and Genealogical Research Papers is Awaiting Further Sorting.

Often the decision to keep and preserve family items is clear-cut, but not always. The item may not have enough monetary or sentimental value, or historical significance, to warrant saving. It may be in such poor condition that salvaging it is impossible. Donating and or disposing of family objects are valid decisions under certain conditions, although it may be hard for patrons to bring themselves to this conclusion. Specific information on donation will be provided later in this chapter.

Personal Reflection: Coming to Terms with Dad's Cedar Chest

Two of the items I chose to keep after my father's death were his tool box and a cedar chest he made in high school. Both were large, heavy items, and rather unwieldy considering my frequent moves. Both currently sit in my family's garage, taking up valuable real estate. I have very sentimental attachments to the tool box. It is a wooden U.S. Army Corps of Engineer's carpenter's box, complete with the original diagram of contents on the inside lid. It is full of all sorts of smells and visual reminders of time spent with my dad and of the stories he told about the box. It was given to him by a person who played an important mentoring, father-figure role in his teen years. Emotionally, I don't see how I could part with the box, so I need to focus on making sure the rusting supports are cared for and that that is it stored in a clean, dry place. This means I have made the conscious decision that that preservation of the original family item is a priority and is worth the time, effort, and cost it will take to maintain it.

The cedar chest is another matter. It was a high school project, made by my father and valued by my family for that reason. I took the chest because no one else would, although no one wanted to see it thrown away, but it had been damaged by frequent moves. The chest is just too large to be useful for most of today's households, but it was a part of our family's upbringing. It provided storage and was a piece of furniture in every house we lived in growing up. The chest could be repaired, but I've decided to take photos of it and document the item by writing down family memories of it. Then I will either find someone in the family who wants to keep the box or give it to a good home. This way, the memory that was important enough to warrant keeping the large beast of a box for years will be preserved and documented, while passing the story of it to each heir.

Sometimes family items that are broken are now "upcycled" or modified, which would not be an appropriate solution in an institution, like an archive. But this can be a useful family solution and certainly is better than storing the box in conditions that eventually destroy it, so no one can enjoy the artifact or the memory. The "limbo" of unmonitored storage, particularly for textiles, wood, and paper-based products, eventually will make a family's decision for them, as the items disintegrate in hostile attic or basement environments. Understandably, making a decision can be difficult ("Someone might want this down the road."). This is why many family attics are stuffed full of family objects. We cannot bear to make decisions about them, but, in the end, doing so may help to bring resolution and preservation, even if the decision is to sell, give away, or repurpose an item. Making decisions about what to keep also provides space, mental clarity, and resources to focus on those items that warrant family preservation. —RLC.

RESOURCES

Codina, Martin. *Liquidating an Estate: How to Sell a Lifetime of Stuff, Make Some Cash, and Live to Tell About It.* Iola, WI: Krause Publications, 2013.

Cooke, Lisa Louise. "What to Keep When Cleaning out a Relative's Home." Lisa Louise Cooke's Genealogy Gems (blog), June 14. 2014, http://lisalouisecooke.com/tag/home-sources/.

Greene, Kelly. "The Pearls Are Mine!" *The Wall Street Journal*, February 4, 2012, http://www.wsj.com/articles/SB10001424052970203920204577195292564700600.

Hall, Julie. *How to Clean Out Your Parent's Estate in 30 Days or Less: A Solutions-Based Guide to Emptying the Home Without Losing Your Mind*. Charlotte, NC: Estate Lady Publications, 2011.

Hall, Julie. *How to Divide Your Family's Estate and Heirlooms Peacefully and Sensibly: A No-Nonsense, Solutions-Based Guide for Equitable Distribution*. Charlotte, NC: Estate Lady Publications, 2010.

Rinker, Harry L. *Sell, Keep, or Toss?: How to Downsize a Home, Settle an Estate, and Appraise Personal Property*. New York, NY: House of Collectibles, 2007.

WHAT IS THIS AND WHAT IS IT WORTH? COMMON QUESTIONS ABOUT FAMILY ITEMS

In addition to documents, patrons may also ask questions about artifacts. They may have just discovered a diary, an old photograph, or a painting in the attic. Perhaps an estate was just settled, and new items were bequeathed to their family. Motivations for bringing family objects to the library include a desire for valuations, general curiosity to learn more about an item, and a desire to understand how to preserve and protect family objects. The potential in such interactions for providing good library services and for encouraging interest in the local studies collection should not be overlooked, but careful criteria should be established for the range of information to be provided in each instance. Unless the institution has a person/policy in place to accommodate such requests, generally the staff in an institution should not provide any value estimations or information that patrons interpret as authentication of an item. Instead, patrons should be referred to a vetted list of resources that can provide further information on qualified professionals in the area.

VALUATIONS AND AUTHENTICATIONS

Patrons often desire information on the value of their family objects, or items they may have acquired at a sale. A number of resources in combination can be suggested. Antique and collectibles price guides can provide a baseline for determining general values of an item. Large numbers of works on all sorts of antiques, books, tools, and household collectibles exist that provide enumeration of identification numbers, year of manufacture, variations in style, color, packaging, etc., as well as photographs and drawings to assist in identification. Some appear annually and cover all manner of items, such as *Kovel's Antiques and Collectibles Price Guide,* a print resource, as well as other online information at www.kovels.com. Other resources address specific types of collectibles or antiques, ranging from those covering centuries of production, such as the *Complete Price Guide to Watches* by Gilbert, Engle, and Shugart, or one which covers very specific time periods or short-lived collectibles, such as *The Milk Glass Book* by Slater and Chiarenza. Many public libraries already own such price guides.

Patrons should be cautioned that prices vary widely, depending on current demand and also the condition of an item. A tiny chip in glassware, for example, may render it worthless to a collector. Additionally, market forces continuously change valuations. In the area of glassware, for example, recent remakes of once-popular collectibles, such as Jeanette and Anchor Hocking jadeite pieces from the 1940s and 1950s, may have an effect on the demand for older ones. It is easy to confuse new glassware that is cast in old molds with original glassware. Patrons may be directed to works by experts in the field that differentiate between the sizes, styles, and markings of the reproductions, compared to the originals, such as the *Guide to Fakes & Reproductions* by Chervenka.

Online auction sites often provide "real world" information as to what prices people are actually receiving for collectibles. Sites such as eBay provide the results of ended auctions, while some other auction sites require registration and/or membership fees in order to see ended auction information. It should be understood that fine antiques and items that can easily be faked, such as postage stamps, rarely will trade on these sites, as authentication is required. The sites also may take a fee, so the final prices are not reflective of the monies received for the item in all cases. Likewise local live auctions can be instructive for learning about prices, but live auctions may take a large percentage of the sale price, for example fifteen to fifty percent of the sale price, in order to agree to sell the item. Live auctions demonstrate the notion that demand drives price in real-world exchanges, as items may go for well over or well below their perceived value, and the same type of item may go for widely different prices in different auction settings or on different days at the same setting. Increasingly, online auctions are used as a means of providing ranges of values for antiques and collectibles. However, it is worth noting that on many auction sites, one must have an account or pay to access sales information.

REFERENCES FOR REPUTABLE RESOURCES FOR APPRAISALS AND AUTHENTICATIONS

Care must be taken to explain the role of the appraiser versus an antiques dealer. An appraiser should provide estimations of value that are free of bias that one may find from other sources.[2] The dealer may have a vested interest in making an offer for an item, so the value is relative to demand in his or her specific region and time and is modified in order to reflect potential profit after purchasing an item. Most persons seeking general information about an item may not need a professional appraisal, but some do, particularly those who would like to ascertain the insurance value of an item. They also should understand there is cost involved, that even professional appraisals may vary widely, and that appraisals provide information on market value that is rarely attainable if one is not a merchant. However, some patrons may want to pursue appraisals, so providing the web or physical addresses of national organizations, such as the American Society of Appraisers, could be beneficial. This contact information is provided below in the resources section.

Authentication is a process to verify that an object is genuine, such as a signature of a celebrity or artist. It can refer to formal verification that an item is indeed what a seller is claiming it to be and often involves research into the chain of ownership, or provenance, of an object. Patrons often want help with identifying a family heirloom, but it is not the job of the librarian or archivist, unless the institution has clear guidelines and policies allowing them to do so. Instead, consider creating a resource list for the patron that lists professional organizations related to authentication. It is not recommended that a cultural heritage institution accept business cards or appear to promote one business over another, so the use of a more neutral resource, such as a professional organization site, might be a wiser choice.

CREATE A FACT SHEET FOR YOUR AREA

In order to save time and to provide consistent information, it is useful to create a resource guide for the patron. The Internet public library has put together a wonderful pathfinder called "Antiques and Collectible Appraisal" at http://www.ipl.org/div/pf/entry/48439. Examples such as this one provide a great starting place for the creation of a guide for local regions. Consider adding information that is easily found in local library collections, and links to verified information about items that may be of particular interest in a local setting. Were there manufacturers in the area of items that are now collectible? If so, links to reputable information cataloging their items would be useful.

When considering linking to or acquiring additional resources to help families evaluate their private collections, there are many organizations that may be of help. Many family heirlooms are handicrafts, such as quilts and handwoven or sewn garments. Others are metal farm implements, weapons, and other tools. Cultural heritage professionals at local museums, historical societies, archives, and libraries may have lists of possible contacts and experts in the area. For any manufactured items, whether by hand or machinery, try looking at resources listed by professional organizations, clubs, and guilds.

RESOURCES

American Society of Appraisers, http://www.appraisers.org.

Chervenka, Mark. *Antique Trader Guide to Fakes & Reproductions*. Iola, WI: Krause Publications, 2001.

Kovel, Terry, and Kim Kovel. *Kovels' Antiques and Collectibles Price Guide 2015: America's Most Authoritative Antiques Annual!* 47th ed. New York, NY: Black Dog & Leventhal Publishers, 2014.

Library of Congress. "Preserving Your Family Treasures," http://www.loc.gov/preservation/family/.

Williams, Don, and Louisa Jaggar. *Saving Stuff: How to Care for and Preserve Your Collectibles, Heirlooms, and Other Prized Possessions*. New York, NY: Touchstone, 2005.

THE PERSONAL ARCHIVE: TEACHING SKILLS FOR FAMILIES TO PRESERVE THEIR OWN ITEMS

Because documents and heirlooms may live for generations within private hands, the archival profession, libraries, and other cultural heritage institutions are recognizing personal archiving as an important aspect of cultural heritage preservation.[3] Private collections may be accessed virtually, as families develop their own digital history sites. The narrative of the past at the local level is also being interpreted more openly by the public as a result of social media. Families should be provided with information to help them preserve original items in a way consistent with current archival methods. They should also be guided to enjoy an original item that is not intended for long-term preservation or to create use copies.

Resources already exist in the preservation and archives literature that easily can be modified for family applications. In the digital realm, the personal digital archiving movement can inform the public about how to manage digital objects, both born-digital and digitized items. In order to assist patrons with such questions, librarians and other cultural heritage staff should become familiar with basic concepts and procedures or be able to point patrons to good instructions on the library website. What are some of the most important questions that library and other information professionals should ask when assisting patrons with personal items?

OWNERSHIP AND COPYRIGHT

Is it theirs? One of the important questions patrons should consider before deciding how to maintain family documents and objects is that of ownership. Family items, especially during the settlement of an estate, can become the subject of very contentious disagreements. If objects are shared among various family members, patrons should not assume that the person who physically holds the object has the right to copy, sell, dismantle, etc. without *prior* permission from other family members. Refer patrons to numerous works by estate sale professionals and auctioneers that give general guidance for negotiating this process that are listed in the first resources section of this chapter. In addition, the University of Minnesota Extension Service sells a workbook that could be used for programming or as a reference work, *Who Gets Grandma's Yellow Pie Plate?™ Workbook*.[4] The websites of major universities in the state or region of the library may also provide advice on estate planning and recommended resources.

The issues of ownership and copyright are separate. Ownership does not necessarily mean that copyright is held.[5] Therefore when inheriting documents, photographs, or artwork, clarification of who holds the copyright, usually the creator, is essential. Understanding the copyright issues relating to photographs can be particularly complex. Whoever takes the photograph owns the copyright to it, whether or not that person is a professional photographer. Therefore, if someone owns a copy of a photograph, and publishes it without permission when its copyright is owned by someone else, it can be a violation of copyright law. How long a copyright lasts depends on several factors. For an explanation, it is best to refer to Circular 15A of the U.S. Copyright Office, "Duration of Copyright" at http://www .copyright.gov/circs/circ15a.pdf, if one would like to reproduce or digitize the items. For example, if someone is writing a book about the family, that person should obtain permission to reproduce images of family items before publication. Permission should also be sought before images are distributed to family members via a photosharing website such as Flickr, or linked to an online tree.

RESOURCES

American Society of Media Photographers. "Photos of Public Buildings," https://asmp.org/ tutorials/photos-public-buildings.html#.VSfP5fldV8E.

Columbia University. "Fair Use Checklist," http://copyright.columbia.edu/copyright/ fair-use/fair-use-checklist/.

"Obtaining Copyright Permissions: Photos," University of Michigan, http://guides.lib .umich.edu/content.php?pid=302339&sid=2478384.

Russell, Judy G. "Copyright and the Photo Negatives." *The Legal Genealogist* (blog), March 4, 2015, http://www.legalgenealogist.com/blog/2015/03/04/copyright-and-the -photo-negatives/.

"Thinking Through Fair Use," https://www.lib.umn.edu/copyright/fairthoughts.

"Understanding Photographic Copyright" Professional Photographers of America, http:// www.ppa.com/about/content.cfm?ItemNumber=1720.

STORAGE ADVICE AT A GLANCE

Diaries and letters provide wonderful insights into the past. A simple search of diaries on auction sites such as eBay demonstrate that there is a collector's value for them, particularly for those dating from the early twentieth century and before. Letters, postcards, wedding invitations, scrapbooks, school notebooks, and artwork may hold sentimental value for a family. Yet these items are can be difficult to store properly. However, with some effort a variety of paper documents may be preserved at home, and the following basic guidelines for storing them come from Abby Shaw, an archival expert at Hollinger's Metal Edge, a leading archival supply company.[6]

- *Any* container or storage method is better than none. The goal is to keep out dust, insects, and light.
- Acceptable temporary storage methods include plastic storage tubs, Ziploc bags, file folders, and envelopes.
- The basement and the attic are the worst places in a home to store materials because extreme temperatures and dampness are the enemy. Storage in parts of the home that are temperature controlled the majority of the year (40% to 50% relative humidity), and out of direct sunlight are the preferred locations, such as under a bed, or in a closet of a bedroom or a study.
- More archivally-sound permanent storage methods will be needed. One hears a lot about acid-free enclosures, but the best archival enclosures are also lignin-free and sulphur-free. Some archivists also recommend that they are buffered. Such enclosures are generally not available at even office supply stores, but can be mail ordered from archival supply firms.
- Any plastic enclosures such as sleeves should be made of polyester film, such as polyethylene or polypropylene. Some with multipockets are acceptable. They should come from an archival supply source, because cheaper versions available from discount stores sometimes off-gas and are not desirable.
- Try not to stack archival boxes more than three deep.
- Try not to touch items unless necessary, and then only at the edges. Make sure hands are thoroughly clean. Cotton gloves can be used, but only if they are extremely formfitting, as brittle old documents can easily catch and tear on them. Gloves made of nitrile can also protect archival items from the oils and hidden dirt on hands.

Letters are often bundled together with rubber bands, ribbon, or string. Tight rubber bands can damage the edges of the letters. Ribbons contain dyes and/or acids that can harm the letters over time. Metal fasteners such as staples and paper clips will eventually rust. It is best not to fasten documents with anything. If it is desirable to group them, it can be done in a number of different archival enclosures:

- Clear polyester sleeves are good if you have the funds and they need to be viewed. If they are folios, they can be unfolded to view the whole letter if the folds are not too fragile. Otherwise, store the items folded. Sleeves can then go into folders and a box, or just into a box.

- If a folder and box system is used, there are many different types of boxes possible. The box can be flat, or upright, have a lid, or a drop front. Just make sure with the upright box, that the folders cannot slump (either the box must be full or spacers must be used). A file folder is better for labeling because it has a tab. Folders for drop front boxes are flush, which do not allow for labeling.

GETTING TRAINING FOR PRESERVATION AND STORAGE

If staff members wish to acquire more training in sound archival practices, there are fortunately many places to receive such training, even for nonprofessionals:

- library and information science program courses
- seminars given by state libraries/archives, usually aimed at information professionals
- seminars given by professional organizations and societies for a mixed audience
- free webinars sponsored by a variety of not-for-profit groups

Several more sources of information are listed in the Resources below.

CONSIDERING DONATIONS

Descendants may not want to take on the curatorship of family items when another family member has passed away when they lack the proper storage space or conditions for successful long-term curation. One "solution" is putting family items out on the curb with the trash, a lamentable, but oft-occurring scenario. If family members turn to an institution to help them figure out where family items might be donated, a piece of the historical record is saved, and the family may be entitled to a tax credit depending on the value of the donation. Where should patrons look to donate?

- If the items center around a family or families in a specific geographic location, then contact institutions there first. If that fails, then try the state archives, library, or historical society.
- Although it is several years old, the print guide called *Directory of American Libraries with Genealogy or Local History Collections* by P. William Filby may help identify collections that would accept family papers.
- archives of a college or university that a family member attended
- Library of Congress

Patrons also inherit the task of figuring out what to do with a relative's genealogical notes, sources, and related books and maps. Few individuals think to make a provision for these materials in their wills, although that can be done and should be encouraged. The research might be accepted by the following institutions:

- Genealogy Library Center, Inc., Tremonton, Utah, http://arleneeakle.com/pages/library.shtml

- Allen County Public Library Genealogy Center, http://www.genealogycenter.org/ Donate.aspx
- The Family History Library, https://familysearch.org/learn/wiki/en/Donations
- Library of Congress, if it is in the form of a published book, http://www.loc.gov/rr/ genealogy/gifts.html
- Daughters of the American Revolution (DAR) library in Washington, DC, or the library of another heritage society
- Other specialty collections such as the New England Historic Genealogical Society. http://www.americanancestors.org/support/donate-materials/

RESOURCES

Archival Products Suppliers, https://docs.google.com/document/edit?id=1LDtK EsEPoq47w3JkjXothrjA4rEiahS7QrCB0w7A3YA&hl=en&authkey=CMvzmJYF.

Association for Library Collections & Technical Services, American Library Association. "Preservation of Family Photos: Here There and Everywhere," accessed April 23, 2013, https://www.youtube.com/watch?v=I_moGnyaRKc.

Council of State Archivists. BACE: Basics of Archives Continuing Education Program, http://www.statearchivists.org/arc/bace/.

Crow, Amy Johnson. "4 Things To Do Before You Donate Your Genealogy," Ancestry.com blog, February 20, 2014, http://blogs.ancestry.com/ancestry/2014/02/20/ 4-things-to-do-before-you-donate-your-genealogy./

Haskins, Scott M. *How to Save Your Stuff From A Disaster: Complete Instructions on How to Protect and Save Your Family History, Heirlooms and Collectibles.* Santa Barbara, CA: Preservation Help Publications, 1996.

Hopkins-Rehan, Dottie, Senior Archival Curator, Illinois Secretary of State's Office. "The Basics of Paper Conservation," https://www.youtube.com/watch?v=dcb3JwPjDjA &feature=share&list=UUIA1SUSwkOGuN4Phf-e9gWg&index=1.

Levenick, Denise May. *How to Archive Family Keepsakes: Learn How to Preserve Family Photos, Memorabilia and Genealogy Records.* Cincinnati, OH: Family Tree Books, 2012.

Louisiana Archives and Manuscripts Association. "Archival Training Collaborative." Updated June 17, 2011, http://louisianaarchivists.org/atc/archival-training-resources -online.html.

Mannon, Melissa. *The Unofficial Family Archivist: A Guide to Creating and Maintaining Family Papers, Photographs, and Memorabilia.* [United States]: Melissa Mannon, 2011.

National Endowment for the Humanities, and White House Millennium Council (U.S.). *My History Is America's History: 15 Things You Can Do to Save America's Stories.* Washington, DC: National Endowment for the Humanities: For sale by the U.S. G.P.O., Supt. of Docs., 1999, http://archive.org/details/myhistoryisameri00nati.

Northeast Document Conservation Center. "Caring for Private and Family Collections." 2013, http://test.nedcc.org/assets/media/images/Pres_Fam_Collections_2013.pdf.

Raab, Nathan. "Donating an Archive? A Book Collection? Get an Appraisal." April 16, 2011, http://www.forbes.com/sites/booked/2011/04/16/donating-an-archive-your -book-collection-get-an-appraisal/.

Ritzenthaler, Mary Lynn, and Diane Vogt-O'Connor. *Photographs: Archival Care and Management.* Chicago, IL: Society of American Archivists, 2006.

Smithsonian Institution Archives. "Preserve Your Treasures: How to Store Your Photographs," accessed November 17, 2010, https://www.youtube.com/watch?v=geqVsJJK5rs.

Society of American Archivists. "Donating Your Personal or Family Records to a Repository," http://www2.archivists.org/publications/brochures/donating-familyrecs.

U.S. National Archives. "How to Preserve Family Papers and Archives," http://www .archives.gov/preservation/family-archives/.

U.S. National Archives. "Preserving Family Memories and Preserving Personal Digital Files – YouTube," accessed March 16, 2015, https://www.youtube.com/watch?v=jDFoW5dMyjg.

SCANNING

After the gathering, identification, and organizing of documents, there remains a final task: scanning. This can be done for several reasons. First, scanning provides a copy of a physical document that will capture the image before more deterioration of the document occurs and, despite the best possible storage conditions, is inevitable. Second, scanning allows the storage of a large number of images in a small amount of space. Scans can be copied and shared much more easily than physical documents. Finally, scanning of photographs and documents can be attached to online genealogical trees, which support and enhance the information contained in them.

If you will be assisting patrons with scanning, you should be aware of the following:

- Scanning documents and photographs is very time-consuming, so it may be a good idea to send them to a company that specializes in this.
- The optimal scanning resolutions are 600 dpi for photos, 300 dpi for documents, and 3,200 dpi for slides and negatives.
- Adjustments can be made to the scans, such as color balancing (old photos tend to go blue), and deepening the shadows under the tone to make overexposed images much clearer. Software programs like Adobe Photoshop and ArcSoft PhotoStudio give good results. Sumo Paint is a free online image editor.
- The backs of documents and photographs should be scanned if they contain information, even if the information does not make sense now. The information could hold valuable clues for identification and dating.
- It is a good idea to include borders in the scan, because even when they do not contain dates, their shape may help to date photographs, and may at least show which photographs in a group of many were taken about the same time.
- Redundancy in the storage of digital files is essential—two, three, or more locations in physically separate spots prevent a single disaster such as a fire or hurricane from destroying your digital heritage.

The format best used to scan old documents is not a clear-cut matter. However, a general rule of thumb is to scan in a high-resolution, lossless format. This means the image, when edited, will not break down and begin to pixelate. It is important to save and preserve an archival copy, such as a tagged image file format (TIFF). Once you have an archival copy in a high quality lossless format, then a copy can be made in a different format which is a smaller, less cumbersome size, for sharing on websites. A common use format is JPEG, which is lossy, so any editing of the photograph will begin to break down the image, but one can always make a new JPEG from the archival file. Another more compact format is PNG, which is also lossless and widely supported by browsers.

In cases of large or oversized photographs, one might use a digital SLR to shoot a digital image of it. These cameras can save in Raw or TIFF formats for an archival original of the photograph. Some professionals like the Raw format because these files can be manipulated to the greatest extent. For ideas about how digital images can be used in recording family history in graphically pleasing ways, please see the chapter entitled "Record It: Preserving Family and Community History."

LIBRARY SCANNING POLICIES

Some aspects to include in your policy are:

- Will patrons be allowed to operate the equipment on their own?
- Will the scanner be used for materials held by your institution only, or will patrons be allowed to use it for personal documents and photographs?
- Will patrons be charged to use the scanner?
- Will patrons need to reserve the scanner for a specific length of time, or will it be used on a first-come first-served basis?
- Will flash drives be sold to those patrons who forgot to bring one?

PERSONAL DIGITAL ARCHIVING

What do families do once they have either created a digital file by scanning, or increasingly, once they have accumulated born-digital family items, such as digital photographs, family documents, emails, etc.? Happily, there are clear instructions already available to cultural heritage institutions that want to assist patrons with their family digital objects. This movement, called "personal digital archiving," has broad support in libraries and archives, with a great deal of programming and other information already available for use. The Library of Congress website on personal digital archiving provides excellent guidance to those just beginning in this area. The website provides ideas for institutions to lead families in programs for storing and maintaining their digital family files.[7]

TO-DO CHECKLIST

- Make a fact sheet for your area with information about sources of local information for obtaining appraisals.
- Consider purchasing antiques price guides, guides to personal archiving, and works on the identification of old photographs for your institution.
- Seek information/training on archival best practices for storing old documents and photographs, in order to better assist patrons.
- Create/adapt a photographic release form if your institution wants to create/augment a collection of local interest photographs.
- Plan and implement programs, possibly with other local institutions, dealing with the care and storage of family documents and heirlooms, or keep track of where such programs occur in the vicinity to refer patrons there.

RESOURCES

Ashenfelder, Mike. "Personal Digital Archiving: The Basics of Scanning." Library of Congress blog. March 27, 2014, http://blogs.loc.gov/digitalpreservation/2014/03/personal-digital-archiving-the-basics-of-scanning/.

Ashenfelder, Mike. "What People Are Asking About Personal Digital Archiving: Part 1." Library of Congress blog. June 17, 2013, http://blogs.loc.gov/digitalpreservation/2013/06/what-people-are-asking-about-personal-digital-archiving/.

Ashenfelder, Mike. "What People Are Asking About Personal Digital Archiving: Part 2." Library of Congress blog. July 3, 2013, http://blogs.loc.gov/digitalpreservation/2013/07/what-people-are-asking-about-personal-digital-archiving-part-2/.

Baldrige, Aimee. *Organize Your Digital Life: How to Store Your Photographs, Music, Videos, & Personal Documents in a Digital World.* Washington, DC: National Geographic, 2009.

"How to Preserve Old Photos Without Losing Your Mind," http://www.glowimagery.com/how-to-preserve-old-photos/.

Payne, Rich, and Leo Saidnawey. "Choosing the Right Scanner." Association for Information and Image Management E-Doc Magazine 21, no. 5 (2004): 21–23.

"Preserving Family Memories and Preserving Personal Digital Files – YouTube," accessed March 16, 2015, https://www.youtube.com/watch?v=jDFoW5dMyjg.

Taylor, Maureen A. *Photo Organizing Practices: Daguerreotypes to Digital.* United States: Picture Perfect Press, 2014.

Universal Photographic Digital Imaging Guidelines Coalition. "The Guidelines," http://www.updig.org/index.html.

CONCLUSION

The information found in home sources is a crucial part of our historical record, and by helping families deal with and preserve these sources, we are rescuing that precious historical record! Every attic and basement might harbor untold treasures that document individual, family, institutional, and community stories. Weave enough of these stories together, and a picture of a nation emerges. Of course, the basement and the attic are just where the treasures should not be stored. The next chapter discusses in detail strategies for handling those visual gems, family photographs.

PROGRAMMING IDEAS

Because so many individuals and families are faced with the tasks outlined in this chapter, this is a perfect subject area on which to base programs. Some possibilities are listed below.

1. Personal Digital Archiving

Someone presents on best practices for organizing and storing digital files. That someone could be a tech-savvy staff member, or a guest speaker. It might even be possible to obtain someone for free who works with a local computer business. The Library of Congress thinks this topic is so important that they have devised the following kit that contains instructions and support materials for librarians to host public programs about it. The Personal Digital Archiving Day Kit is found at http://www.digitalpreservation.gov/personalarchiving/padKit/index.html.

Schedule: About one hour and 15 minutes.

Start by explaining the importance of careful storage and backups for digital photographs. Give an example of how someone has lost years' worth of photographs when a hard drive fails. Spend the majority of the session discussing the following options for making backups: external hard drives, flash drives, The Cloud, box accounts, photosharing accounts, and online trees. Spend the remainder of the time fielding questions from the audience.

2. Antiques and Collectibles Show and Tell

This program could be patterned on the popular television series "Antiques Roadshow.^{TM}" People sign up ahead of time in order to show their family treasure at the event, and to explain what they know about it. Then an expert, such as an owner of local antiques and estate sale business, provides even more information about the items, along with a ballpark appraisal.

Introduce the appraisers, and give information on their backgrounds/how they acquired their expertise. Then have the person who brought in the object spend about five minutes describing it and its provenance. Next, the expert will spend about ten minutes giving the background of the object and its value. Do this with four or five different objects, as time permits.

The final minutes will be devoted to explaining where information can be found in both the institution and online, about storing and valuing family heirlooms. For example, the Northeast Document Conservation Center has prepared handouts for cultural heritage institutions who are putting on programming related to the preservation of family collections. One example is listed here: https://www.nedcc .org/assets/media/images/Pres_Fam_Collections_2013.pdf.

Additional Ideas

- Hold a program about how to clear out a household which is presented by various experts including an appraiser, a professional organizer, and a lawyer.
- Hold a program that demonstrates good archival methods for paper documents.

NOTES

1. "Preserving Family Treasures," http://www.loc.gov/preservation/family/.

2. American Society of Appraisers, http://www.appraisers.org/find-an-appraiser, 2015.

3. See, for example, Richard J. Cox, *Personal Archives and a New Archival Calling: Readings, Reflections and Ruminations* (Duluth, MN: Litwin Books, 2008). *eBook Academic Collection* EBSCO*host*, accessed July 9, 2015 and Donald T. Hawkins, ed. *Personal Archiving: Preserving our Digital Heritage* (Medford, NJ: Information Today, 2013).

4. Marlene S. Stum, *Who Gets Grandma's Yellow Pie Plate?*[TM] *Workbook* (Minneapolis, MN: University of Minnesota Extension Service, 2011).

5. United States Copyright Office. "Copyright Basics," Circular 1 (Washington, DC: US. Copyright Office, 2012).

6. Abby A. Shaw, e-mail message to author, September 11, 2014.

7. Personal Digital Archiving Day Kit, Library of Congress, http://www.digital preservation.gov/personalarchiving/padKit/index.html, accessed May 5, 2015.

Chapter 5

PICTURE IT: GATHERING, ANALYZING, AND STORING FAMILY PHOTOGRAPHS

"In the family photographs that we cherish so, we are able to 'freeze' time, to 'stop' it, and in this way to control it."

—Catherine Noren[1]

In addition to paper documents, most families have generated significant collections of photographs, which in addition to being valuable for sentimental reasons are visual documentation of family and community history. The management of such collections can be challenging due to their volume alone. Patrons often come tottering into the library with a box of old family photographs jumbled together that they have uncovered as part of the research process, or that they have inherited from another family member. This chapter has ideas to help patrons properly store their photographs, to help them identify the photographs' subjects and time periods, and also to provide them with research suggestions when they are not lucky enough to have a collection of family photos to work with.

ENHANCING ACCESS: ORGANIZATION

Initially sort photographs according to two categories: contemporary, defined as photographs that have images of living people, versus the antique, photographs in which all the people pictured are deceased. In addition to being a handy way to divide the collection, this distinction is made because family history information that is published usually only includes facts about deceased individuals in order to protect the privacy of living family members. In the same way, visual documentation that is shared publically, such as being attached to online family trees, should only contain images of the deceased, unless permission is obtained from the living family members to add their images.

If photographs are dusty, they can be brushed with a very soft, clean brush, similar to the type used to apply face powder. Slide them into polyester sleeves, and write the identity of the subjects either on a sticky note on the exterior of the sleeve, or by writing on the sleeve with a special pen, or by making a note on an acid free slip of paper with pencil and placing it in the sleeve with the photograph—these are all acceptable temporary measures. If the location of where the photograph was taken and the date or approximate date are both known, also record this information.

Then sort the photographs by branches of the family. It is easy to sort when there is only one person in a photograph, but what about when there are multiple people? Here are a few options:

- All photographs of one nuclear family can be placed in one container. When the children in this family start families of their own, then they go into a separate container. This can apply to paper or digital files.
- One family group photograph can be duplicated and a copy, or a note describing the individual's presence in the group photograph, can be placed in each individual's file.
- All photographs of an extended family can be placed in the same file, but the photographs can be organized into subfiles by time period or by event.

Information about the proper storage methods for photographs will be given later in this chapter.

If actual names of the subjects in the photograph are not written down, sometimes clues are written on the backs or margins of photographs, such as an address. Paying attention to such clues, and then putting them together with information already known about ancestors, such as addresses, occupations, etc., may help identify the subjects in the photographs. It usually helps to put together photographs that were part of the same roll of film, and/or photographs that were from the same time period; they will be the same shape because they are in the same format. Anything which remains, i.e., unidentified photographs, may be placed in a separate container to be worked on again later. Discourage patrons from discarding photographs that they cannot initially identify, because they may eventually do so with assistance.

Unfortunately, not every single photograph is a work of art. Photographs that are blurry, or have the heads of the subjects cut off, should be discarded unless they are the only known images of an individual. Duplicate photographs can be given away to family members or discarded. If some of the photographs are not personal in nature, and do not have meaning for anyone in the family, patrons should consider donation. Examples are a collection of landscape images taken on a trip, or a collection of images taken on the job. If any other part of the photograph collection will not be curated by a family member, then assist in finding an institution for donation. See the section in Chapter 4, "Considering Donation," for ideas about where they could be placed.

Photographs that have been placed in photograph albums require special consideration. Most photograph albums offer poor storage conditions, such as highly acidic black paper pages, or the "magnetic" photograph albums, where the pages have lines of adhesive to hold the photographs in place. Remove the photographs if possible without damaging them. Photographs attached with paper photograph corners often pop out readily, but sometimes photographs have been glued. If the latter is the case, these pages can be scanned in their entirety, and because pages can contain written identification that should be preserved, this is a good idea anyway.

Framed photographs should be removed from the frames if possible because they are not an archivally sound place to store a photograph. Usually the glass does not contain a coating to filter out harmful ultraviolet rays, and the cardboard backing is highly acidic. If a framed image is desired, it is a better idea to frame a photocopy of a photograph. Another problem is that sometimes the fronts of framed photographs become stuck to the glass over time. The glass and the photograph can be placed into an unsealed plastic bag, and then stored in the freezer for one or two days, which may dry the photograph finish enough to allow separation. A dull knife might be used to gently pry a corner of the photograph loose from the glass. If the photograph will still not separate, then it can be scanned through the glass.[2]

Slides and negatives must also be evaluated. There may or may not be paper copies of the images they contain in the collection, but both of these formats can also be scanned. The digital images produced by a scanned negative are often superior to those produced by a scanned photograph.

A final format to consider is home movies, which should be inventoried, and are discussed further in the preservation section of this chapter.

SHOW AND TELL

If the family photographs are not identified, urge the owner to take immediate action to consult other family members. This is a time-sensitive task because the family members who are able to help with this project are often older, and they will not be able to assist indefinitely when poor health, failing memory, or death intervene. Photographs can be examined at family picnics and other get-togethers. If the photographs are fragile, it is better to bring photocopies or scans of them. Scans of photographs can be sent via email, or posted on photosharing websites.

Starting a group on Facebook or another social media website for the purpose of sharing and identifying photographs is also helpful. If identifications are made, it is better to make notations on a separate paper, or to write the identification on polyester film storage sleeves, not on the photographs themselves. Inks can bleed through and damage photos. Using sticky notes directly on individual photographs is also a bad idea, because their adhesive may damage them. If a family member insists on labeling the back of the photographs, have him or her do it lightly in pencil.

TRACKING DISTANT RELATIVES TO HELP WITH IDENTIFICATION AND PHOTOSHARING

- If relatives' names are already known, try online telephone directories such as whitepages.com. A simple Google search under an individual name might also help, because it often links to business contact information. Reversed names, and name variants, such as including a middle initial, should be tried, as well as spelling out the entire name completely.
- Obituaries, often available online if they are from the last decade or so, usually name surviving children and grandchildren.
- Consult books that offer good advice on tracking living people.
- When names of distant relatives are not known, queries may be posted on surname message boards, or on one for a geographic area, like those at rootsweb.com, and usgenweb.com.
- Some researchers also have had success when they placed an ad in the newspaper of the locality where family was last known to reside. This is particularly recommended for small towns.

When contacting relatives that are not well-known, writing a letter rather than telephoning might be the best first approach. It gives the relative time to digest the situation, and helps them to feel more in control. Many people are now wary of unsolicited telephone calls for good reason. The letter should explain the background of the person seeking the information, and their connection to the family, the specific connection to the person they are writing ("We are third cousins, etc."), and state the research goals. Please consult the sample photograph request letter in Appendix A: Forms.

Facial recognition software is a new tool in the family historian's bag of tricks, and there are several types to choose from; some are free while others are available for a fee. The software can help match the facial features of an individual in an identified photograph, with those in other photographs, even if the subject is older or younger in the other photographs. This can be handy when there is a large group of digitized but unidentified photographs to sort and identify. Caveat: the software is not foolproof, and is only as accurate as the initial identification of the photo that it is using as its basis of comparison. Examples of this type of product include: Picasa, Fotobounce, EclipseIR^{TM}, and the subscription website myheritage.com.

If all efforts to identify individuals in photographs within the family fail, suggest to patrons that they can post images online in the hope that someone else will be able to help. Identification can sometimes be achieved through crowdsourcing. See one incredible example at http://harryandedna.com, when a large collection of slides belonging to an anonymous married couple was purchased in a junk shop by a stranger, who proceeded to scan and upload hundreds of them onto Facebook. People from all over the country contributed observations about clues found in them, which ultimately lead to the identification of the couple, and to making contact with their descendants.

DATING OLD PHOTOGRAPHS

Educated guesses as to when a photograph was created can be made by looking at several factors:

- Physical details of the photograph, including its size and format, will indicate a range of years when it was produced. See Table 5.1 for brief descriptions of photographic formats.
- Any information about a professional photographer found on the photograph can date it to the time period when the photographer was in business, which can be ascertained through city directory listings.
- The style of clothing worn in the photographs can be tied to specific time periods.
- Other background details that can be observed in the photograph, such as sidewalks, type of street paving, electrical and phone wires or lack thereof, transportation, and buildings. When these amenities appeared in a community can usually be specifically dated, so that the photograph must have been produced afterwards. Photographic curator Albert K. Baragwanath suggests that institutions can develop a list of such information for their community in order to date local photos.[3]

Other markings:

- Multiple other details such as gold lines, types of edges, type of cases, and color of cardstock, can all help identify when photographs were produced.
- Photographs taken during the Civil War by a photographer on the Union side had a tax stamp affixed to them between August 1, 1864 to August 1, 1866. If it is a one-cent stamp, the photograph was taken after March 1, 1865.
- Some photographs have an "NPA" insignia on their back, which stands for National Photographic Association. The photographers were registered with this organization, and it was supposed to denote that the photograph was of a higher quality. This emblem was used only during the years 1868–1876.

Table 5.1

Major Nineteenth Century Photographic Formats at a Glance

Format	Dates	Description	Sizes
daguerreotype	1839–late 1850s	silver-coated copper plates which were treated with iodine vapor, exposed to light, and then developed with hot mercury	various
ambrotype	mid 1850s	a collodion image fixed to a glass plate whose back was either painted black or placed against a black background	various
tintype	1856–1920s	photographic images on black-painted tin, which could be contained in cases until about 1868 or so	various
carte de visite	1858–1895	photos printed on single or multi-ply paper whose edges were first squared, later rounded	2.5"×4"
cabinet card	1866–1910	also printed on paper in a larger format than CDVs	about 4"×7"
real photo postcard	1903–1930s	a photo that is developed onto paper with a pre-printed postcard backing	about 4"×6"

• Photographs produced with roll film (from 1889 on) may have roll numbers stamped on the back. They help identify group photographs that were on the same roll of film, and often that were taken at the same time and place.

For sources of more information, and examples of various photographic formats, please see the Resources section below.

PHOTOGRAPHER'S IMPRINTS

Professional photographers usually placed their imprint on the backs of photographs, but as time passed, they sometimes appeared on the fronts instead. These imprints often contain both the names of the photographers and the city where they worked. They were initially simple, but became more ornate, until about 1885, when there was a divergence—when some photographers went back to a simple imprint, and some continued elaborate styles. City directories and local histories can be checked to see what year a photographer was in business at a given location. This will provide a range of years during which the photograph could have been produced. Photographer ads in old newspapers are also helpful to establish when and where a photographer was in business.

Figure 5.1
Photo from the Author's Collection.

The photographer for Figure 5.1, Louis W. Friesleben, is listed in Chicago city directories at this address between 1906 and1914. The child, Francis Johnston, was born in 1906, and since he appears to be under age five, the approximate date of the photograph is likely 1909–1910. His mother's parents were German immigrants, as were the photographer's, and both families resided on the South Side of Chicago.

TWENTIETH-CENTURY PHOTOGRAPHS

In the early decades of photography, photographs could only be taken by professionals because of the specialized equipment and chemicals that were required. That factor, coupled with the long exposure times, meant that early photographs were almost always formally posed, the subjects frozen in solemn expressions. Props might be given to the subjects, especially to children to keep them still, or to women, to bring to add interest and elegance to the picture. Backdrops varied from painted scenes to plain ones. Pricier photographers prided themselves on better quality, more artistic renditions, and may have had fancier sets and props. Later on, as the technology changed and the exposure times shortened, photographs became slightly more casual, though were still taken in studios. Friends might go into a parlor for a picture together, even in their working clothes. A photograph which appears to show a group of siblings might really be a group of friends. The lesson here is to be careful about making assumptions about the people in photographs. The subjects in a photograph may not be related, they may be wearing borrowed clothing, and they could be shown in fancy settings that did not reflect their true status in life. Photographs can deceive the viewer.[4]

In 1900, the first camera was sold that could be owned and operated by amateur individuals: the Brownie was manufactured by Eastman Kodak. Suddenly, photographs were no longer limited to sittings with professional photographers. A new informality and freedom in photographs was made possible, and because the cost of this camera was modest, almost anyone could be a photographer.

Technological advances in photography were rapid in the twentieth century. Dating photographs based on their physical characteristics can be difficult because the size of negatives and finished photographs often varied, and because photographs developed from celluloid negatives could be enlarged, so that the photograph's size did not

Figure 5.2
Photo from the Author's Collection. The Wavy Edges of this Photo, and the Hairstyles of the Subjects, Help to Date this Photo to the Early 1950s.

necessarily correspond to the negative's size. The following is a listing of some characteristics of photographs from this time period and their dates which can help with dating process:

1889	Kodak markets the first transparent roll film.
1900	Brownie cameras produce 2¼" square prints.
1901	Brownie 2 cameras produce 2¼×3¼" prints.
1920–1940	Art deco motifs appear on photo borders and folders.
1926–1931	Smaller-sized photographs had a border of double open lines on sides.
1935–1940	Some photographs had chevron-like designs on the borders.
1936	Kodachrome, the first commercially viable color film was introduced.
1948–2001	Polaroid "instant" photographs were produced.
Early 1950s	Wavy borders are found on smaller pictures measuring 3¼"×2½." See Figure 5.2.
1960s–1970s	Photograph borders often contained dates on the front of the photo.
1970	Photographic paper is replaced with resin-coated, or polyethylene paper.
Mid 1980s	Fuji Photo Film Company, based in Japan, starting marketing film and photographic paper in the United States.

Reading Photographs

Studying the details of people in photographs such as composition, expressions, postures, physical relationship to others, etc. can yield information about their subjects. Writing down the details and the analysis can be very useful. The National Archives and Records Administration (NARA) has devised a series of "document analysis worksheets" for this purpose that are available online, not just for photographs, but for a variety of documents and ephemera: http://www.archives.gov/education/lessons/worksheets/.

CLOTHING

If the identity of the person is in an old photograph is not known, it might help to **date it as narrowly as possible** so that likely candidates in the family can be identified. Studying details of the clothing worn in photographs can help pinpoint that date. Keep in mind that men's fashions are difficult to differentiate, even between decades, and that elderly women may be wearing out-of-date clothes. Also, the clothing of young people for several decades from the late twentieth and early twenty-first centuries, the ubiquitous t-shirt and jeans, are hard to differentiate. However, young women have always tended to wear current fashions that can help to gauge a time period. For this reason, it is useful to consult reference books and websites about the history of everyday clothes and fashion. Several examples are listed in the Resources section below. The website called "Dating Historic Images" is particularly helpful.

DATING BY DETAILS OTHER THAN DRESS

- Details in the photographs, such as street signs, or street numbers, may help identify ancestors by their addresses.
- If there are automobiles in the photograph, the make and model of the car can help identify the time period.
- If there are urban amenities like streetlights, sidewalks, and paved streets visible in the photograph, one can investigate when these things appeared in the community in order to determine the earliest date at which the photograph must have been taken.
- The same technique can be used for the background location of the photograph. For example, the photograph may be at an amusement park, hotel, or restaurant. During what time period did that venue exist?
- A website called imageidentify.com claims to be able to identify all the objects found in a photograph.

NONFAMILY SOURCES OF PHOTOGRAPHS

When researchers cannot find anyone who has preserved photographs within their families, they should not give up hope. They still may find a photograph in many nonhome sources such as:

- Old photography websites—e.g., www.deadfred.com, www.ancientfaces.com, and familyoldphotos.com. Look at www.cyndislist.com under "Photographs & Memories."
- Photographs that are attached to online trees at websites such as Ancestry and Family Tree at FamilySearch.
- Newspaper articles—check the local library in the town where the family lived and online newspaper databases, such as ones at the Library of Congress, FamilySearch.org and vendors such as newspaperarchive.com and ancestry.com.
- School yearbooks—there are now online digitized collections at Internet Archive, ancestry.com, and at eyearbook.com.
- Employment file/identification card.
- Periodicals published by an employer.
- Naturalization certificates after 1929.
- Alien registration cards—most for World War I were destroyed, but the ones for World War II, which began to be issued in February 1942, still exist. Locations include Immigration and Naturalization Service files, or Department of Justice Files at National Archives and Records Administration (NARA) in College Park, Maryland.
- Passport applications: Photographs have been required with applications since December 21, 1914.
- County histories/biographical encyclopedias.
- Websites and museum exhibitions for the works of noted photographers who worked in areas where their families lived.

If no type of photograph of an individual can be located, researchers may find a **physical description** in various types of documents such as military papers of various kinds, employment papers, and funeral home records.

Besides photographs of *ancestors themselves*, what other types of photos/images can be used to enhance family history research?

Figure 5.3

If Ernest Hemingway's family had never preserved a photo of him, at least the U.S. Government did. This is his passport photo, Dated July 21, 1923. (http://research.archives.gov/description/192693, accessed April 3, 2015)

- Their **homes**—a fairly current image might be found using Google Street View, or a period image may reside at a historical society.
- **Churches**—be careful here because many congregations have had multiple church buildings, even changing locations of the building. Try to find an image of the church as it looked when the ancestors worshipped there.
- They may be able to find a picture of a **religious leader**. Some denominations kept very good records, and have even published biographies of their officiants, and/or published periodicals.
- **Businesses** that ancestors owned/where they worked—ads may have appeared in the local newspapers or area directories.
- **The town where they lived**—picture postcards, photographs in history books, or at archives.
- **The landscape** around them.
- **Places where ancestors socialized**, including fraternal organization halls, parks, and "opera houses."

Such historical images can be found in many places, online in digital collections, at cultural heritage institutions, and in private collections, but be aware that such images may be copyrighted, not just by their creator, but also by the institution that now owns them. Therefore, permission may be needed to use the images in research and/or writing. More information on using postcards and old photographs in research can be found in Chapter 8, "Mining the Riches."

RESOURCES

In addition to the titles listed here, one may search WorldCat for books that cover photographers, who worked in specific geographic areas, such as Toba Pato Tucker's *Heber Springs Portraits: Continuity and Change in the World Disfarmer Photographed*. Albuquerque, NM: University of New Mexico Press, 1996.

American Antiquarian Society. "Ambrotypes," http://www.americanantiquarian.org/ambrotypes.htm.

Brown, Robert O. *Collector's Guide to 19th Century U.S. Traveling Photographers*. Forest Grove, OR: Brown-Spath & Associates, 2002.

"The Cabinet Card Gallery: Viewing History, Culture and Personalities Through Cabinet Card Images." Blog at WordPress.com, http://cabinetcardgallery.wordpress.com.

Center of Southwest Studies, Fort Lewis College. "Tips for Determining when a U.S. Postcard Was Published," https://swcenter.fortlewis.edu/finding_aids/images/M194/PostcardDating.htm.

Clark, Gary W. *19th Century Card Photos KwikGuide: A Step-by-Step Guide to Identifying and Dating Cartes de Visite and Cabinet Cards*. [Carlsbad, CA]: PhotoTree.com, 2013.

Costume Institute, Metropolitan Museum of Art. "Fashion Plates from the Digital Collections of the Thomas M. Watson Library," http://libmma.contentdm.oclc.org/cdm/landingpage/collection/p15324coll12.

The Daguerreian Society. "Facts About Daguerreotypes," daguerre.org/dagfaq.php, accessed November 3, 2015.

Dalrymple, Priscilla Harris. *American Victorian Costume in Early Photographs*. Mineola, NY: Dover Publications, 1991.

Doyle, Marian I. *An Illustrated History of Hairstyles 1830–1930*. Atlgen, PA: Schiffer Publishing, 2003.

Frisch-Ripley, Karen. *Unlocking the Secrets in Old Photographs*. Salt Lake City: Ancestry Publishing, 1991.

Gagel, Diane VanSkiver. *Windows On The Past: Identifying, Dating, & Preserving Photographs*. Bowie, MD: Heritage Books, 2000. Print.

Gernsheim, Alison. *Victorian & Edwardian Fashion: A Photographic Survey*. Mineola, NY: Dover Publications, 1981.

Hinckley, Kathleen W. *Locating Lost Family Members & Friends*. Cincinnati: Betterway Books, 1999.

Kodak. "History of Kodak," http://www.kodak.com/US/en/corp/kodakHistory/, accessed March 19, 2015. The corporate website contains timelines with information about when their various cameras and photographic materials were developed and marketed.

Landscape Change Program, The University of Vermont. "Dating Historic Images," http://www.uvm.edu/landscape/dating/index.php.

Library of Congress. "Daguerreotypes," http://memory.loc.gov/ammem/daghtml/daghome.html.

Library of Congress. "Liljenquist Family Collection of Civil War Photographs," http://www.loc.gov/pictures/collection/lilj/.

Mace, O. Henry. *Collector's Guide to Early Photographs*, 2nd ed. Iola, WI: Krause Publications, 1999.

MacLeod, Don. *How to Find Out Anything: From Extreme Google Searches to Scouring Government Documents, a Guide to Uncovering Anything About Everyone and Everything*. New York, NY: Prentice Hall Press, 2012.

Nickell, Joe. *Camera Clues: A Handbook for Photographic Investigation*. Lexington, KY: University Press of Kentucky, 2010.

Ockerbloom, John Mark, ed. The Online Books Page. "Serial Archive Listings for Godey's Lady's Book," http://onlinebooks.library.upenn.edu/webbin/serial?id=godeylady.

Palmquist, Peter E., and Richard Rudisill, eds. *Photographers: A Sourcebook For Historical Research*, 2nd ed. Nevada City, CA: Carl Mautz Vintage Photography & Publishing, 2000.

Palmquist, Peter E., and Thomas R. Kailbourn. *Pioneer Photographers of the Far West: A Biographical Dictionary, 1840–1865*. Stanford, CA: Stanford University Press, 2002.

Palmquist, Peter E., and Thomas R. Kailbourn. *Pioneer Photographers From The Mississippi To The Continental Divide: A Biographical Dictionary, 1839–1865*. Stanford, CA: Stanford University Press, 2005.

Pénichon, Sylvie. *Twentieth-century Color Photographs: Identification And Care*. Los Angeles, CA: The Getty Conservation Institute, 2013.

Playle's Online Auction. "How to Identify and Date Real Photo Vintage Postcards," http://www.playle.com/realphoto/, accessed November 3, 2015.

Pols, Robert and Federation of Family History Societies. *Dating Twentieth Century Photographs*. Bury: Federation of Family History Societies (Publications), 2005. This book contains helpful dating charts based on both the physical characteristics and content of photographs.

Reilly, James M. *Care and Identification of 19th-Century Photographic Prints*. Rochester, NY: Eastman Kodak Company, 1986.

Taylor, Maureen Alice, ed. *Dating Old Photographs, 1840–1929*. Toronto, ON: Family Chronicle, 2004.

Taylor, Maureen Alice, ed. *More Dating Old Photographs, 1840–1929*. Toronto, ON: Family Chronicle, 2004.

Taylor, Maureen Alice. *Uncovering Your Ancestry Through Family Photographs*. Cincinnati, OH: Family Tree Books, 2005. Print.

The Victorian Web. "What Victorians Wore: An Overview of Victorian Costume." Last modified January 25, 2015, http://www.victorianweb.org/art/costume/index.html.

KEEP AND PRESERVE: STORAGE
OF PHOTOGRAPHS

The same optimal storage conditions for documents also apply to photographs. Heat and humidity are the enemies of photographs, as well as mold, dust, and insects. Place them in an environment that is temperature controlled much of the year, approximately 40 to 50 percent relative humidity, NOT in the basement, the attic, or the garage. Closets in a spare room, or under bed storage work well.

Any storage container is better than none; however, plastic containers that close tightly may trap moisture in with photographs. The most desirable long-term storage container is an archival box that is acid-free, lignin-free. Some archivists also recommend that they are buffered, i.e. contain calcium carbonate, which absorbs acidity in the items being stored. There are many possibilities for how those photographs are enclosed and arranged within the box:

- Place the photographs in transparent sleeves made of polyester film, especially if they are in poor condition. Then you can buy a special pen to identify the photograph on the sleeve. Avoid writing on the photographs themselves to identify them, but if it must be done, pencil lightly on the back. Never apply adhesive stickers directly on photographs, which contain harmful acids.
- Group several photographs inside an acid-free flap envelope or file folder. It is ideal to include no more than five photographs, and to separate them with buffering tissues. Then place the envelopes/folders inside an archival box. There are many styles of envelopes, folders, and boxes that are available through archival supply companies, some of which accommodate old styles of photographs quite well.
- Old photographs that are permanently attached in photographer's folders should be enclosed in an acid-free envelope or folder to keep the acids in the old cardboard from affecting other photographs in the collection.

Attention should be paid to color photographs, because the only way to keep them from fading is to provide cold storage, and few individuals have access to this type of storage. Scan color photographs as quickly as possible before further deterioration occurs. Some scanners can autocorrect to compensate for some fading.

Home movies are not just fading fast, particularly if they are color, but may also have become so brittle that they will break apart when they are loaded into a projector. If possible, they should be digitized and transferred to DVDs, and/or digital files. Many such companies perform this service for a variety of home movie formats, including 8MM, Super 8, Beta, VHS, and mini-VHS. After this process is complete, it is possible to store the digital files in a Dropbox or on a Cloud. However, it is important to keep the originals if possible, because as technology changes, it will be necessary to migrate the images to new formats as they develop, and it will be desirable to be able to copy from the originals. The original formats also likely will outlast many of today's surrogates, but the images on them will not be accessible unless they are migrated to another new viewing format. The same storage condition rules that apply to old photographs and documents also apply to old films.

CONCLUSION

The staff at a variety of cultural heritage institutions can help individuals and families to preserve family photographs, a task in which even those who are not avid family historians usually see the value. Guidance could help prevent valuable photographs, another piece of our shared cultural heritage, from being discarded. The next chapter will discuss how institutions can provide better access to a wide variety of materials including photographs.

PROGRAMMING IDEAS

Community and Family Photo Scanning Night

The institution uses the event to acquire local images for a digital collection. Care must be taken to encourage participants to only bring in those images that are in the public domain, or that have a copyright release form signed from the copyright holder. The session will last from one and a half to two hours.

Before the session begins, make sure enough scanners are on hand to have only four persons per scanner group, if feasible—it may be possible to borrow some. Have the session preregistered, to insure everyone will be able to have scanning time. Permission forms/releases should be available so that the institution has clear, legal permission to add the images to their collection. The institution will archive and index the scans.

Explain how the institution is going to use the images, where they will be displayed, how they will be accessible, and the importance of this activity in documenting the history of the community. Review the mechanics of scanning. Explain the release forms.

Then small groups will undertake scanning of up to several photos each onto flash drives. Try to have additional staff, and/or knowledgeable volunteers to assist. Wrap up the program by sharing at least some of the scanned images on a screen with the entire group over refreshments, if allowed in the institution.

Note: If a more elaborate version of this program is desired, the National Endowment for the Humanities (NEH) has announced the Common Heritage program, whereby grant funding is available to underwrite a day-long version of this type of event, even to small and medium-sized institutions that have never sought a grant before: http://www.neh.gov/grants/preservation/common-heritage.

Additional Ideas

- Hire an expert to give a presentation on digital photo restoration.
- Hold a program on photo identification tips.
- A program on the proper storage of photographs would be popular.

NOTES

1. Catherine Noren, *The Way We Looked: the Meaning and Magic of Family Photographs* (New York, NY: Dutton, 1983), 5.

2. Heloise, "Ask Heloise," *Good Housekeeping,* Feb. 2013: 139. *Home Improvement Collection.* Web, accessed June 27, 2015.

3. Albert K. Baragwanath, "Dating Photographs," *Curator: The Museum Journal* 20: 47, doi: 10.1111/j.2151-6952.1977.tb00527.x.

4. Michelle Facos, *An Introduction to Nineteenth Century Art* (New York, NY: Routledge), 201.

Chapter 6

THE NEGOTIATORS: ASKING AND ANSWERING QUESTIONS

Helping researchers with their genealogical and local history information needs is an important aspect of providing family history services. The beginning of this book highlighted the fact that an institution does not need a large collection in order to provide this type of reference service, or indeed, any collection at all. What **is** required are information providers who have an enthusiastic attitude and some information about what these researchers are looking for, as well as some knowledge of the common difficulties of family history research.

THE MINDSET: WHAT INFORMATION PROVIDERS SHOULD BE THINKING IN ORDER TO BETTER HELP RESEARCHERS

It is a fact that since the arrival of Google, the demand for reference services has dwindled.[1] Individuals can easily look up many facts on their own that they used to depend on reference staff members to provide. However, the surge in the popularity of family history research may provide the opportunity for reference departments to regain patrons, if they are smart enough to give their staff members adequate training, and to let the public know that they are offering this type of assistance. Patrick Cadell, in a speech on family history services at the International Federation of Library Associations and Institutions conference in 2002, referred to the information professional as "that best of all finding aids."[2] Indeed, that is true if the librarian, archivist, or volunteer behind the desk has a good attitude about helping family historians. The following section is a discussion of ingredients in the mindset required to provide successful family history reference service. Perhaps information staff could keep in mind this series of mantras, or guiding principles, so that they can act as truly wonderful finding aids.

> Mantra: "It is exciting to watch history come alive for researchers."

First, because the link between history and family history is so strong, an interest in **history for history's sake** is essential. Every life story is part of the greater fabric of history. It is our privilege to help patrons assemble and document these stories. The research techniques used by family historians are quite similar to those used by microhistorians, or scholars who ask "large questions in small places."[3] Another apt designation of this type of researcher is a generational historian.[4] This type of history is intensely personal and important to the researchers, many of whom have never entered a library before. They may be interested in understanding more about history in general along with their family histories, but they may not have been exposed to much historical information outside of school.

> Mantra: *"I am going to enjoy the process of working with researchers, and not always look for the conclusion of the process."*

Another key element of the mindset is being **process oriented**, not end-product oriented. In traditional reference, we work to define, and locate very specific information to satisfy short-term queries. A patron desires a statistic, a used car price, a book on Asian cooking, and we supply it. But in genealogy reference, the process is what is important. Genealogical research is usually ongoing for years, decades, even a lifetime. The successful answering of one genealogical query usually generates a host of others. This fact can be irritating to traditional reference staff, who are accustomed to completing a transaction with one patron and then quickly moving on. Genealogy staff members need to get used to spending more time with each patron, and embracing repeat customers, who, after all, provide higher usage statistics, and perhaps some degree of job security. It is easy to acquire a "get them out the door as quickly as possible" mentality, especially when lines form at the reference desk, but that urge should be fought. More on this strategy will be discussed later in this chapter.

> **Mantra:** *"I come to learn as well as to teach."*

Let's start by getting rid of the us versus them attitude. Some library staff members, and other types of workers who deal with the public, subconsciously or consciously, enjoy the power that their position confers upon them. Some information providers know the intricacies of navigating their collections, their online catalogs, and even the Internet; they control the dispersal of information from their collections, and treat their patrons as supplicants asking for crumbs from the rich banquet of their knowledge. This attitude is undesirable for many reasons; one of them is that the field of family history encompasses so many diverse subjects that it is impossible for anyone to be a complete master of it all. Consider that knowledge of foreign languages, naming customs, handwriting analysis, the law, and many other subjects are all helpful in family history research. It is inevitable that the attempt to appear omniscient will result in the staff member becoming unmasked, much as Toto pulled back the curtain to reveal, not the Great and Powerful Oz, but a fumbling charlatan. A much better approach is to **work collegially, *with* the patron**, explaining how and where to find the information during the entire interaction. After all, many reference transactions require the staff member to learn alongside the patron.

Researchers will ask for help with many challenges, such as the interpretation of old handwritten documents such as this baptismal certificate in Figure 6.1. Information providers do not need to be experts in these tasks themselves, but they will need to be experts at tracking down both information and subject experts to assist researchers.

Figure 6.1
Baptismal Certificate. Used with Permission.

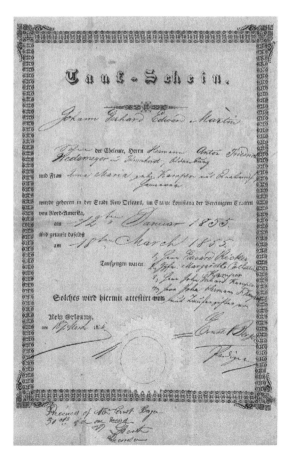

Mantra: *"I do not have to be an expert genealogist in order to provide good genealogy service."*

Information professionals may be reluctant to work with genealogists because they feel intimidated by a complicated and difficult- to- master research field. The Melbourne, Australia public library surveyed their general reference staff and discovered that the majority of them felt intimidated by the prospect of local history reference because it was perceived as a specialty that they did not know anything about.[5] Reference providers need to be reminded that it is not necessary to possess all knowledge related to the field, just the knowledge about how to find it. This can be accomplished with some training and practice.

THE PATRONS

"Genealogists are known to be very vocal in their desires for library service."
—Dahrl Elizabeth Moore[6]

Most genealogists are hobbyists, but there is a broad range of experience, research ability, and goals amongst them. Some of these patrons are content stringing some names together and making a tree. Others will spend years doing intensive research to put together true family histories, which explore all historical and cultural aspects of their ancestors' lives, and produce fully documented scholarship. Some work independently, and others like to collaborate, and are active in genealogical organizations. All of these approaches, and many in-between, are valid, and deserve support by information providers.

A small percentage of researchers are professionals who do research for hire. Some of them may be certified in genealogy through one of two certification programs. One is run by the Board for Certification of Genealogists (BCG), and the other through The International Commission for the Accreditation of Professional Genealogists (ICAPGEN). They may also belong to an organization called the Association of Professional Genealogists (APGEN). None of this guarantees that these researchers provide good and/or reasonably priced service to customers. Many research institutions will provide a list of professional researchers in the area upon request, but most also provide a disclaimer that they cannot endorse the services of any professionals on the list. Sometimes patrons will need to be referred to a professional, especially when they live outside of the area and cannot come to do research themselves, or when the difficulty of the research exceeds their ability and patience.

Research has revealed information about the habits and preferences of genealogists:

- Genealogists in archives prefer to ask a staff member for guidance rather than reading information about how they should use the resources of the institution.[7]
- Genealogists early in their careers tend to use a narrow range of resources, but expand that range as their experience and confidence level increases.[8]

- Genealogists want to find names in records to locate information about individuals and families, but a significant amount of information in libraries and archives is arranged by geographic area, which means that often they do not have easy access points to information.[9]

A wide variety of issues can frustrate researchers. To help them make the most of their time spent at a cultural heritage institution, try to prepare researchers before they arrive:

- Post on your website the kind of information that the patron should come prepared with, and where that information might be located. For example, see "New to Genealogy" on the Allen County Public Library Genealogy Department website. Gather more ideas from "A First-timer's Guide to Archival Research," *NGS Magazine,* April–June 2013, vol. 39, no. 2.

- Provide a link to a how to prepare for your research trip article online. An article "A Trip to Bountiful Genealogy Research" is a good example: http://www .archives.com/experts/macentee-thomas/a-trip-to-bountiful-genealogy-research .html.

- Post a short video tour of the institution and its resources on the institution's website or links to it as a helpful way to prepare researchers ahead of time.

- Distribute handouts with this information; you might not be able to educate patron online before their first visit, but you can before subsequent ones.

THE REFERENCE INTERVIEW

"The quest for family history fascinates and confuses."

—William A. Katz[10]

The most challenging aspect of genealogical research is that there is not one right way of doing it. One researcher, a retired doctor, asked one day in frustration, "Where is the formula that I can use to do it right?" Of course, the answer is "There is no such thing." Everyone, depending on his/her locality and individual family, must discover a unique research path. The Reference & User Services Association (RUSA) does not have specific guidelines for negotiating genealogy reference questions, although they have other sets of general reference guidelines that can still be helpful. The RUSA History Committee has a genealogy subcommittee which publishes separate guidelines for collections and the education service providers should receive in a library school genealogical course. The latter does outline some information on what should be taught about providing genealogical reference.[11] Their local history subcommittee has guidelines, but they only discuss the local history collection, not reference provision.[12]

The skill levels of genealogists vary greatly, which makes our job of negotiating their reference questions challenging. One factor is in the information provider's favor: almost all genealogists are highly motivated to succeed. They have become not just interested, but fascinated, and even downright obsessed, by figuring out their families' pasts. All genealogy patrons also have in common the fact that even though they have different motivations and backgrounds, they are all trying to accomplish the same goal, to find their own unique story. In order to discover it, they all must locate, examine, and evaluate a combination of written records, physical items like photographs and family heirlooms, and oral traditions. Like paintings done in the pointillism style, family history research is comprised of hundreds of tiny, very specific facts.

WHERE TO START: THE GREETING

As with a general reference interview, nonverbal communication is just as important, if not more important, than what is said to those seeking help. Open body language and a pleasant, smiling demeanor state that you are interested in requests and eager to assist. Some reference providers advocate standing as the patron approaches to reinforce this impression, and roving reference, or going to the patrons instead of making them approach a staff member seated at a desk, can also be effective.

The first statement that staff members make to researchers could affect the course of the entire interview. Asking "Hello, how may I help you?" is such a wide open question that often the patrons will start rambling. Also, this wording puts the burden on the patrons to articulate exactly what they want; and that often is not possible at first because many approach information providers without any clear research goals, or the knowledge of what is needed to achieve their research goal.

A better opener is "Hello, what may I help you find today?" This approach nudges them in the direction of asking for something specific. Most researchers will not ask a reasonably focused question at first, but that is why the process is called negotiation, because often the actual information need is hidden and must be uncovered by an exchange of information on both sides.

ESTABLISHING THE CONTEXTS

Similar to the expression, "It takes money to make money," it takes information to get information. The absolute minimum information that the patron must provide to get started is a name, preferably a full name, and a location, as specific as possible. However, the research will commence more easily if even more information is solicited. So the reference provider must ask questions, sometimes many questions, to obtain a solid base of information about the family, and to establish the following three contexts:

- **geographical context**: where the ancestor lived
- **chronological context**: when the ancestor lived
- **socioeconomic context**: the ancestor's status within his or her community

Carefully crafted questions will keep the reference interview on task. If open questions are used such as "Tell me what you know about the Bakers?" the interview could be prolonged as the patron relates endless details and anecdotes, most of them irrelevant and confusing.

Here is a hypothetical example. A patron says he wants information about the Baker family and that they lived in southern Illinois. The reference provider needs to find out if that information can be refined and augmented. Here are some sample questions that might work:

- Can you supply the full name of your grandfather who grew up among these Bakers?
- Do you know the county in southern Illinois in which they lived?
- Do you know the name of the town or township within the county where they lived?
- What was your grandmother's full name?
- Was your grandmother's family from the same community as your grandfather's?

Other questions will help bring out details about the family members that will aid in the search, especially if the surname is a common one.[13] These could include questions about what they did for a living, and their religious and/or ethnic background. The idea is to put together a profile of known clues about the family, even if the clues have not been verified. Even unsubstantiated family legends and traditions usually have some kernel of truth, but in a small percentage of cases they can be completely incorrect. However, asking additional questions about the family's background can help ascertain whether or not you are locating members of the *correct* Baker family in records.

- What did the Bakers do for a living?
- Were they rich, poor, or in between?
- Where did they worship?
- Do you know their ethnic background?

Discovering precisely *where* the ancestor lived, or geographical context, can be tricky because boundaries have a tendency to move around over time, just as the ancestors did. Also, place names can change over time, and families tend to remember the name of the largest community *near* the place their ancestors lived, not the precise community they lived in. The trick is discovering not just that the Bakers lived in Macoupin County, Illinois near Gillespie, but what this area was officially called when the Bakers lived there. You can try searching the Internet, but you may need to try specialized geographic sources. What to consult:

For U.S. Locations:

    Atlas of Historical County Boundaries, http://publications.newberry.org/ahcbp/. This interactive website hosted by the Newberry Library's Dr. William M. Scholl Center for American History and Culture has been compiled based on meticulous research in old state statutes and historical maps. It allows a researcher to pinpoint the various official geographical designations that a U.S. location had by year.

    Geographic Names Information System (GNIS) United States Geological Survey, http://geonames.usgs.gov/index.html. This site contains documented place name variations.

    Old U.S. Post Office Guides. The titles vary somewhat over the years, but there is a large collection of these on Google Books. They help not only to verify old place names, but to identify the community near the ancestor where he or she was likely to have received mail, and possibly to have shopped, traded, and socialized as well. This corresponds to information on some old U.S. Censuses that designated the post office that served those being enumerated, and which helps nail down a more exact residence for those who lived in rural areas outside the boundaries of cities and towns.

For other world locations:

    Harding, Les. *Dead Countries of the Nineteenth and Twentieth Centuries: Aden to Zululand.* Lanham, MD: Scarecrow Press, 1998. This gazetteer covers countries from around the world that no longer exist.

    The JewishGen Gazetteer (formerly called Shtetl Seeker), www.jewishgen .org/Communities. This database was originally designed to locate Jewish communities, many of them located in areas of Europe with rapidly changing borders, but in actual practice it pins down country names and borders for European communities whether or not they are/were considered Jewish.

In addition to the resources above, articles on a variety of websites can be helpful to identify old place names and border changes. If using Google, it may be necessary to search one of the foreign versions of the site if information on a foreign country is desired. For example, going to www.google.de will limit the hits to those in the Google search engine based in Germany.

Some tricks may help establish the chronological context which is not always known by the patron. It may be possible to ask questions to hone in on an approximate time period. One good method is to try to relate family events to how old the patron was when they occurred. Another is to relate them to an event in history whose date can be ascertained. For example:

- Do you know at least an approximate time period when your grandfather lived there?
- Do you remember how old you were when he died?
- Did your grandfather fight in any wars?

The patron may not remember the exact date on which his or her grandfather was born, but may remember that the birth occurred when a great-grandfather was just about to leave to fight in World War I. This would give you an estimated date of 1917–1918 for the birth of his grandfather.

Another aid related to when the ancestors lived is to sketch out a timeline of a life span, and then next to it, sketch timelines for the major available record groups in the community, such as various vital records. The two or more timelines juxtaposed will reveal in which record groups that information on the ancestor can be found.[14]

What to suggest if the patron comes up blank on information that establishes the contexts:

- Do some legwork. See if, with the details the patron does know and a quick search of online family trees, census records, local histories, and vital records, some facts turn up which could help nail down any of the three contexts.
- Refer the patron to home sources. Ask if the patron either has brought any family papers, or has any at home that could be searched for clues.
- Tap the oral traditions. Ask if there is anyone in the family who might be able to provide some of the missing details.

NEXT STEP: NARROW THE FOCUS

Only after these contexts are established should the next step occur, narrowing the focus. Then even more questions will be exchanged. Negotiating the typical family history question is not a fast process. An unfocused query, not asking where a specific type of resource is located, rather asking what the institution owns about a specific family, may take fifteen to twenty minutes to negotiate or more. That is okay as family history reference simply cannot be delivered at a fast-food pace. It takes time to establish the correct research contexts, to narrow the focus of the question, to identify sources to consult, and to provide instruction as all of these steps are occurring.

Here is a sample of the types of questions that challenge reference providers to narrow them, as well as some coping strategies. The terms for various types of questions in this section are not meant to be disrespectful of our patrons, but simply are a shorthand method to indicate the type of challenge they represent.

The first, The Newbie, is the patron who "has no idea where to start...". This patron appears with no plan or documentation, but with a vague goal of "finding out about my family" or "doing genealogy."

- Lead the patron to a copy of a basic how-to genealogy book that can be checked out. Your institution should own it in multiple copies. If your institution does not circulate items at all, hand the patron an annotated bibliography of recommended titles to borrow or purchase elsewhere.
- Hand the patron a copy of an in-house brochure that summarizes the institution's genealogy holdings, a genealogy pathfinder.
- Give or sell the patron copies of family group sheets. Explain how to fill them out with what the patron knows, or provide written instructions for doing so. This is NOT always intuitive. Then help to begin finding sources to back up facts or to fill in holes by finding additional facts.
- Distribute a packet which includes the materials mentioned above, but also might contain a map of the collection, a basic advice sheet on beginning genealogical research, a list of helpful websites, and more.
- Tell the patron about the "One Quarter Rule." Everyone has four grandparents. Have the patron choose a line going back through *one* of them as a place to begin the research. This narrows the research to a manageable amount, at least down to one quarter of the family. Explain that trying to work on too many lines at one time is confusing.
- Refer the patron to local how-to family history classes and programs.
- Give the patron information about joining the local genealogical society.

The Newbies are time-consuming, no doubt about it, but they are coming in to see us because we have wisdom to share. We are the research experts. So get them started with one, or all of the above steps, and then go back to check on their progress.

The second type is The Gusher. This patron "knows" a lot of information about the family, and is eager to share it, *ad nauseum*. There is usually not a hint of a question to be found in the entire monologue. Try to switch the exchange from a verbal one to a written one, at least until the basic contexts of the question can be established.

- One technique is to attempt to fill in a pedigree chart based on the information that is pouring forth from the patron. This is somewhat akin to trying to cap a gushing oil well, but may help make sense of the verbal onslaught.
- Another technique involves when the patron pauses for breath, ask if the patron has seen your Family History Reference Question Form, and quickly produce it. This form is designed to force the patron to focus a small amount of what might be known in the direction of a specific question. Ask the patron to fill it out before you attempt to proceed with the reference interview. Work from the vague and labor intensive, towards a focused and manageable information request.

The third patron is The Confused. This patron asks if you have a specific source, such as Ancestry.com, and then flounders, obviously overwhelmed. This patron does not necessarily want to access this website, but feels it appropriate to ask for something, anything. Any question is unlikely to reflect what is truly needed.

- Ask, gently, if there may be something else that needs to be searched and let this question initiate a dialogue.
- Guide the patron to the original requested source and return after a couple minutes to say, "I just thought I would check to see how you are doing."
- Stroll in the patron's general direction later. Smile encouragingly. This will help the patron to get up enough nerve to try again.

The fourth patron, The Optimist, asks to see "the book" that has all the information on his or her family, the Browns. Perhaps this patron has heard from a family member that someone has written a book, or simply hopes that one has been written. This person is *searching* for information that has already been compiled by someone else. It is logical to begin by finding out if anyone else has ever published research on a given family. However, a published monograph may or may not exist for this family, and even if such a book does exist, the information may not be well-researched or sourced.

- Search for genealogies by checking WorldCat under the surname, the reference work *Genealogies Held by the Library of Congress*, as well as Google Books, Internet Archive, and FamilySearch for digitized genealogies. If the surname is a common one, it may still be possible to narrow to a likely publication by also searching for allied surnames that are less common, or to also add geographic location as a search limiter, i.e., to see if any books on the Brown family cover Browns from Loudun County, Virginia.
- Help the patron determine if research on the family has been published in some format other than a book. Search for an article in a local history/genealogy periodical by checking *The Periodical Source Index (PERSI)* and other indices. Search through some online family tree websites. Search your institution's family files, if that is appropriate.
- Show the patron how to evaluate any source of information about the family. Good information lists specific sources from where the information came, and is logical. An individual's mother should have a birthdate that occurred roughly 15 to 45 years before the individual's birthdate. If the birthdate of the mother occurs after that of an alleged child, there are problems with the information. Unbelievably, these kinds of gaffes are found in online family trees all the time.
- If searching fails, then instruct the patron on how and where to post queries on message boards. See "Message Board Etiquette."
- Explain the difference between **searching** and **research**. Searching is finding information compiled by others, while researching involves pulling and analyzing information from sources oneself.

The fifth, The Disorganized Patron, comes in with lots of enthusiasm and overflowing files bulging with papers. This patron just needs "one more minute" to find the thing you were going to be asked about, one the patron started looking for ten minutes ago. This patron needs help with organization, desperately! Finding information is just half the battle. Analyzing it, and organizing the results, is the other half.

- Suggest books, articles, and websites with organizing strategies.
- Chat about how genealogical software programs store and organize data.
- Ask if the patron has heard about research logs. Forms for this purpose can be printed off the internet for free. They help researchers keep track of what sources they examine, when they examined them, and what the results were.
- Remind the patron that analyzing sources is even more complex than organizing them. If you do not have time to teach some basics, then refer the patron to books which can. Emily Ann Croom's *The Sleuth Book for Genealogists* is a helpful title. More titles are listed in Appendix A, "Annotated List of How-To Family History Titles."

Next, the Wounded is a highly emotional rather than an objective researcher. This patron comes in with a question motivated by a desire to grapple with a difficult family situation. A good example of this is an adoptee searching for information on the birth family, but it may also involve having a criminal in the family tree, a suicide, illegitimacy, or some other touchy issue. Elizabeth Yakel writes, "genealogists are emotional and their emotions inspire and propel research."[15]

For this patron, **librarian as therapist** is the hat you may need to wear. One surprising thing about family history is that even when the events involve family members who are long gone, who the patron has never even met, the actions of their ancestors can conjure up many emotions., not all of them pleasant. A researcher once related how she met a member of another branch of her great-grandfather's family via a message board. They were part of his first family that the great-grandfather had abandoned in another state before moving to Indiana to found another family that the researcher is part of. The members of the first family were still upset a few generations later that they were the ones left behind.

- Make sure that the reference interview is conducted in a low voice, in as private a location as possible.
- Ask the emotionally distraught patron if it would be easier to ask the question via email and offer your direct email address if your institution uses an online reference form. Have tissues handy if the patron begins to cry.
- Reassure the patron that any information being shared will be treated with the utmost confidentiality. Information providers have this obligation along with clergymen, lawyers, physicians, and other counselors.
- Make sure that any referrals you make are to places that will actually have and are able to share information this fragile patron needs. Call or email ahead if necessary.
- Offer an outlet if this patron is interested in sharing concerns with others. The International Blacksheep Society of Genealogists hosts a listserv where researchers can share tales of their dastardly ancestors: http://ibssg.org/blacksheep/.

The Monopolizer is the patron who asks a never-ending series of questions and shows little willingness to do any independent work. There may be good reasons for this behavior including excitement, loneliness, or true ignorance of how to use the institution and its resources. However, because other patrons may be waiting for help, a line must be drawn in the sand.

- Explain that the time that you can spend right now with the patron is at an end, but that he or she is welcome to leave another question in writing. This may be a good time to encourage the patron to fill out the reference question form.
- Schedule a personal research consultation if allowed by your institution. Spending an hour analyzing this patron's research needs, and then drawing up a list of specific tasks may provide the needed guidance.
- Cite the reference policy as a reason to move on to the next patron. Some policies state specific time averages that can be spent on individual questions. Others may state how many "pieces of information" can be provided to one patron at one time. Regardless of what the policy is, try not to use it like a club, but as a gentle restrainer of excess enthusiasm.

The Shootist is the patron who asks an impossibly broad question such as, "Do you have anything about the Smith family?" This patron is "shooting in the dark," hoping that a staff member will agree to check every possible source in the collection for any mention of anyone with this surname, that is, to do all his or her research. Some patrons ask this type of question out of naïveté about what is involved in providing an answer, and others may be gunning for someone else to completely compile their family histories for them. Regardless of the motivation, this question will need to be narrowed to a considerably smaller target.

- Try to find a focus by providing a source checklist form and have the patron indicate which documents have already been located for a family group or individual, and which still need to be tracked down.
- Use the question "If there were just one thing that you could locate today, what would that be?"

IDENTIFY SPECIFIC RESOURCES TO MEET THE RESEARCH GOAL

After the first few steps are complete, it is time to actually identify sources in the institution's collection, and also online, that will help answer the query. Because such a wide variety of sources are used by local studies researchers, this step can be challenging to the information provider who is new to this type of research. Another challenge is that a single type of record sought by the researcher, or its finding aids, could be located in multiple places. Chapter 8 of this book, "Mining the Riches" is an overview of the main types of records used, and provides insight into how they can best be accessed and analyzed. Another aid is to start by identifying and studying the sources that are used for research where your institution is located.

Some institutions have put together locality guides which are written overviews of their communities' sources. These are tremendously helpful for both staff members and researchers, and detailed information on what they contain is in Appendix B.

As mentioned earlier, no one can master all aspects of family history research, and the odds are very good that at some point you will receive questions that you and your colleagues cannot handle on your own. Help is available by "calling in" the virtual staff members!

- Use a brain trust. One place to try is the GENEALIB listserv. Family history librarians from around the country read the posts, and it is very common to see members post questions asking for advice on how to help patrons with specific research problems. Usually answers are posted within the working day. Also turn to the help line at the Family History Library (FHL) in Salt Lake City, Utah. They have a toll-free number, 1-866-406-1830 and it is staffed with trained volunteers 24 hours a day. Callers are routed to the specialized department that is best able to handle each particular question. The volunteers are able to view the contents of most FHL microfilms from their computer screens in order to help callers. Technology and the FHL are wonderful aids!

- Share a question involving local families with members of the local genealogical/historical society, with the patron's permission. Someone else might be researching the same family line, or know something or someone that helps.

- Check in, with an official town historian in New York[16] and Connecticut. This is an appointed position, often unpaid, that is not well defined. Some town historians actually have records that they manage while others focus more on genealogy, some more on local history, and some on both. The Association of Public Historians of New York State website may help locate them: http://www.aphnys.org/. Connecticut has an online directory called "Towns, Cities and Boroughs–Officers and Statistics," and the "municipal historian" is listed along with the other town officers under each town section.[17] The websites of individual towns may also list town historians and their contact information.

- Search in Eastman's Online Encyclopedia of Genealogy which is an easy, free place to check on the meaning of terminology: http://www.eogen.com/.

- Post a genealogy-related question on this website: http://genealogy.stackexchange .com/.

- Contact local volunteers found on The Random Acts of Genealogical Kindness website which allows researchers to contact those who will do searches and who probably possess expertise on research in their locality. It is a global organization: http://www.raogk.org/.

If the information provider decides that the question cannot be answered with the institution's resources, all is not lost. First, **negative research results** are a very important part of the research process. Researchers need to keep track of what they cannot find in different sources, not just so they do not accidentally recheck the same sources later, but so they can refocus their search strategies. For example, are there no family marriages in Grainger County, Tennessee? Maybe the next step is to check neighboring Jefferson County.

Second, even if specific records cannot be supplied, perhaps crucial **background information sources** can. A history of the state or the area of research which sheds light on migration patterns, settlement areas, or ethnic and religious communities will help the patron to jumpstart the research process.

Indexing versus Records

It should be noted that there is a big difference between using indexing and studying actual records. Beginning researchers are often confused by this concept, so it is important that staff help them to understand it. More and more indexing of various types of records is appearing online in both subscription and free genealogical websites. This indexing is a fantastic research aid, allowing researchers to know, with good probability, if their ancestors' names appear in certain record groups. However, many beginning researchers think that the online database containing the indexed names is the only source they need to consult, not realizing that they should still track down the actual record itself. Indexing is not a source of genealogical information, but an aid to track down a source of genealogical information. Researchers should not be citing an index as a source in their research. Some online indexing does connect to digitized images of the records themselves, but much of it does not.

There are good reasons for researchers not to rely solely on indexing:

- An index will not have every piece of information on a record. In fact, usually a lot of information on the record is passed over.

- Indexes are not perfect. Often the names are misinterpreted by the indexer and placed in the index under the wrong spelling, or typos occur when the index is created or transferred online, or names are missed entirely and not included in the index at all.

- An index is another step removed from the original information. If the researcher trusts the date that someone has supposedly transcribed from a record, but that date turns out to have been copied incorrectly, then problems will ensue.

Another issue that needs attention is understanding the scope of indexing in online databases. Often, databases are labeled with a very broad title, such as "Marriage Records of South Dakota." But if one reads the description of the database, it turns out that only certain counties in the state of South Dakota are included and only for very specific, varying time periods. Just as it is prudent to read the prefaces of print reference sources, it is also prudent to carefully read the descriptions of databases. Make sure patrons access this information to help them make sense of why or why not they have success searching the database.

ATTENTION TO DETAIL

Here are some more concerns that should be addressed as information providers work with their patrons. The first two bulleted paragraphs are essential.

- Supply the patron with the specific titles of sources you have checked, even if they do not ask for them. Patrons need to know this for their research process, even if you did not find what they requested, or had negative results. Remind patrons that they should record information sources so that they know where it came from later, and so other researchers can recreate their research, if desired.

- Label the back of any photocopy or supply with any scan you send to a patron the complete citation of the source, because they need to be able to cite this in their research. For example, if you send an obituary, make sure it has the complete name of the newspaper as it was during the time the obituary appeared. Remember that newspaper names change over the years. Do not label it the "Centerville Bugle," its current name, if the newspaper was called the "Daily Bugle" when the obituary appeared in 1930. Also make sure that you include the date of the issue, the page number, and the column number. Likewise, supply the volume number and issue number, along with page numbers for magazine/journal articles. This seems like common sense, but many institutions fail to provide this information to patrons.

- Contact the patron later if you cannot determine places to check for the requested information while the patron is with you, and you think of additional places after the patron has already left. After all, the patron's research will be ongoing for years. That is why it is a good idea to obtain **contact information from every patron** regardless of whether the exchange has been in-person or long distance. Some institutions have sign-in books that at least will gather that information from patrons walking through the door, and helps to keep a head count of users.

- Integrate all library services into the research process such as interlibrary loan, placing holds on material, and referrals to other departments within your institution, if it is a large one.

- Direct a patron to the best staff member to help with their research needs. Most researchers would be willing to wait to talk with a staffer who knew the most about a particular topic, such as a type of ethnic research, than deal with a less knowledgeable staffer immediately.

- Make sure that any usage of proprietary databases to answer queries falls within the guidelines of your site license.

- Keep track of questions asked by frequent patrons. That way, the next time they come in and get a different staff member, the staff member can check his or her file to see what the patron has been working on lately, the sources tried, etc., so the wheel does not have to be reinvented.

- Use the Reference Effort Assessment Data (READ) scale as a good resource for thinking about the depth of the queries, your answers, and the overall types of questions you are getting at the institution: http://www.readscale.org/.

SENSEI: THE ROLE OF TEACHING

Once sources are retrieved, instruction may be necessary to teach the patron how to use them, and how to record and interpret the information. The question arises of how much teaching should information providers provide to patrons. The answer for those who work with local studies patrons is: a fair amount. *Sensei* is a Japanese term that means a combination of a teacher, leader, and counselor, and that is what researchers need when they turn to a cultural heritage institution. Those staff members who do not feel comfortable teaching should reconsider whether they really want to assist family historians. It cannot be assumed that patrons have a handle on basic library skills, such as how to search the online catalog, how to locate an item by its call number, and how to compare subject headings, much less that they understand some of the typical tasks involved in family history research such as interpreting old handwriting, making sense of legal documents, and assessing sources for accuracy. Some genealogists have been out of school for many years, and have not been library users in the past.

Librarian Pamela J. Cooper did a study of about 600 members of genealogy societies in Florida and determined that about half of them had never used the online catalog at their home libraries.[18] Always ask if assistance and/or instruction is needed before you send a patron off to complete a task. Always do this in a business-like manner; never register surprise if a patron exhibits uncertainty as to how to do something. Be prepared to suggest sources of education/training for patrons. Classes on research skills, computer usage, and the Internet may be necessary for the patron to progress. These may be found at community colleges and senior centers, not just in the library. In addition, there is a tremendous amount of how-to genealogical information that is available online for free to which patrons could be referred.

THE LAST STEP: REFERRALS

Because no single institution could possibly ever contain all the information that researchers need, it is often necessary to make referrals. If staff members cannot find a piece of information for the patron within their walls, they should figure out **where the needed information is**. A quickly tossed-off referral that is a guess, sending the patron scampering in the wrong direction, is research sabotage. Websites of other institutions should be checked to accurately direct the patron to the next stop in the research process. If it is not clear from a website if the needed information is available at another institution, a quick telephone call to a colleague at the other institution is in order. Locating digitized books, or the processing of an interlibrary loan request may also be in order. Never just shrug your shoulders and say to the patron, "Sorry, we can't help." You should always end an interaction with a patron on a positive note, offering some proactive type of assistance, because we are our institution to the patron. If they come away from interacting with us with a good feeling, then they feel good about the institution. Some librarians like to always give the patron something tangible: a preprinted chart, a pathfinder, a photocopy of helpful chart, etc.

SUCCESSES AND FAILURES

All family history researchers must go through a learning curve as they begin to locate sources and interpret the information they contain. All of them will make mistakes at some point, even if they read several how-to genealogical books. This is a completely normal. It is helpful for the staff members who help genealogists to understand what these mistakes are in order to get researchers back on track. A list of them can be consulted at FamilySearch: "Rookie Mistakes," http://family search.org/learn/wiki/en/Rookie_Mistakes.

Conversely, it is also helpful to have a sense of what makes successful researchers successful. Below is a summary of widely disseminated research advice. Feel free to share it, but remember that the researchers may have trouble understanding and following the advice before they have been researching for a while and have made a few mistakes.

- Start recording information about one's self first, and then systematically work backwards through the generations. Progress from the known to the unknown. Do not try to skip backwards several generations.
- Rely on more than one source to establish a fact because sometimes sources contain errors and that single source you found may be flawed. Use several sources, as many as you can find.
- Consult transcribed and abstracted records, but then follow up by finding the original record or its facsimile, if possible. Transcribed and abstracted records can contain errors.
- Check the spelling of names which were often misspelled, mangled, or changed on documents for a variety of reasons.
- Check for both first and middle names; sometimes people used them interchangeably.
- Pay attention to misinformation. It may hold a clue to what the correct information really is.
- Treat the memories of family members initially as unproven theories.
- Search the female lines as well as male lines.
- Check the pre-1850 U.S. Census information even though it is sparser than later records; the information still has value.
- Rely on facts rather than assumptions. Assumptions can greatly hinder research progress.
- Check ancestors' neighbors as they matter. Community webs can be as important as kinship networks.

TO-DO CHECKLIST FOR NEGOTIATING FAMILY HISTORY REFERENCE QUESTIONS

- Change your body language as the patron approaches. Stop other tasks, look up, and appear receptive.
- Smile and ask, "What may I help you find today?"
- Listen. It may take a while; it is okay to take notes while doing so.
- Prepare and ask questions to establish the three basic contexts.
- Find any sources to help establish contexts when your patron does not know enough to provide them. The patron may need to consult relatives and/or home sources to better establish contexts.
- Ask more questions to try to help the patron establish a specific research goal, if he or she does not already have one.
- Try to determine if what the patron is asking for will truly provide what is needed. Ask: "And you want to know that because. . .?"
- Identify sources of information in your collection and/or online that may help the patron to meet the goal. Another useful phrase is "Let me get you started by. . .".

- Refer the patron to a variety of other institutions such as government offices, libraries and archives, cemeteries, etc., and websites that also keep information to help meet the goal.

Personal Reflection: When the Shoe Is on the Other Foot

For about thirteen years, I was used to being behind the desk, controlling the reference interactions. During that time, I completely forgot what it was like to be a patron. Then I left my reference position, and began researching my family history, mostly long distance. I quickly became shocked at how powerless I felt. Would the staff member I was interacting with decide to share information or not, and, if so, how much would he be willing to scan and email or photocopy and mail? Sometimes, the answer was a generous amount. Other times, it was just a little, far less than what I wanted or needed. Sometimes the answer was none. Many times I phoned or emailed a question and the library never contacted me with an answer, or even to say "We don't have an answer."

The genealogy reference service I have received has ranged from superlative, such as the librarian who drove into a rural area at the end of a work day to check out the spot I suspected where an ancestor was buried, to the wretched as when the department head of a local studies collection at a major public library "lost" my question on his desk and never called me. After I called back two weeks later to inquire, an underling exposed the erring boss, and never apologized for the gaffe. But at least he wrote down the question—again. Some of my experiences have made me question how we currently deliver family history service. We often act as the jailers of information rather than as its liberators. This chapter offers ideas how we can improve reference service and empower researchers. —NWM

RESOURCES

Croom, Emily. *The Sleuth Book for Genealogists*. Cincinnati, OH: Betterway Books, 2000.

Dollarhide, William. "Find a Place, Find an Ancestor," http://www.genealogyblog.com/? p=22008, accessed April 13, 2015.

Francis, Laurie S. "The Genealogy Reference Interview." *PNLA Quarterly* 68, no. 3 (Spring 2004): 13–15, http://www.pnla.org/assets/documents/Quarterly/pnla_spr04.pdf.

Kaplan, Paul. "How Public Librarians Can Provide Basic Genealogy Instruction." *Illinois Libraries* 86, no. 4 (Spring 2007): 16–20.

Parker, J. Carlyle. *Library Service for Genealogists*. Detroit, MI: Gale Research Company, 1981.

Ross, Catherine Sheldrick, Kirsti Nilsen, and Marie L. Radford. *Conducting the Reference Interview*, 2nd ed. New York, NY: Neal-Schuman Publishers, 2009.

"United States Record Selection Table," https://familysearch.org/learn/wiki/en/United _States_Record_Selection_Table.

ADMINISTRATIVE ASPECTS OF PROVIDING FAMILY HISTORY REFERENCE

MANAGING THE WORKFLOW

Many institutions cannot afford to staff local studies reference rooms with a dedicated reference librarian, even for partial hours. How then can the institution still provide assistance?

- Provide very good websites, resource guides, pathfinders and signage. These can go a long way towards guiding researchers when personal help is not available.
- Offer a "room use" training every few months, so researchers who plan to use the resources on a regular basis can be trained together.
- Collaborate on how-to research programming with another institution. Perhaps encourage the local historical society to host its next genealogy workshop in the institution, demonstrating how to use the resources.
- Emphasize the training modules and help features for each of those resources when onsite or remote access to subscription databases are provided.
- Consider using the services of volunteers. There is a discussion of how to work with them later in this chapter.

What if the institution has staff members, but they are very busy, and feel harried? Here are ideas for maximizing their effectiveness on the desk.

- **Divide the questions** if the department is staffed by more than one person. One staff member can handle the practical questions such as how does the scanner work, where is the change machine, and please show me how to load this microfilm. The other staff member can deal with the more in-depth reference queries.
- **Triage the questions.** Emergency room staff handle cases based on what they are, not strictly on the order in which they arrived. Because genealogists typically have lots of patience, local studies staff can do the same thing. The patrons will wait a few minutes extra for help with an involved question while the information provider leads someone over to the surname files. This way the easy questions are answered quickly, and then the in-depth ones are answered in a more leisurely fashion. As a result, the patrons will feel better taken care of by the staff. In addition, patrons can start filling out reference question forms while they wait for staff to return.
- Encourage patrons needing in-depth assistance to sign up for **a reference consultation**, rather than just showing up any time you are open. Limit the appointment to an hour, and try to schedule it during a less busy time of the week such as Saturday mornings. Even though it seems like a lot of time to spend with one patron, much can be accomplished in such a session. A research plan and to-do list can be generated which will keep the patron working independently for some time. It will also eliminate the need to have that patron approach the desk repeatedly, and ineffectively, because he or she is spinning his or her wheels.

PROVIDING LONG DISTANCE REFERENCE

Answering long distance genealogical questions works quite well, especially when the patron has a focused question. Many local studies departments are beginning to scan and email a limited number of pages of information directly to patrons rather than having them submit interlibrary loan requests through their home libraries. This more direct method may be quicker and more cost effective for all parties involved. But patrons who do not have such a focus may or may not be able to be helped via telephone. That is because a fair number of patrons have a mass of documents, ephemera, and photographs that they are having a hard time sorting and inventorying in order to understand what exactly these sources tell them, and what information they still need to find. When the caller is local and in that situation, they should be encouraged to come to the library, if possible. If the caller is long distance (and a growing number are thanks to researchers finding institutional websites), encourage the caller to consult information on organizing genealogical records.

Sometimes, the written questions that are submitted are misleading, and do not clearly indicate the patrons' needs. It may be possible to perform a sort of written reference interview to clarify via an exchange of emails, texts, or via chat. Some queries may justify a telephone call to the patron in order to speed up this process.

The amount of time and level of detail that the institution is willing to provide via telephone, email, U.S. mail, text, chat, or Skype, should be outlined as part of the overall genealogical reference policy. (More information on reference policies on the section in this chapter called "The Reference Policy: Finding a Way To Be Positive.") The one ironclad rule regarding long-distance reference should be this: researchers who have made the effort to travel to your institution in person should be taken care of first. This seems like common sense, nonetheless many institutions and businesses that serve the public do not follow it, and often interrupt a transaction with a customer standing in front of them to answer the telephone, not just to record a telephone number, but to spend a lengthy time period assisting the caller.

FAMILY HISTORY REFERENCE IN ACADEMIC LIBRARIES

Faye Phillips points out that local history materials can be in a self-contained special collections department, or as a part of reference or a public services division, and that a university archives is an important keeper of local history: "Records such as minutes of board meetings, public relations activities, alumni organizations, fundraising ventures, and student affairs document the involvement of citizens in the institution, and its impact on community affairs."[19]

Because many universities are public and tax-supported, they should be serving anyone in the community who wants to use them. Unfortunately, many citizens are intimidated by the size and complexity of many academic collections, and so they fail to utilize them for their local studies research. This could be rectified with some effort on the part of the staff. Certainly not every staff member working every public service desk in the academic library is going to be a family history expert, but one or two staff members could work to produce a pathfinder to aid determined researchers.

This pathfinder should list all the major parts of the university collection where local studies materials are located, which will probably include several different departments. For maximum exposure, the pathfinder should be posted on the institution's website, and also be available in hard copy. Writing the pathfinder would be would be an ideal task for a graduate student to complete, particularly if the institution houses an information science program. Even if it did not, a graduate student in history could also write it. Here are some ideas for the types of sources it could include:

- An index to historical periodicals, such as *America: History and Life*
- An overview of newspaper holdings, print, microform, and digital
- Call number areas for telephone, city and rural directories
- U.S. and state census records available on microfilm and digitally
- Location of maps
- Local records such as militia rolls, tax lists, school censuses
- Historical records such as *Records of ante-bellum Southern plantations from the Revolution through the Civil War: Series J, Selections from the Southern Historical Collection, Manuscripts Department, Library of the University of North Carolina at Chapel Hill*
- Biographical reference sources and *Biographical and Genealogical Master Index*, in print and/or online versions

The institution may want to also offer a publicized tour once or twice a year that would show people where the materials are located. Local history and genealogical societies would be eager to participate. Again, this is a great project for a graduate student, and so would not take up much staff time except to review and approve the student's work.

BARRIERS TO GOOD GENEALOGY REFERENCE

Like all types of information, more and more family history resources are appearing online. Most patrons are going to conduct some of their research with computers, and some may think, mistakenly, that everything they need is online. A quiet minority is not computer literate, does not own a computer, and may be highly resistant to using one in the library. Staff must make sensitive decisions regarding reference service, weeding, and collection development based on this knowledge, and must stretch the boundaries of service parameters to accommodate these folks. Some reference tools such as print indexes may now seem redundant, but may still be used by some patrons for this reason. More on why all print indexes should not be automatically discarded in Chapter 8 (see the section on the census records). A number of other factors also hinder patron access to local studies services:

- The collection is only open during business hours, guaranteeing that patrons who work 9:00 a.m. to 5:00 p.m. will be unable to perform any research, and that genealogy is a pastime for retirees, and for almost no one else.

  > "Archives that limit access to archival materials, archivists, and finding aids on nights and weekends present significant barriers to non-professional genealogists. Archives provide full service during the daytime, but provide less service after 5 p.m., the time when most hobbyists visit. Consequently, novice genealogists who need the most help often get the least."[20]

- No item circulates, not even "how-to" titles. There is a tendency to make any genealogy/local history materials non-circulating. Some of these titles are old and possibly even rare, but not all of them. How about buying one copy for reference, but a second copy to circulate, of contemporary, reasonably priced items? The newer local history titles in paperback published by Arcadia Publishing come to mind as a good candidate for this practice.

- Reference is handled by a general reference staff who have never received any specialized training in local studies reference.

- The collection does not have a manned service desk. Patrons must seek assistance from a general reference desk in a distant part of the building, and these staff members may or may not have any knowledge of the local studies materials. No signage directs patrons to the general reference desk.

- No information is provided to guide independent usage of the collection when staff members are not available.

- Uncataloged materials and finding aids are present in the collection. However, their provenance, existence, scope, and usage are only known by one staff member who is about to retire. The idea of recording and sharing such institutional information amongst all staff members is called **knowledge management** in the business world, and cultural heritage institutions should practice it.

- Fees for services are going to discourage some researchers, regardless of how reasonable they are.

All of these potential barriers to service should be factored into decisions about the collection and staffing, but especially when drafting the genealogy reference policy.

THE REFERENCE POLICY: FINDING A WAY TO BE POSITIVE

Libraries and archives often set limits on the amount of assistance that they provide to patrons, and these limits are usually in the reference policy statement. Often, these are placed in a prominent location on the institution's website. The limits, which can be quite specific, are the staff's attempt to protect itself from patrons who basically ask that all their research be done for them, rather than asking focused questions. They are also an attempt to give some service to all patrons, rather than have the staff time monopolized by a single patron for indefinite periods of time. All of this is quite understandable, but sometimes results in very restrictive policies which are a double-edged sword. Reference policies allow staff to limit service, but they can also prevent them from working with patrons in a flexible and creative manner. If service policies are sensitively worded, problems can be avoided. Here are some paraphrased examples of actual service policies that are somewhat unfriendly.

- Only minimal searching of the online catalog, local biographies, and indexing of major local histories will be performed.
- Photocopy requests will be filled only when an exact citation is provided.
- We do not perform extensive research photocopying projects, compile family lineages, determine parentage, or locate missing persons.

The extreme negativity of these statements is obvious. The first idea that they communicate is what the staff will NOT do. While it is understandable to have some limits, stressing the negative upfront sets a very unwelcoming tone which is intimidating for many local studies patrons, many of whom are not seasoned researchers. Policies can have encouraging words:

- The expert staff of the _____ Collections provides assistance and information to users from all over the world in person, by telephone, postal service, or e-mail. No appointment is necessary. Tours of the _____ may also be arranged.
- The reference staff is eager to assist you in locating local history and genealogy information. We can provide photocopies for patrons who request information to be mailed to them. The charge for this service is $.10 per page plus postage. We also can scan and email files of requested information if desired. Donations are accepted. You can also search the _____ through our Digital Archive.

The emphasis here is almost completely on what staff WILL do. The wording is vague on purpose, allowing staff some room in interpreting it. Notice that these policies do not state that questions will be answered in the order in which they came in, because that is not always the most efficient way to handle them.

Some libraries curb service to those living outside the boundaries of its taxing district. The logic is that they should not serve those whose tax dollars do not support their institution. However, establishing generous service parameters is quite important. Besides the fact that it is the right thing to do for a democratic institution, institutions should serve everyone because there could be benefits, not just for the library or archive, but for the whole community. The link between genealogy and tourism is a proven one. (Please see Chapter 1 for more details.) Serving long-distance patrons to the best of one's ability may attract them to the area as visitors, which means they will spend money on hotels, restaurants, parking meters, and cheesy t-shirts. And there just may be an outside chance that a patron will decide to donate or will some money to the institution that served him or her so well with a very personal research request.

There are more aspects to consider before drafting that reference policy. As stated earlier in this chapter, the role of genealogy reference staff as educators is crucial. Be prepared to have at least half of the exchange with the patron spent on teaching. Extensive educational needs should be handled with referrals to written information and/or classes and programming.

All genealogy patrons, regardless of research goals and abilities, should be given the same level of service. If this is the goal, then necessarily all researchers will be given the same minimum level of service, which is a carefully conducted reference interview which establishes contexts of the information sought, narrows this information to a reasonable amount, and establishes a specific plan to seek the information.

Because this is not a cookie cutter process, establishing time limits is quite difficult. If the exchange with one patron is taking an unusually long time, there are techniques, already discussed earlier in the chapter, to help draw it to a conclusion, or at least to defer part of the information request to a later time. It is not unreasonable to tell patrons with more difficult questions, "We will work on this one as time permits." Staff should assist researchers with all reasonable requests to locate and analyze sources that will help to prove family history information. There is a difference between "assisting with" and "completing all research for. . .". If you make this distinction in your reference policy statement, then you should not have to identify specific types of questions that you will not answer. Keeping all these considerations in mind, a purposefully vague and generous reference policy will best serve both information providers and researchers.

Here is a hypothetical policy that embraces this philosophy:

> The _____ is happy to **assist with** family and local history research, via in-person visits, telephone, email, or U.S. mail. This process works best when you ask us specific questions, such as: locating an obituary based on a death date, locating an individual in a specific U.S. Census, or locating information on a specific ethnic group or geographical location.
>
> If your question needs to be focused, a staff member will work with you to do so. If we do not have the information you seek in our collection, we will suggest other places where it may be located. We try to answer questions promptly, but some questions will take longer than others, and we appreciate your patience as we strive to give you the best service possible.

Then the institution can fill in the details about how much to charge for the photocopies and scans, and other practical parts of the policy.

VOLUNTEERS

Family history volunteers work in many types of institutions. Family History Centers (FHC), part of the wonderful, free information provision system of the LDS church, are entirely run by volunteers, not all of them church members. The training that these volunteers receive can be variable, and the knowledge level and research experience that each has is uneven. But this can be the case with professional information providers as well! Volunteers who run genealogical and local historical society collections often find themselves coping with little or no professional guidance. They do the collection development, cataloging, conservation, book repair, reference service, grant writing, and fundraising all on their own.

In addition to working in bricks and mortar facilities, volunteers are active online, compiling databases of information such as USGenWeb and Genealogy Trails, doing free searches, often called "lookups," for individuals, and collaborating on massive indexing projects like ones at FamilySearch and Ancestry. Volunteer and "crowdsourced" projects will continue to have an important role in making sources accessible to researchers, and in guiding them in the research process.

IDEAS FOR FINDING AND USING REFERENCE VOLUNTEERS

A large number of institutions with paid staff, such as libraries, archives, and museums, use volunteers in many capacities. These include compiling finding aids such as indexes, labeling and processing some materials, maintaining clippings files, and even conducting tours and providing reference help. Librarians on the genealib listserv, which is short for Librarians Serving Genealogists, have posted many positive comments about how much their volunteers accomplish. However, it does require some staff time to manage volunteers, so their labor is not entirely free. Another aspect of using volunteers to ponder is exactly how what they will do meshes with the duties of paid staff. This is yet another area in which it is wise to have a written policy, which can be referred to when such questions arise. Countless libraries have put theirs online. Here are some thoughts on how to work with volunteers:

- Try to create collaborations to recruit volunteers. Contact local history and genealogy groups, but also preservation groups, history round table members and any other history-themed groups. Their members will receive valuable training to do better research, and the institution receives people to guide other people.

- Choose avid users of local studies collections, often seniors, but do not forget about youth. Tap into high school and college students, especially those interested in history who are looking for an impressive volunteer credential. Potential Eagle Scouts also need to complete a major project.

- Train volunteers. A staff member can do this, hopefully en masse, but later the training of new volunteers could be assigned to seasoned volunteers.

- Assign volunteers tasks such as inventorying nonfragile items, indexing, and compiling written information to be used in how-to materials, which can be completed during slow times at the desk.

- Provide a binder containing written guidance for the volunteers because it may not always be easy for them to find a staff member who can answer their questions.

- If volunteers get stumped, have them write down and forward queries for staff to answer later. They can also try the help line at the Family History Library at 1-866-406-1830.

- Volunteers deserve to be recognized from time to time. An award ceremony or social gathering in their honor can be simple in scale, but it is important for them. Also, highlight volunteers in the institution's newsletter or publicity.

RESOURCES

The National Council of Nonprofits, https://www.councilofnonprofits.org/tools-resources/volunteers.

VolunteerHub.com is the website for software that manages volunteer hours.

VolunteerMatch.org matches nonprofits with volunteers and is free to use.

Willhite, Jim. "A Day in the Life of a Librarian for a Genealogy Society." *OLA Quarterly* 11, no. 4 (Winter 2005): 14–15. *Library & Information Science Source*, EBSCO*host*, accessed February 17, 2015.

TECHNICALITIES: USING GENEALOGICAL SOFTWARE, ONLINE TREES, MESSAGE BOARDS, AND APPS

ONLINE FAMILY TREES

Online family trees are an amazing source of free information for researchers, but with one giant caveat. Sloppy researching, searching, and borrowing of information, leads to bad information being posted online. Check out the Public Trees link on Ancestry.com, where one can see that the same unsourced, sometimes questionable information has been reposted to multiple trees without verification. That being said, valuable clues can be found in online trees which can then be used to try to complete actual research. The proliferation of this type of online information will eventually allow local studies collections to discontinue the storage and maintenance of bulky surname files, and already some institutions are maintaining lists of links where information on their local families can be found online.

Personal Reflection: Teaching Tenacity

If there were just one thing that I could teach patrons, it would be tenacity, the idea that they should not give up when the first, or even the second or third, methods of finding the information that they want did not pan out. Often in family history research, it is necessary to use creativity and ingenuity just to procure information, not just to analyze it. One example is my mother's search for an ancestor's grave marker. She knew from both the death certificate and the obituary that the ancestor had been buried at Mount Greenwood Cemetery in Cook County, Illinois with the rest of her family. But when she walked out to the area indicated by the cemetery record, no trace of the marker was there. Carefully, she compared the description of the burial location to the physical location. Then she returned to the cemetery office, explained the problem, and requested that a maintenance worker return to the area with her. Back they went, and after a few minutes of probing the ground with a long-handled tool, the maintenance man hit something hard. He carefully scraped the sod away, and there lay the missing marker, which he dug up and placed back into the correct position. A less determined researcher than my mother would have walked away not understanding where the missing marker was.

Another example also has to do with cemeteries and church records. My father-in-law was born in Jasper County, Illinois, a rural area in the southeastern part of the state. One weekend we wanted to go to a reunion that was being held at the church he attended in his youth, called The Bend Christian Church. This country church had not operated in many years. It was not located in a town, but in an unincorporated area of Ste. Marie Township. It was not found in any phone directory, on any map, or in our GPS. Because it was many years since my father-in-law had visited the area, my husband and I knew that we needed directions. Finally, inspiration struck. I knew from my father-in-law's recollections that there was a small cemetery close to the church on a bank of the Embarras River. Surely the local funeral director would know the location? I Googled, then telephoned, and had a lovely chat with the funeral director, who gave me very precise directions to the old church. He also knew every member of my father-in-law's extended family who had stayed in the area. We met many of them when we arrived at the reunion. What a good thing that we persevered and attended, and took many photos, because a few years later the church burned to the ground.

But the story does not end there. The church records were not present the day of the reunion, and no one seemed to know where they were. This haunted me for some time. A few years later, I was in contact with a distant cousin of my husband, a woman who was also related to the group who had attended The Bend Christian Church. She kept calling and urging us to visit because, as she told us, "I have lots of stuff." It was never clear what that "stuff" was, but because she was persistent, and I knew that she was elderly and in poor health, I convinced my husband to head back to southern Illinois. When we arrived, I discovered that among other treasures, such as lots of very old photographs, she had digital photographs of the missing church records that she had taken years before! The current location of the originals is still unknown. Now, I plan on transcribing that information and submitting it to USGenWeb, so it is never lost again.

Researchers need to understand that often more than a single email or phone call or Google search is needed to locate information. Sometimes lots of walking and/or driving is involved! Information is often neglected, hidden, mislaid, offline and unindexed, but it is waiting for someone to rediscover and share it.—NWM

Each type of site operates somewhat differently. Some only allow researchers to upload or input information, but then it cannot be altered in any way. Some are collaborative, and allow researchers to augment and change the information. Regardless of how they run, they all allow researchers to upload their information in the form of a GEDCOM file, which is the standard type of computer file for genealogical information. That means that researchers who have used a genealogical software program to organize their information, will be able to extract the information from their program, regardless of which one they used, and fairly easily upload it to the online family tree website of their choice. Some of them allow one to build a tree online by inputting the information manually.

Below is a list of some of the main websites which host online trees. New ones appear frequently. For an updated list of all such websites, consult www.cyndislist.com under the heading "The Collaborative Family Tree."

- www.rootsweb.ancestry.com—free site sponsored by Ancestry.com
- Ancestry.com—Public and Private Trees
- WeRelate.org—sponsored by Allen County Public Library
- Family Tree on familysearch.org—new and constantly improved
- Geneanet.com—European emphasis

MESSAGE BOARDS AND THEIR ETIQUETTE

Message boards definitely have their uses. Before they were invented, researchers had to submit queries to genealogical and local history print publications, hoping that someone else who was researching the same family lines would see it and respond. The most famous publication for this type of searching was *Everton's Genealogical Helper,* now defunct. Now genealogists simply need to post queries on message boards. They exist in many places, but probably the most used message board is on www.rootsweb.com, a free website run by Ancestry.com. Messages can be posted on boards related to geographic location, surnames, or special topics. Remember that gathering information this way is searching, not researching, and that the information taken from others may not be good, particularly if it is not sourced. Users of message boards should keep the following in mind:

- The heading on the message should be labeled as specifically as possible so that other researchers do not have to open and then read the entire message to ascertain whether they can help or not. For example, "Searching for Grandma" is a terrible heading, because it is much too generic; instead use "Mabel Mae Thomas of Ottumwa, Iowa."

- The query should provide as much specific context as possible, such as full name, parents' names if known, at least approximate birth and death dates, and geographic location. The query should state whether the information is family lore or documented.

- Email addresses in queries should be the kind that will last forever. It is common to find inactive email addresses in these posts, which is frustrating for others.

- Researchers should reciprocate with information when someone has shared with them, if possible.

APPS

Many apps are available for genealogy; and new ones are constantly appearing. Some are free and some are not while some are initially free, but then charge an annual fee in order to connect with some type of online database. They are available from the online stores affiliated with the various types of mobile operating systems, and fall into the following basic categories:

- Apps that allow you to input genealogical information into a tree.

  Examples: Ancestry's Tree to Go, RootsMagic To-Go

- Apps that allow you to read information you have already stored in a genealogical software program.

  Examples: RootsMagic To-Go, FamilySearch Tree

- Apps that interface trees with social media websites.

  Examples: We're Related Facebook, Famicity

- Apps that perform a special function, such as capturing information on grave markers, analyzing information that is already in your tree, or retrieving facts to bolster your family history research.

  Examples: BillionGraves, Relative Finder, Wolfram's Genealogy & History Research Assistant

- Apps for genealogy games.

  Examples: Family Village Game, Family House

RESOURCES

To find genealogical apps:

"Mobile Devices' iPad, iPhone, and iPod Touch," http://www.cyndislist.com/mobile/iphone/.

Reviews:

Eaton, Kit. "Trace Your Family Tree, from Roots to Green Shoots." *The New York Times*, on-line ed., February 12, 2014, accessed June 1, 2015, http://www.nytimes.com/2014/02/13/technology/personaltech/trace-your-family-tree-from-roots-to-green-shoots.html?_r=0.

GenSoftReviews, http://www.gensoftreviews.com/index.php?sel=1&new=&lic=all&pla=hand&type=util&sort=, accessed June 1, 2015.

MacEntee, Thomas. "7 Genealogy Facebook Apps." *FamilyTree Magazine*, July 2011, http://familytreemagazine.com/article/7-genealogy-facebook-apps.

CONCLUSION

Providing family history reference service is a necessity for a wide variety of informational and cultural heritage institutions, such as libraries, archives, local history societies, and even museums. It behooves the information providing and cultural heritage communities to serve these researchers as generously as possible. A well-trained staff member is the most helpful aid to genealogical reference that an institution can provide. The best way to acquire that training is to walk a mile in the patrons' shoes. Do some genealogy and family history research, not only to learn the techniques, but to understand what researchers experience when they contact many types of institutions seeking guidance and information. The next chapter covers ways in which even very small institutions can work to provide improved access to local studies materials for researchers.

PROGRAMMING IDEAS

It may seem like programming is something over and above the normal services that a local studies department provides, and that trying to plan programming is going to consume a lot of time and effort. Yet carefully done programming is an opportunity to showcase and teach an institution's resources on a very efficient scale, and it does not have to be complicated. For example, is it more desirable to teach twenty patrons separately how to use Ancestry.com, or to spend a little time planning a program that teaches twenty patrons simultaneously how to use Ancestry.com? If no one on staff is prepared to conduct such a program, it is possible to hire a professional lecturer. Many are listed on the website of the Association of Professional Genealogists: http://www.apgen.org/.

1. "Ask Granny"[(c)]

"Ask Granny"[(c)] is a great example of a program that shows people how to use family group sheets, and pedigree charts. It is designed specifically to help senior citizens to capture family information to share with their families, but the structure of this program could be duplicated to work with just about any group. This award-winning program was devised by Judy Russell and Greg Crane, and a free set of materials plus detailed instructions is available from them via email. This program is already in the bag! For more information, please consult the follow places online:

Photos: https://sites.google.com/site/askgranny2010/
Facebook: https://www.facebook.com/askgranny
Newsletter: http://newsfromaskgranny.blogspot.com/

To obtain a kit, please send a request to: ask.granny.us@gmail.com.

2. "Showcase of Genealogical Software"

In this program several types of software are explained and demonstrated, and it should be aimed at researchers at any skill level who are looking for a software program. The program will last for one to two hours depending on how many software programs are discussed. Also plan on 15–20 minutes to cover one type of software.

Members of the local genealogical community are canvassed to find users of several different software programs who would give a short talk on the software that they are familiar with. A device to allow a computer to project onto a large screen is needed. This program could be jointly sponsored with the local genealogical group.

Additional Ideas

Programs that highlight and teach a single source, or group of sources:

- Teach how to use a specific website/database, whether that is subscription based, or free. Examples are American Memory (from the Library of Congress), Ancestry, FamilySearch, Fold3, and GenealogyBank. A volunteer from the local Family History Center may be willing to teach the FamilySearch class for you. Most of the subscription websites provide online information about how to use their sites, and a review of this material can help to structure a group presentation.
- City directories: including what is the scope of your holdings, what types of information is typically found in them, and how that information can be analyzed and organized.
- How to search census records using the resources in your collection.

Programs that teach a research or recording technique:

- How to do background historical research. Include how to search WorldCat.org in this program because it is a well-kept secret to many patrons.
- How to plan your research.
- How to organize your research.
- How to write genealogical citations according to the standard guide *Evidence Explained: Citing History Sources from Artifacts to Cyberspace* by Elizabeth Shown Mills.

NOTES

1. Richard E. Bopp and Linda C. Smith, eds., *Reference and Information Services: An Introduction* (Santa Barbara, CA: Libraries Unlimited, 2011), 21.
2. Patrick Cadell, "Building on the Past, Investing in the Future through Genealogy and Local History Services," *International Genealogy and Local History*, IFLA Publications 130, Ruth Hedegaard and Elizabeth Anne Melrose, eds. (Munich, DE: K.G. Saur, 2008), 24.
3. Charles W. Joyner, *Shared Traditions: Southern History and Folk Culture* (Urbana, IL: University of Illinois Press, 1999), 1.
4. Genealogist Elizabeth Shown Mills coined this term. See "Genealogy in the 'Information Age': History's New Frontier?" *National Genealogical Society Quarterly*:

Centennial Issue 91 (December 2003): 260, http://www.ngsgenealogy.org/galleries/Ref_Researching/NGSQVol91Pg26077GenealogyHistory.pdf.

5. Shirley Bateman, "Innovation In Local Studies Collections and Programs: How Melbourne Library Service Is Fostering Community Pride," *Aplis* 25, no. 1 (March 2012), 14, *Library & Information Science Source*, EBSCO*host*, accessed February 17, 2015.

6. Elizabeth Moore Dahrl, *The Librarian's Genealogy Notebook: A Guide to Resources* (Chicago, IL: American Library Association, 1998), ix.

7. Ann D. Gordon, *Using the National Documentary Heritage: The Report of the Historical Documents Survey*, 1992.

8. Elizabeth Yakel and Deborah A. Torres, "Genealogists as a Community of Records," *American Archivist* 70, no. 1 (SPRING/SUMMER 2007): 93–113.

9. Wendy M. Duff and Catherine A. Johnson, "Where Is the List with All the Names? Information-Seeking Behavior of Genealogists," *American Archivist* 66 (January 2003): 85, doi: http://archivists.metapress.com/content/L375UJ047224737N.

10. William A. Katz, *Introduction to Reference Work, Volume I: Basic Information Services*, 8th ed. (New York, NY: McGraw Hill, 2002), 372.

11. RUSA, "Guidelines for a Unit or Course of Instruction in Genealogical Research at Schools of Library and Information Science," revised 2004, http://www.ala.org/rusa/resources/guidelines/guidelinesunit. (These guidelines are currently being revised.)

12. "RUSA Guidelines for Establishing Local History Collections," revised 2012, http://www.ala.org/rusa/resources/guidelines/guidelinesestablishing.

13. Researching individuals with common names can be challenging, especially when there are multiple individuals bearing the same name in one community. See "Sorting Individuals of the Same Name," in *The FamilyTree Problem Solver* by Marsha Hoffman Rising, pp. 151–172.

14. For more information on this strategy, see "Visualize Time Lines for Available Records," in *Crash Course in Genealogy* by David R. Dowell, pp. 55–56.

15. Yakel and Torres, "Genealogists as a Community of Records," 93–94.

16. Amanda Erickson, "New York's Curious, Century-Old Law Requiring Every City and Town to Have a Historian," from the Atlantic CityLab, September 12, 2012, accessed June 1, 2015, http://www.citylab.com/cityfixer/2012/09/new-yorks-curious-century-old-law-requiring-every-town-have-historian/2954/.

17. Denise W. Merrill, Connecticut Secretary of State, http://www.ct.gov/sots/cwp/view.asp?a=3188&q=392446.

18. Librarian Pamela J. Cooper conducted a survey of five Florida genealogical societies and received over 600 responses. She posted the results of the survey on the Genealib listserv on April 8, 2013 at Mailman.acomp.usf.edu/pipermail/genealib/2013-April/020937.html. In addition, she presented a program at the 2013 National Genealogical Society Conference in Las Vegas entitled "Online Catalogs: A Bridge to Successful Research."

19. Faye Phillips, *Local History Collections in Libraries* (Englewood, CO: Libraries Unlimited, 1995), 7.

20. Duff and Johnston, "Where is the List with all the Names"?, 81.

Chapter 7

MAXIMIZING ACCESS TO FAMILY HISTORY MATERIALS

It is often difficult for new volunteers, patrons, and even librarians to understand how to locate materials in the family history collection. The link between the searcher and the resource can appear in many forms, such as a record in a library database, a descriptive document in an archive or historical society, or an index in a heritage room. Methods for providing access to materials are vast for the local studies collection because these resources vary so much in their formats. This chapter provides a basic overview of access methods to local studies materials. Volunteers, librarians, and others new to the family history environment will benefit from the explanations.

It also will be useful to those who are experienced in creating some types of access methods, but who need an introduction to other approaches. This is particularly important when attempting to collaborate with other institutions by sharing resources or reference services among collections. The chapter is especially intended for those volunteers and professionals working with collections that are partially or fully uncataloged. The chapter provides guidance as to how to proceed in choosing the appropriate method for representing the items and where to get the proper training or other support needed to do so. There are also tips for innovative cataloging and use of existing web materials.

THE SEARCH FOR INFORMATION IN A FAMILY HISTORY COLLECTION

"In the best of all possible worlds, all information regarding the subjects in the local history collection would be in a computer database, and patrons could simply search for their topic online."

—Faye Phillips[1]

Faye Phillips' desire for cataloging of local history materials, expressed twenty years ago, at the onset of the Internet generation, has, sadly, still not been fully realized. So many local collections contain gems for family researchers. In addition to the standard published items, there may be photographs of their family homes, neighbors, and relatives, diaries, letters, and other items of interest. But, sometimes, these items may be difficult to locate because the items are not cataloged. This means that the only way to access the material is to browse or be shown the item by a knowledgeable staff person in the institution. What happens when an item is cataloged? A record of that item appears in a place one would expect to locate a list of available materials, like a library online catalog. Cataloging does not just provide the name of the item, but also some description of what the item is about, or subject access.[2]

When considering how to best provide access to these items, one should consider a wide variety of research needs. Family historians and genealogists, in particular, need to be able to locate information using *names*. Other users, such as architects, consult local resources in order to recreate the look of a city block or a particular building façade, so their access needs are by *location*. Committees planning a centennial celebration come seeking photographs and stories of the town. Professional historians may need to pore over documents relating to major industrial, political, economic, and social events tied to the area. All of these users seeking contextual information will need *subject access*. They should be provided with efficient, detailed, and consistent access tools for the collection. In reality, however, the family history collections in libraries, historical societies, local archives, and other cultural heritage centers often lack clear access methods. Many have mixed methods of organizing or "cataloging" their collections and still others have no description at all of parts of their collections. So how do the managers and librarians in these collections take stock of their materials and provide reliable, but timely access?

WHAT'S IN A WORD?

The process of making items accessible is often called *cataloging*. This word serves as a general term in any cultural heritage setting to mean items in the collection have been examined and described in a manner that is consistent with norms in this setting. Good cataloging provides subject access points and physical descriptions. A book in a library is considered cataloged when it has been examined and described according to standard formats, usually for use as an online cataloging record. In other information settings, such as archives and historical societies, different words may be used for this process of describing and making items available. In archives, *representation* is a common term used, as well as *archival description*. The process of cataloging in an archive involves more extensive description of multi-item collections, so the method of describing them reflects that complexity. Archival description often appears in a *finding aid* that may be accessible online or in paper format.

Another common term for providing access to local family items is *indexing*. An index may be a list of names or subject terms from a single item, such as a county history, or it may span a wide variety of resources not available at the library, such as cemetery records. Indexing is an extremely important way to organize and represent information for local studies collections and is often carried out exclusively by volunteers.

Cataloging of digital online resources is done by recording information in specific formats, called *metadata schemas*. Metadata really just means information about the item, such as the name of the photographer of a family photograph. By following a set of rules to input this cataloging information in specialized software, the metadata can be shared and searched on the web, which constitutes a powerful tool for family research. Each of the above methods for cataloging will be further described in the following chapter, but first a look at the types of institutions that house family history collections will provide some understanding of the cataloging methods employed in them.

STANDARD INSTITUTIONAL APPROACHES TO PROVIDING ACCESS

Many cultural heritage institutions provide access to local special collections including historical societies, public, academic, and other libraries, heritage societies, genealogy clubs, archives, museums, and museum libraries. The manner in which items in these institutions is catalogued differs significantly. Terminology differs by location as well. Below are outlined some of the primary methods for organizing and representing information in each setting.

- **Libraries:** When cataloging books, serials, and other items, librarians describe major information about the work, such as the author, title, publication date, and the name of the publishing house. The record resides in a computer system or on a printed card (card catalogs are still used in some libraries). The electronic records are created using a coded record, usually a Machine Readable Cataloging Record, or MARC format record, which originated at the Library of Congress.[3] Typically, catalogers create records to represent each item or serial using the original or copy cataloging. Rules for the formatting of information in a MARC record follow strict guidelines, established by the Library of Congress. These records are needed to provide access to the item's information in the library's integrated library system. Items typically are individually described, although for serials, one record per serial is created. Likewise, digital libraries and other collections can be cataloged with one record to provide access to the collective resource. Additionally, the cataloging of online resources can be in a library's workflow, particularly in areas such as local history and genealogy. Links to the online resource are included in the cataloging record. Discovery is aided by the use of controlled vocabulary, usually Library of Congress subject headings.[4] Persons cataloging a collection must have an understanding of the language of family and local history collections, in order to describe the item consistently.

- **Archives:** For archives, one encounters the term "representation" or "archival description" more often than cataloging. Collections are described to reflect the original order and to maintain the grouping of items donated. The description is in a document called a *finding aid* that exists as a document, for example, .doc, .pdf on a website, or encoded to appear on the Internet using Encoded Archival Description (EAD).[5] Archivists are aided by a variety of software such as ArchivesSpace, Cuadra STAR Archives, and CollectiveAccess, to catalog collections, create online finding aids, and to better integrate subject terms for discovery.[6] The guiding professional organization for the archival field is the Society of American Archivists (SAA), which publishes works on arrangement and description of archival collections.[7] Within archives, one may find other methods of cataloging materials that do not arrive at the archive in cohesive record groups. Archivists also may create MARC records to provide access to their collections in online catalogs.

- **Historical societies, historical museums, and museum libraries:** Some historical societies and museums, such as those affiliated with state historical commissions, may use the archival methods described above. Others, particularly smaller organizations, often use software such as PastPerfect to catalog specific collections, photographs, or postcards.[8] The program is also very well-suited for objects and artifacts, such as collections of historic garments, since it allows for a thumbnail image along with the cataloging information. Though is most suited as an item-level cataloging tool, it is possible to use PastPerfect to reflect archival finding aid methods of organization and representation as well. Lois Hammill's recent manual on archival organization and description for lay persons discusses how to manipulate the PastPerfect fields to reflect the more complex organization of materials seen in archival approaches.[9] Historical societies often utilize a number of other tools, such as *indexes*, and *vertical files*.

- **Digital libraries:** Collections of materials that one may access online are often referred to as *digital libraries*. This may be a collection of items one would find in a normal library setting, but available digitally. Large academic libraries with access to databases, reference items, books, and other items in full-text format might be called a "digital library." In these examples, traditional library materials, usually under copyright and with vendor support, are provided virtually. But sites may also often have digitized unique elements such as faculty scholarship in large academic libraries or digitized postcards from the local history room of a small public library. These online collections in libraries may also be referred to as *digital libraries* or they also could be defined as *digital collections*. In either case, original cataloging must be performed on the items. They tend to be housed in separate *digital repositories* either on-site or on a remote site from the parent institution. They often are described using cataloging terms created for digital objects, such as Dublin Core, a set of "elements" or descriptors that allow the cataloger to describe individual digitized items.[10] The information that is put into the elements is called *metadata*. Most of the description refers to the original item, though some administrative data refers to the digital object. Dublin Core tends to be used at the item level, though there usually are Dublin Core records for each collection as well. In addition, many digital collections have a MARC record created for access in a local library catalog or WorldCat. Digitized collections will be further explored in Chapter 9.

MAJOR CATALOGING METHODS FOR FAMILY HISTORY ITEMS EXPLORED

What cataloging methods are best suited to local collections? The answer depends on the setting, staff support, volunteer base, and the methods already in place. In reality, a variety of methods are often used in one setting in order to maximize access. For example, a local history room in a library may use catalog records for the book items, PastPerfect for photographs, vertical files for ephemera, and an index to the local newspaper obituaries produced by volunteers at the library. As methods are evaluated, it may be that the collection can be migrated to some representations to new formats and platforms. This is particularly true when beginning a digitization project. Often, items that were described at the folder or box level will be described at the item level in Dublin Core or another metadata set in order to put the digitized item, such as a photograph, into the digital collection. The following overview of major methods will provide introductory information on how different access is provided for local history materials. Additionally, resources on each method and training opportunities will be noted.

LIBRARY CATALOG RECORDS

Librarians create online and paper catalog records for individual items or serials. Typically, the record describes a book, audiovisual, map, or serial item and the record exists in the library catalog. For online catalog entries, librarians create MARC format records that contain extensive descriptive information, such as author, title, publisher, size, number of pages, etc. of an item. The record allows for subject headings that can be specific to a local area:

- Louisville (Ky.)–History.
- Louisville (Ky.)–Genealogy.

Even if a family history collection does not utilize standard cataloging records created by librarians, it is useful to be aware of Library of Congress subject headings, which may also be used as a controlled vocabulary (or basis for a local controlled vocabulary) in such programs as PastPerfect and for indexing. It is also good to provide a list of common headings for the local area to users who are searching the library catalogs, PastPerfect subject areas, or other online indexes that may have Library of Congress subject headings.

The ability to tailor a catalog record to the local arena offers much potential for accessing these unique items. Certainly the unique publications of small historical societies and genealogical societies benefit from records that can be searched in major library collections. The use of name and subject authority for these records provides excellent access points and useful information for local projects. The following record (Figure 7.1) is an example of a catalog record produced by the Library of Congress for a local history item.

Figure 7.1

Record for a Local History Item in the Library of Congress Online Catalog.

When is it appropriate to use catalog records for the local collection? In a library setting, it would be ideal to have a catalog record for every item, serial, or archival collection such as photographic, postcard, manuscript, etc. This includes:

- High school annuals
- City directories
- Local newspapers
- Local histories: Sometimes these works are published by small presses, by vanity presses, or self-published by the author. These too should be included in the library catalog. As long as they have been accepted into the collection, they need representation like any other book.
- Family genealogy books or notebooks: These items are represented individually so they can be searched by family name or location.

Catalog records can be used to "collect" all of the other representation methods in your collection. For example, if there is a local paper index to obituaries in the collection, it would be wise to include a reference to that index in the library catalog. Here is an example entry (Figure 7.2) for an index to other items.

Catalog records can be created also for digitized collections. This can be especially useful for remote patrons who are doing searches on local collections. Entry should be established through links on the library web page as well, but a catalog record can provide continuity and can also be added to the WorldCat online catalog for added discovery of the digital collection. Here is an example of a catalog entry to a digital collection on WorldCat (Figure 7.3).

Figure 7.2

Record for a Local Index in the Library of Congress Online Catalog.

Archivists also may create MARC records, which provide discovery for archival collections. The MARC format record is not able to deliver the level of description of materials in archival groups to the extent that a finding aid is able because the finding aid is a much longer representation. However, the MARC record provides

Figure 7.3

Record for a Digital Collection in WorldCat. © 2015 OCLC Online Computer Library Center, Inc. Used with OCLC's permission. WorldCat is a registered trademark/service mark of OCLC.

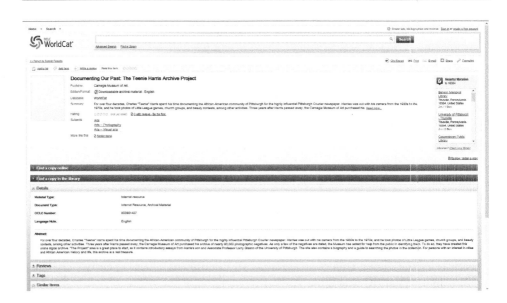

Figure 7.4

Record for a Manuscript Collection in the Library of Congress Online Catalog.

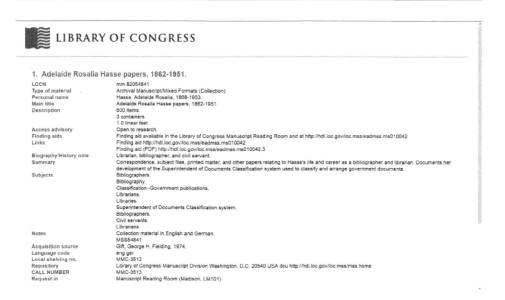

access through the assignment of subject headings that are searchable on WorldCat and in a local library catalog. In the case of the Adelaide Rosalia Hasse papers at the Library of Congress, there are several subject headings, a brief description of the manuscript collection, and links to the full finding aid in web text or pdf formats.

It is important for those working in local historical societies and for volunteers in family history collections to understand the value of library catalog records in order to locate items they may want to link to in their finding aids, guides, or online catalog records. Records in the WorldCat database provide excellent access to information on items of interest. It is beneficial for any group that is researching available local studies items to undertake consistent and regular searches of online catalogs, such as the Library of Congress and WorldCat in order to discover relevant resources that are being added.

What Is WorldCat?

WorldCat claims to be "the world's largest network of library content and services. WorldCat libraries are dedicated to providing access to their resources on the Web, where most people start their search for information."[11] Maintained by OCLC, member libraries upload MARC records of their holdings which create an online record of information about the item and a mapping of locations where one might find this item. Many formats are catalogued in WorldCat, including both traditional format books, serials, CDs, films, as well as a wealth of digitized materials, including photographs, documents, oral histories, and other items relevant to family history. WorldCat can be accessed two ways, at worldcat.org by anyone with Internet access and through the website of an institution such as a library or archive. Access to WorldCat requires a password that is supplied by the institution. The advantage of entering WorldCat this way is that interlibrary loan requests can be placed by the user directly, whereas this cannot be done at www.worldcat.org.

How is this information on catalog records useful for volunteers and others working in local collections? First, many local collections exist in libraries, but the local publications have never been cataloged. This may be because of a backlog in work, because no-one felt capable of doing original cataloging, or because there was a dispute over who owned and should catalog the materials. If this scenario sounds familiar, it would be advisable to examine the options for obtaining help in cataloging the materials, so they appear in the library's online catalog. Here are steps to getting help with creation of online cataloging records:

- If volunteers are primarily responsible for the materials in a library local history room, which lacks cataloging for the book collection, try approaching the library to request that this cataloging be carried out.

- If librarians at an institution recognize that cataloging should occur, but do not have the ability to undertake original cataloging, try looking for outside support. Perhaps there are small grants to be used for such purposes. Perhaps there is training available through the state library, which would teach librarians to create or modify a record for local resource use.

- For cultural heritage institutions with finding aids in EAD, HTML, or PDF format but do not have access to a means to create a MARC record, OCLC offers a service that will add records to a large database by harvesting the finding aids on the institution's website. OCLC's ArchiveGrid provides a service that allows for automatic and continuing harvesting of the institution's finding aids (to reflect revisions) into the ArchiveGrid database.[12]

- If there are no options for collaboration with libraries, small institutions may want a user-friendly software to catalog its book collection. Many software programs exist that will create an online cataloging database record that will display book information and provide user searches. The systems create the records easily for books with the International Standard Book Numbers (ISBN). LibraryThing.com will allow an organization to set up an account. The search feature allows one to search over 700 library and other databases, in multiple languages. Once an item is located that is desired to be "cataloged," one adds it to one's own library. This allows the organization to search for other copies of the same book and use that information to create a database record. Patrons may search the collection using a dedicated computer onsite or via a URL that can be provided on the organization web page. LibraryThing is only for books (up to 5,000 titles) and does not provide features like circulation that full library integrated systems do, but it is a quick and easy way for very small organizations to provide access to the list of their current books. There is even the option for a home page where one can put announcements about the organization. The software is colorful and allows social media applications, like tagging and Twitter. And it is inexpensive—only $25 for lifetime membership.[13] Other software/sites of note include PrimaSoft.com, ResourceMate.com, Shelfari, Collectorz.com and, for churches, cross-products.com.

RESOURCES

Chan, Lois Mai. *Cataloging and Classification: An Introduction.* Lanham, MD: Scarecrow Press, Inc., 2007.

Joudrey, Daniel N., Arlene G. Taylor, and David P. Miller. *Introduction to Cataloging and Classification.* Santa Barbara, CA: Libraries Unlimited, 2015.

Taylor, Arlene, and Daniel N. Joudrey. *The Organization of Information.* Westport, CT: Libraries Unlimited, 2009.

LOCALLY DRIVEN INDEXES AND DATABASES: AN INTRODUCTION

Indexes take many forms and serve a variety of purposes. Indexes are lists of terms in alphabetical order that provide a link back to another source. A **back-of-book index** is a familiar example. Most back-of-book indexes provide both subject and name entries. Some provide additional geographic and placename lists. Family collections use indexes in many more ways than the traditional book index. When genealogists and historians transcribe the information from tombstones and compile them into a book that provides alphabetical name listings with additional information, that work can be considered an index. When a list of names is created from local newspapers, with links back to the specific issue and page, this is called a **name index**. Indexing provides consistent entry into collections of resources, such as a collection of photographs, postcards, collections of books, and other resources. Websites can be indexed, as can artifacts.

What formats and technologies are used for family history indexing? Traditionally, books were the staple form of genealogical indexing and that tradition has not yet entirely been abandoned in smaller historical societies. Increasingly, databases are used to retain indexing information in order to provide searching and web access. So, at the local level, one may find indexes that are generated into a traditional-format paper index, a digital version as a .doc or .pdf, or online, searchable indexes. For searching online, one expects access to a variety of digitized or interactive online resources. Online genealogy and family history databases like Ancestry.com and FamilySearch.org are providing digitized versions of many older paper indexes, as well as newly-created indexes to resources, such as the U.S. Census.

LOCALLY-DERIVED INDEXES: OBITUARY

One of the most common indexes found in local studies collections is an index to obituaries from the local paper. These may take the form of clipping files from the newspaper, index cards with citation information, spreadsheets, databases, Word files with lists, and information stored on a CD-ROM. It is important to note that even if the local newspaper becomes available in digitized format, the maintenance of indexes can provide valuable access. The software that provides searching of digitized newspapers uses optical character recognition (OCR), to match the search word typed in to the words in the paper. Often, for historic newsprint, OCR does not work perfectly, though in recent years, the level of accuracy, even for historic fonts has been fairly good.[14] Even so, many digitized historical items do not have high rates of accuracy for full-text searches, therefore relevant information may be missed and often there are numerous "false hits," which need to be sifted through and may be discouraging to a patron. Additionally, errors may occur in the spelling of names which indexers are more likely to recognize and correct at the time of the index creation. There are even situations where a name search would lead to erroneous information that was reported and then retracted.

Indexes to obituaries have a variety of formats ranging from a simple listing by last name, death date, and place, and citation to the original obituary, to a full transcription of the obituary. If the index provides only the death date and name, but not the citation to the original obituary, this is less valuable to the researcher. Some indexes include a reference to the microfilm reel number that contains the full text of the obituary. Providing a full transcription may have copyright concerns, so, unless there is an agreement with the copyright holder, or the item is in the public domain meaning published before 1923, then it is wise to give only the main facts and the citation.

LOCALLY-DERIVED INDEXES: CEMETERY

Cemetery indexes provide access to information associated with the burial or interment of individuals in the local area. These resources may exist as published volumes, often written by organizations such as local historical societies or the Daughters of the American Revolution (DAR). Though not a traditional index, one also may find cemetery information in database format that is searchable on the web or in a full-color, interactive website with digitized transcriptions and GPS coding of tombstone locations.

The information covered in the indexes ranges from a strict transcription of tombstones to a more complete record of death, using associated files in the cemetery offices. Information one might find recorded from tombstones includes:

- Names of deceased
- Titles, such as Rev., Col., Dr.
- Dates of birth and death
- Names of spouses and children
- Epithets

Additional information one might find in a cemetery index includes:

- Cause of death
- Names of relatives, including maiden name of wife
- Physical ailments

In the past, this information has been gathered and stored at the local level, but the Internet has made it possible to offer global access. Find A Grave is the most prominent example of a website that is an international cemetery index. It was begun in 1995 by Jim Tipton, someone who had the hobby of visiting famous graves, and wanted a place to record the information and that of other hobbyists.[15] He subsequently expanded the site to include information on any grave, and then the genealogists jumped on board. Both individuals and organized groups have used it as a way to record local information. The online format allows not just a transcription of the marker's information, but also digital photographs and additional information about the individual and his or her family, such as short biographies and digitized obituaries, as well as links to other family members' listings. Many other websites also list burial information such as BillionGraves, Cemetery Junction, Interment.Net, and the USGenWeb Tombstone Transcription Project. DeathIndex.com provides links to a number of such sites.[16] The possibilities for information professionals at local studies sites to use these online resources include the following:

- Link to a list of such sites on the local studies web page.
- See if any persons who are active in the county-level pages are in the area and might want to communicate with the local studies center volunteers.
- Provide links from the local index to outside pages for the same persons.

Because in most cases these online resources are not vetted by library or archival professionals, the information should not be presented as the local studies center's work or information. Credit should be given to those who created these sites perhaps with a note that the information cannot be guaranteed by the local studies collection. Users will the need to verify any information for themselves when linking to external sites.

OTHER TYPES OF RECORDS THAT MAY BENEFIT FROM AN INDEX

Name indexes refer to lists of any names in a text. *All-name indexes* provide similar lists, paper or database, to several resources. For example, some local studies collections provide what is called an all-name index which covers several newspapers. This may be an index to obituaries in a local newspaper. It may cover the stories in the paper or advertisements as well. The all-name index might also be created to cover a variety of other local resources including county histories, many of which were originally published without an index. Some local groups then created their own and published them as a supplementary volume or as part of a reprinted county history. Genealogies and cemetery records have also been added to local indexes of historical materials.

The Wisconsin Name Index is a great example of such resources. It has been compiled since 1870 by Wisconsin Historical Society librarians and staff. The current version exists as an online index, providing name searching for information covering 150 county and local histories, as well as directories, encyclopedias, scrapbooks, and other serials, ranging primarily in date from 1870 to 1970.[17] The categories draw from a database of 150 county and local histories, dozens of professional directories and biographical encyclopedias, more than 60 scrapbooks containing 30,000 obituaries, and selected articles in Wisconsin magazines and newspapers. Most items were published from 1870 to 1970. The Name Index functions in a larger database that allows for searches across many other genealogical indexes. A browse feature can be modified by county and year.

Likewise, another great example of an all-name index exists at the Champaign County Historical Archivesin Urbana, Illinois.[18] The site provides an amazing array of indexed resources, including newspaper articles, books, directories, yearbooks, oral histories, municipal and county records, maps, images, personal collections, and more. The searches by name, subject, or title allow the researcher to locate citations to specific articles and records that match the search terms, and there is a way to order the full item online. The extensiveness of these examples demonstrates the power of online access to indexes for the researcher. Though the information in the citation is generally not digitized, the path to accessing that information is made clear on the site.

As seen from these two examples, local studies collections can benefit from additional indexes to any items in the collection that may not have name or subject entry. Additionally, joint projects between historical societies, libraries, archives, and organizations that may hold family history documents, such as churches, could benefit from joint indexing projects for items that are not scheduled to be digitized in the near future. A subject index would take a great deal of time, but a simple name index for family history purposes is not nearly so time-consuming. Here are some ideas of other materials that could be included:

- city, rural, and regional directories
- property tax lists, and lists of other special fees such as dog tags, and merchant licenses
- 1890 census of Civil War veterans and their widows
- local histories
- content from local newspapers, especially lists of people who have letters at the post office, and vital events
- school personnel and enrollment records
- church records
- social and fraternal organization records
- voter registration lists
- municipal and township office holders lists
- records from institutions such as poorhouses and orphanages
- names from wills and promptly filed probate records from that year
- court cases

Additionally, historical societies may keep address files on historic structures in the area. It would be useful to create a reverse directory index of addresses and the names associated with them. This is particularly helpful for researchers working on house or property histories, but also wonderful for the family historian, who would like to see photographs or written information about a building where ancestors lived or worked.

Multiple resources exist to aid in the "how-to" of indexing. One may consult the *Chicago Manual of Style* (16th ed.) for a starting guide to formatting and consistency of name construction. For the construction of the actual index, specialized programs exist that create back-of-book indexes, such as Sky Index Professional^{TM} and

CINDEX.[19] These programs provide support for indexes one sees at the back of a book, (BOB) index, and may not be worth their cost to a small institution with other indexing needs. One may index using databases, such as FileMaker Pro, Microsoft Access, and Microsoft SQL server, particularly if there are techsavvy individuals at the institution (or grant monies) to make the database interface with the library or institution website. A wonderful discussion of how to migrate an older index into an interactive, online database can be found in Kerry A. Fitzgerald's description of the *Grand Haven Tribune* indexing project. The article provides insights into the steps volunteers and others might take without knowledge of databases and the time when the project coordinators should seek help for database design.[20]

VERTICAL FILES

Vertical files have been the "catchall" storage for one-off, unique, and oddly-formatted items that do not seem to otherwise fit into collections. Ephemera, such as brochures, ticket stubs, circus flyers, sales receipts, pamphlets, and others often find their way into a filing cabinet with folders arranged in some local method. The arrangement may be from A to Z, by topic or title. They may be arranged by family name, or company or business names. They may be arranged by address, in the case of photographs and documents related to structures in town. The difficulty with such files is access. Few visitors these days expect to be browsing file cabinets for possible information on families and local history even if they are mentioned on the institution's website. While the materials in these files continue to be relevant, the manner in which access is provided should be updated.

Many institutions are finding ways to provide information about vertical file items through indexing and cataloging.

- The Tulsa City-County Library (OK) has created catalog searching access vertical file headings. Name and other searches can help patrons to locate files of interest that they can view at the library.[21]
- The Warren-Trumbull Public Library (OH) has taken a very simple, yet effective approach by posting a list of the vertical file subject headings on their web page.[22]
- The West Virginia Division of Culture and History has an online, searchable database of their vertical files.[23]

The following are suggestions for upgrading access to vertical files that do not have satisfactory subject or name access:

- Provide a rudimentary listing of the folders or organization and provide this explanation or list in digital format on a website. If the institution does not have one, then collaborate with another institution that does. A hard copy should be kept on site.
- Provide a major name index, not an all-name index, to the materials included in the files. Place this index online.
- Consider subject access for some items. In a library setting, there are resources for cataloging pamphlets, such as the Wilson Pamphlet Index.

- If items are cataloged by subject, make sure there is also a way to browse the files. Vertical files by their nature contain unpredictable information. Often researchers need to browse topics in order to discover relevant materials.

The options for tying together digital and traditional ephemera and other vertical file items are vast. It is up to each institution to decide upon the best approach, but staying abreast of digital innovations may save some time and provide better access and support for patrons.

FINDING AIDS

As stated earlier in the chapter, the standard method for describing archival records and manuscripts is the finding aid. Compared to standard library bibliographic records, these documents are usually lengthy representations that describe not just the contents of archives, but the relationships of items within an archive. These guides reflect a good deal of complexity within one archival grouping, like a records group or a family manuscript collection. In other words, it would be difficult to create individual representations for each item in a set of papers that arrived from one family, so the finding aid describes the items as a group.

Additionally, finding aids reflect a guiding concept in archives, that of *respect du fond*, which means maintaining the integrity of a collection by documenting and preserving the grouping and often the organization of the materials as their creator(s) arranged them. It also means there is an attempt to establish an understanding of the context and importance of these items by providing background on the creator(s). A finding aid allows for extended writing about the family which donated the items, and it reflects the organization of the papers after they are processed into files and boxes by listing the folders and boxes with short descriptions. Archival finding aids often do not list a description of every individual item, such as photographs or letters, though they may. This is referred to as an item level finding aid.

Finding aids can exist as paper guides, available on-site. Many of these guides, however, have been converted to a digital format through either the process of digitizing or through a markup process to make them more accessible on the web. Others use a process of marking up the document with a series of programming codes in order to make them machine readable. One common method of marking up a finding aid is through the use of Encoded Archival Description (EAD). Increasingly, archival software is able to take data input into its fields and produce an encoded version of the finding aid.

It is important for volunteers, librarians, and researchers to understand how finding aids can provide extensive access to local family history information. Archival collections in historical societies and library family history collections may benefit from the detailed treatment of the finding aid, which correlates to the arrangement and description of collections together, rather than as individual items. Some of the possible inclusions of the finding aid that are real strengths for family collections are:

- Listings of family names
- Biographical notes
- Chronologies
- Description of related photographs, letters, and memoirs together
- Activities of known family members, such as writers, politicians, scientists

PASTPERFECT

Many historical societies and small archives use the PastPerfect program to catalog their collections. As pointed out above, it is possible to manipulate the PastPerfect fields to create collection-level records; however, the program is also used as one tool in a suite of representations for local items. Particularly when a family history collection is located in a library setting, where the book items may be catalogued using library cataloging records, the PastPerfect and other database programs may be used for specific items, such as photographs, postcards, and objects. If the standalone version of PastPerfect is used, then steps must be taken to make the information available to researchers. The program may be running only on a staff computer and assistance to the catalogued collections may be only through staff.

PastPerfect Online has recently increased the access to catalogued collections (or specific items in the online "exhibit") via the Internet site. PastPerfect has many merits, but it takes considerable training to use the program in a consistent manner. For example, there are several options for selecting terms from controlled vocabularies, such as Library of Congress Subject Headings (LCSH), to describe subjects and objects. The widely-used controlled vocabulary of the American Society for State and Local History, Nomenclature 3.0, is a standard feature on the program. This list of common terms needed to describe museum objects has evolved into a helpful tool for the family history collection. Overall, PastPerfect offers much functionality for small local studies collections, however its effectiveness is strengthened when workflow manuals are created that reflect specific institutional needs.

INNOVATIVE ACCESS

Local studies collections now should actively create methods for storing or linking to born-digital information. This includes family web pages and digitized items relevant to the local collection. Whenever possible, links to fully digitized versions of family history materials should be located and linked to in a catalog record or with the use of a pathfinder. This is especially important for facilities that do not have access to major databases with many of these items, such as county histories, city directories, and newspapers.

It is also advantageous to be aware of family websites and other resources that are created for local families, including genealogical and family history sites. Such items also may warrant a systematic approach, such as a catalog record or notation in a guide. Perhaps allowing family members to upload a link and a short explanation of their site to a blog would be an easy way to keep track of such items without taking staff time. Pages created about local history, sites with local historical statistics, listserv entries with details about local families, among others, are more elusive candidates for a vertical file, were they in paper form. Creative solutions to electronic access for both traditional and born-digital "vertical file" items can be seen in OCLC's use of its "Question Point" resource to store links to odd bits of Internet information that may come in handy in the reference world.[24] At the institutional level, a variety of bookmarking, social media tagging, and citation managers might be used, as well as databases, but the information as to where and when to access such methods should be obvious to the casual reviewer of the local studies website. Here are some digital approaches to solving the dilemma of access:

- Choose one interesting item, traditional or digital, per week to showcase in a blog. Describe the item and give examples of who might be interested in it and why.
- Create a group library in Zotero or another bibliographic management program for historical society or local studies volunteers to populate with digital ephemera related to family and local history. Make this "library" public and available to interested patrons.
- Invite families related to the local area to submit their family blogs, websites, and other digital information to a list of local links.
- Create an Omeka.net site for local family history. Supply information on the institution's website as to the information sought to populate basic family pages that can be linked to other sites.

Cataloging outside information that is related to your collection's content is a marvelous way to expand your collection, learn about the cataloging methods of similar collections, and integrate resources of others into programming, outreach, and services. Increasingly, scanning the digital environment to identify items of relevance to collections is a part of the reference librarian's job at academic and other libraries.

RESOURCES

Browne, Glenda, and Jon Jermey. *The Indexing Companion.* New York, NY: Cambridge, 2007.

Carmicheal, David W. *Organizing Archival Records: A Practical Method of Arrangement & Description for Small Archives.* Lanham, MD: AltaMira Press, 2004.

Cleveland, Donald B., and Ana D. Cleveland. *Introduction to Indexing and Abstracting,* 4th ed. Santa Barbara, CA: Libraries Unlimited, 2013.

Cox, Richard J., and Debra Day. "Stories of a Pleasant Green Space: Cemetery Records and Archives." *Archival Issues* 33, no. 2 (2011): 88–99.

De Keyser, Pierre. *Indexing: From Thesauri to the Semantic Web.* Oxford, UK: Chandos Publishing, 2012.

Falk, Patricia, and Stefanie Hunker. *Cataloguing Outside the Box: A Practical Guide to Cataloguing Special Collections Materials.* Oxford, UK: Chandos Publishing, 2010.

Hamill, Lois. *Archives for the Lay Person: a Guide to Managing Cultural Collections.* Lanham, MD: AltaMira Press, 2012.

Hunter, Gregory S. *Developing and Maintaining Practical Archives,* 3rd ed. New York, NY: Neal Schuman, 2015.

Intner, Sheila S., and Jean Weihs. *Special Libraries: A Cataloging Guide.* Englewood, CO: Libraries Unlimited, Inc., 1998.

Millar, Laura A. *Archives: Principles and Practices.* New York, NY: Neal Schuman, 2010.

Omeka. www.Omeka.net, Corporation for Digital Scholarship, Roy Rosenzweig Center for History and New Media.

Pearce-Moses, Richard. *A Glossary of Archival Records and Terminology.* Chicago, IL: Society of American Archivists, 2005, http://www2.archivists.org/glossary.

Roe, Kathleen D. *Arranging and Describing Archives and Manuscripts,* 2nd ed. Chicago, IL: Society of American Archivists, 2005.

Stewart, B. "Getting the Picture: An Exploratory Study of Current Indexing Practices in Providing Subject Access to Historic Photographs". *Canadian Journal of Information & Library Sciences* 34, no. 3 (2010): 297–327.

Theimer, Kate, ed. *Description: Innovative Practices for Archives and Special Collections.* Lanham, MD: Rowman & Littlefield, 2014.

Zotero. www.Zotero.org, Roy Rosenzweig Center for History and New Media.

EVALUATING AN INSTITUTION'S ACCESS TO FAMILY HISTORY RESOURCES

The first part of this chapter provided very basic overviews of common cataloging methods in a variety of settings. The purpose was to orient volunteers, researchers, and cultural heritage professionals to those methods not used by them or familiar to them. Understanding the way other institutions may treat the same types of materials facilitates collaborations and research. The next section provides a set of steps one may take to evaluate the current condition of one's access methods and to think about ways of improving access. It also highlights guiding principles for access to local collections.

A first step is to evaluate the current state of the collection and the potential partners for future efforts, in other words, to take a step back and look at the collection. You will need to answer these questions in order to understand how to proceed with providing better (or any) access to materials:

- When was the collection established?
- What were the reasons for its inception?
- Where is it housed?
- Are there multiple owners of the materials who may all be different from the owners of the location where it is housed?
- Who are the "stakeholders" in maintaining this collection?
- Are there planning documents that guide the collection? This is rare, but a great goal.
- Who staffs the room?
- Are there trained librarians or others who have taken training seminars in cataloging or using archival and museum software?
- What is the current support base?

Collect all the known information about the collection's history, processing, leadership, and access.

Perhaps the answer to this question is the most important of all. Who manages the room: volunteers or staff? It is very important to understand who works in a local collection. If there are volunteers, are these persons committed to provide collection access? If so, for how many hours a week? Do the volunteers answer to anyone in the organization or related institutions? In other words, do they participate in a larger vision of how the organization should run? If there are paid staff, do they answer to the owners of the collection or to an institution that houses this collection or are these likely to be the same? Are there provisions for the replacement of volunteers when they retire or leave? Is the volunteer base adequate to provide reference? Are there strong working partnerships with other organizations to reduce redundancy in your area's services? If many of these answers are "no," then some thought should go into the sustainability and effectiveness of the family history collection. Perhaps providing great access digitally to a collection might make more sense than continuing cataloging methods that rely on a person on-site to deliver the reference information. The evaluation of cataloging methods used by nearby organizations can be useful as well, since there may be opportunity to share information digitally.

Users? Are there records of recent usage for the room? Have reference inquiries shifted from on-site to phone and email? Do users ask for access to subscription databases that your institution does not provide? Keeping a record of any requests and usage statistics can provide strong evidence to submit to a board or friends group for special funding needs. Even doing a short, six-week study of usage, combined with a user preference survey would provide valuable insight into ways the collection is used and might be catalogued better for easier access.

Potential funders? Are there local grants that might make cataloging the collection a reality? Are there volunteers who could write grant applications and assist a cataloger with the contextual information about collection materials? Would a collaborative effort work in local funding?

Take Stock! An Exercise for Those Working with a Local Special Collection

Using the above questions as a guide, develop a reflection session to help establish an understanding of the local collection context and realities for staffing, funding, and use. Collect a group of those interested in the policies and procedures of the room, as well as some representatives of the user base and local researchers. This group will be able to provide feedback and guidance as new plans take shape for the representation and maintenance of the local collection. As the group reviews the following guiding principles for local collection organization and access, it should reflect on how well these concepts are currently achieved in their room and how they might work towards better achievement of these goals.

Guiding Principles for Insuring Local Studies Access
   All collection materials should be cataloged.
   Access methods to all materials should be explained in one place.
   Legacy methods should be evaluated.
   The collection should be visible.

ALL COLLECTION MATERIALS SHOULD BE CATALOGED

All materials in a local studies collection should be catalogued or represented in some manner, whether it is through library catalog records, specialized indexes, finding aids, or a combination of methods appropriate for the materials. Unfortunately, in many library local collections, historical societies, and archives, the problem of "backlog" is one that is still prevalent. Methods to address backlog, such as More Product Less Process, an archival method for streamlining the steps archivists take to process collections, as well as major grants to discover hidden collections of the United States have brought attention to the issue for larger historical societies and archives.[25] But many local collections in libraries and smaller historical societies suffer from a backlog of materials that are in boxes or that are assumed to be findable by virtue of their location in the history room.

In library collections, family history and local collections are often segregated from the rest of a library collection, so traditional cataloging workflows may not have been applied to these contents. Even book items, such as yearbooks, may not be cataloged. In rooms or collections where some items do not appear in the online catalog, there may be a variety of representation methods that have been put together over the years by a variety of individuals and without an overall plan such as:

- a notebook or paper list of items
- databases or indexes that exist apart from the catalog and are not referenced in it
- items such as yearbooks with no catalog records grouped by subject
- vertical files with alphabetical or subject grouping
- rare books or unique artifactual items that are randomly kept in offices or in a safe

Correspondingly, classification and arrangement of items may be nonstandard, such as:

- arrangement, alphabetical by author of family-produced items on a shelf
- simply putting "like" materials together, such as yearbooks, in a designated space
- a cataloging system which could be locally devised adapting the Dewey Decimal System call numbers for special local use and adding Cutter numbers, state abbreviations or postal codes, or codes for type of material

Some of these methods may work, considering the room's context and use, while others, like the grouping of items on a shelf with no other representation, should be updated. It is certainly going to be the case in many institutions that different cataloging or access methods exist for local collection items. That is because different methods may be appropriate for different items. Indexes in particular often need to exist on their own, as access methods to other items in the collection.

ACCESS METHODS TO ALL MATERIALS SHOULD BE EXPLAINED IN ONE PLACE

A list of all cataloging/description methods used for the local collection must be created and made available to the patron. For example, if all local history book items are cataloged in the library's Integrated Library System (ILS), then the patron should be directed to the library catalog to search for them in a pathfinder or guide to the collection, which also gives local subject headings and other tips for searches. If a variety of methods are used, including catalog entries, indexes, etc., then these methods might be accounted for in one landing page on a website or with a paper guide that explains the collection. Such a guide may also be attached as a pdf to a collection. Librarians may want to use LibGuides or another standard form of pathfinder. Archives may need a guide to relevant locations and searching techniques for items of family history interest.

How does one provide clear, usable descriptions of multiple indexing methods?

- Create a web presence, such as a landing page to the collection, even if few of your items exist in digital format. Be sure to include brief explanations of how to search for catalog items, using specific subject terminology. It there are digitized items, link to them and provide access information.

- Create a separate pathfinder or brochure for the collection. It is a great idea to provide a printed copy available on site in the collection, as well as in the form of a downloadable handout from the collection web page.

- Create a map of your library or institution that marks every space where local materials may reside, such as reference, the local history room, the microforms area, and the stacks. The map should be available in printed format and also as a part of the site web page or downloadable from it.

- Create a concept map for your collection. Label the map with answers to "Where do I go if I have a question about. . .?"

- Look at collaborating with other institutions. Because creating these pan resource historical indexes is so labor intensive, duplication of effort should be avoided. It may be possible to roll data collected by multiple organizations into one online index, which would be a glorious research aid owned by the entire community.

LEGACY METHODS SHOULD BE EVALUATED

Many family history collections contain cataloging or indexing methods that are incomplete or not easily used with modern technology. For example, many a good-hearted volunteer began a project, with little or no documentation of the process, and left before the indexing was completed. A card file may exist for some years of obituaries, but a clipping file for other years, or there may be an Excel chart done for only a few years of obituaries as well. These methods are often called "legacy methods," and they provide both opportunities and challenges to the local collection information environment. Undocumented methods may still have high usability and value for the collection, but they may need to be updated or migrated, depending on the circumstances. For example, (1) a local index might be on software, such as a spreadsheet, which requires version upgrades in order to remain usable. (2) An index on paper to newspapers or to the circular file could use updating for more consistent subject terms. (3) A dusty notebook with old typed entries which provide the only listing of the historical room's contents may need to be recreated in searchable format. What are the important features one should examine when evaluating these methods?

- What item does the entry/index/representation cover?

- When was it created? By whom?

- Is there documentation by the creator or other volunteers as to the development and rationales for the tool?

- Does the cataloging method cover all items? If not, what documentation exists or clues as to what was not included?

- Is the original method for creating the index/manifestation still functioning and being utilized? If electronic, can it be migrated to a newer version?

- What are the strengths and weaknesses of this representation method?
- Does the method create a way to search by subject?
- Is this format one that the institution should maintain or should it be migrated to another format?

Once this information has been obtained for each representation method, it is good to create a chart that compares the methods, their overlap, pros and cons, and the difficulty of maintaining versus migration versus cessation/replacement. It is useful to consider a hierarchy of access when analyzing legacy methods. Where do these legacy methods fit into this schema? Should working card files or paper indexes be retained alongside digital surrogates if access to them is easier for some patrons? Please see Table 7.1 for an overview of different access levels in a collection.

When comparing the legacy and other methods of cataloging and indexing, and making a local collection available, how many of the collections fall into the minimal or no access range? Limited access? The goal of many patrons is full access, but that is a dream not to be realized for many years in most institutions. There also may be resistance to planning for full access resources, since there is a perception of income in some institutions from these resources. While it is true that resource searches and sales of indexes published in book format do bring in income for institutions, it is useful to consider the potential for revenue from well-designed local resource portals that have donation buttons on them and from programming that creates goodwill and invites donations for specific projects. If the institution's volunteer base and foot traffic are waning, it may be time to take stock of the collection and its role in the institution and move forward with a new vision of outreach and active participation in the historical and genealogical community.

The best methods of access for the collection should be chosen considering the environment, staff, funding, and other considerations. What are the most important

Table 7.1

Access Hierarchy Chart

Minimal or No Access	• Uncataloged items • Items in remote storage • Damaged items not for use • Rare items not for use
Onsite Limited Access	• Items are partially cataloged or indexed • Items are fully indexed/cataloged, but the index is not easy to use and/or unavailable to the public at all times • Resources are staff-use items that may become accessible during a reference interview, but otherwise not accessible • Resources are fully cataloged/indexed, but only available when local resource room is open or when particular staff are present
Onsite Full Access	• Items are fully cataloged or indexed, including consistent subject access methods • Catalogs and items are available onsite whenever the main facility is open
Full Findability	• Items are described in online catalogs/indexes that are available 24/7
Full Access	• Items are fully digitized and available for free 24/7.

concepts when considering access to local collections? A method of representing a local collection should reflect the abilities and expertise of the typical staff who would be working in the room, unless there have been provisions to fund continuous methods that the body of staff and volunteers may not understand. So, new methods being considered should be **sustainable.** For example, if a local historical society is considering writing a grant to purchase PastPerfect, but there are no dedicated volunteers who will commit to training and using the program consistently, this is not money well spent. It might make more sense to continue paper methods or the legacy database and focus on making the information in that database more accessible.

THE COLLECTION SHOULD BE VISIBLE

Because most of our patrons have computers, the first and most important face of the institution is not the well-stocked facility brimming with materials and eager staff members, but the web page. Sadly, many web pages for local studies departments are skimpy, indifferent affairs that leave end users just as in the dark about the institution's resources and services as they were before they found it. However, the preparation of a detailed, easy-to-use web page will pay off in many ways. The more information that can be front loaded onto the website, the more informed and independent researchers are by the time they come to the facility, or contact the institution with a question. Essential information to communicate, *but which is missing from many websites* includes:

- the scope of the local studies collection, the number of volumes, microfilm reels, shelf ranges, square feet, filing cabinets it contains. Most people cannot visualize what a specific number of square feet means, so use a combination of these.
- location of the local studies department especially in a large, multisite facility
- contact information including a direct telephone number to any available local studies reference staff
- staffed hours of the department, particularly if they are different from the hours of the larger institution
- the ability to make an appointment with a staff member
- the ability to have materials pulled by staff members in advance
- the types of materials housed should be incorporated in the name or at least in the description of the collection
- amenities provided such as photocopiers, scanners, digital reader printer, magnification devices
- links to the online catalog, and the Interlibrary Loan (ILL) policy

Bells and whistles or those really nice items that should be included:

- information on how to prepare for an onsite visit
- a listing of staff members and their areas of expertise
- a photograph of the collection is nice, however, a video tour is much better
- a map of the collection

- pathfinders on various topics, including a locality guide (for more on these, see Appendix B)
- a blog maintained by the staff which highlights programs and new additions to the collection

The web page should include a clear overview of all avenues to the collection, such as:

- Indexes and other finding aids
- Newspapers and other serials
- Digitized collections
- Vertical file locations and indexes
- Cataloging programs, such as PastPerfect
- Photo files
- Link to the library catalog with a brief explanation of how to search using LCSH

Depending on the location, some of these will be highlighted and explained more than others. It is very important that users can understand from one screen all the various avenues to the collection. It does not have to be the case that all items are digitized; rarely would this ever be the case in a local collection. **But all collections must easily be locatable from the online description.** Another concern is that often it is difficult or impossible to locate the part of the institution's website that lists genealogical or local history information. On some websites, no terms relating to this subject are found on the homepage, not even on the dropdown menus. The researcher must attempt a keyword search in the search engine, which sometimes locates the information lurking in an obscure corner of the website, or simply telephone or submit a question via the general reference department in order to determine if the institution has local studies holdings.

A number of great resources exist for designing library websites with low-tech requirements. The Halton Information Network provides great support for members (www.halinet.on.ca). The notion of a Catablog is one that might work for some institutions to either raise visibility of the resources or to even serve as the primary cataloging mechanism for the site as well. Blog postings provide information about key resources in the catalog and raise awareness through social media of the riches to be found there.[26]

WHAT IF CREATION OF A WEB PAGE IS JUST TOO MUCH?

It is still the case that many small cultural heritage institutions do not have websites. For collections in these locations, the creation of a one-page guide to the collection is a useful device to promote the visibility and accessibility of the collection. Another solution is to collaborate with others in the community on a digital portal where the institution with the most support to create digital materials would put information on all the collections that exist in the local area on one site. The information can include directions, a short overview of each institution's collections, and the best days/times/manner of contact. For a full discussion of digital portals, see Chapter 9.

CONCLUSION

Access methods to family history collections can vary considerably in their format and detail, as well as the software needed to create the records. Four primary principles in assessing the state of collection may help provide guidance in evaluating priorities:

- cataloging the entire collection
- providing information on all access methods in one place
- evaluating legacy methods, and
- making the collections visible.

Those in small collections may benefit from partnerships to provide more access. In addition, they may want to better understand the types of family history materials that exist in partner organizations. The following two chapters provide more information on the kinds of resources available in the traditional collection and in digital collections, with emphasis on the potential for digital collaborative efforts.

NOTES

1. Faye Phillips, *Local History Collections in Libraries* (Englewood, CO: Libraries Unlimited, 1995), 84.

2. For good introduction to concepts related to subject access and other cataloging methods, see Arlene G. Taylor and Daniel N. Joudrey, *Organization of Information* (Westport, CT: Libraries Unlimited, 2009).

3. For more information on the evolution of MARC, see *Understanding MARC: Machine-Readable Bibliographic* (Washington, DC: Library of Congress, 2009), http://www.loc.gov/marc/umb/.

4. Library of Congress, "Introduction to Library of Congress Subject Headings," 2015, http://loc.gov/aba/publications/FreeLCSH/lcshintro.pdf.

5. Encoded Archival Description 2002 Official Site, http://www.loc.gov/ead/eadabout.html.

6. For a detailed report on these and other archival management software, see Lisa Spiro, *Archival Management Software: A Report for the Council on Library and Information Resources* (Washington, DC: ACRL, 2009).

7. See, for example, Society of American Archivists. *Describing Archives: A Content Standard* (Chicago, IL: SAA, 2013), http://files.archivists.org/pubs/DACS2E-2013_v0315.pdf.

8. Museum Software Online, http://www.museumsoftware.com.

9. Lois Hamill, *Archives for the Lay Person: A Guide to Managing Cultural Collections* (Lanham, MD: AltaMira Press, 2012), see in particular, Chapter 4.

10. For an overview of Dublin Core development and applications, see Dublin Core® Metadata Initiative, http://dublincore.org/documents/dcmi-terms/.

11. "What is WorldCat?" http://www.worldcat.org/whatis/default.jsp.

12. http://beta.worldcat.org/archivegrid/about/.

13. "Organizational Accounts," LibraryThing.com, last modified September 11, 2009, https://www.librarything.com/wiki/index.php/Organizational_accounts.

14. A recent study of open source OCR programs for historical digitization demonstrates rates of OCR among a variety of open source and proprietary programs to be between 80% and 96%. T. Blanke, M. Bryant, & M. Hedges, "Ocropodium: open source OCR for small-scale historical archives," *Journal of Information Science* 38, no. 1 (2012): 82.

15. "Who is Behind Find A Grave?" http://www.findagrave.com/cgi-bin/fg.cgi?page=whois.

16. "Online Searchable Death Indexes and Records: A Genealogy Guide," http://www.deathindexes.com/cemeteries.html.

17. "About our Wisconsin Name Index," http://www.wisconsinhistory.org/Content.aspx?dsNav=N:4294963828-4294963805&dsRecordDetails=R:CS3508.

18. http://urbanafreelibrary.org/local-history-genealogy/local-history-online.

19. For a list of other back of book indexing programs, see a list maintained by the American Society for Indexing: http://www.asindexing.org/reference-shelf/software/.

20. Kerry A. Fitzgerald, "Reinventing the Obituary File for the Digital Age," In Elaine Williams and Carol Smallwood, eds., *Preserving Local Writers, Genealogy, Photographs, Newspapers, and Related Materials* (Lanham, MD: Scarecrow Press, 2012), 243–253.

21. "Local History in the Research Center," Tulsa City-County Library, http://guides.tulsalibrary.org/content.php?pid=137405&sid=2961876.

22. "Vertical Files," Warren-Trumbull Public Library, http://www.wtcpl.org/index.php/verticalfiles.html.

23. "Vertical Files Database," West Virginia Memory Project, West Virginia Division of Culture and History, http://www.wvculture.org/history/wvmemory/clip.aspx.

24. T. Dalrymple "Just-in-Case" Answers: The Twenty-First-Century Vertical File," *Information Technology & Libraries* 27, no. 4 (2008): 25–28.

25. Mark A. Greene and Dennis Meissner, "More Product, Less Process: Revamping Traditional Archival Processing." *The American Archivist* 68, no. 2 (2005): 208–264.

26. Catablogs, http://publichumanitiestoolbox.wordpress.com/other-tools/catablogs/, see also Cyndi Harbeson, "Promoting Local History through the Catablog," In Williams and Smallwood, *Preserving Local Writers*, 234–242.

Chapter 8

MINING THE RICHES

Whether the local studies collection exists in a library, historical society, archive, or museum, its basic building blocks preserve collective and individual memory and provide valuable resources for the family historian and other researchers. In a typical collection, one may find monographs and periodicals, manuscripts, government documents, various research aids such as indexes and transcriptions, photographs, family documents, and artifacts. In addition, the collections are increasingly enhanced by digital access to materials found onsite, and also to digitized materials from other institutions through online links to digitized collections and subscription databases. The diverse nature of the local collection provides both riches and challenges for the institution housing it. This chapter is a quick and ready reference guide to some of the most common resources and finding aids found in local studies collections, and provides advice on how they can be used and interpreted, and suggestions for finding further information. There are many more types of resources also used in family history research, but the focus in this chapter is on the ones most commonly used by beginning researchers. Throughout the chapter there are tables which contain summaries of how to locate records in various formats.

PERIODICAL PUBLICATIONS

CITY DIRECTORIES

Unique in their ability to capture a time period in the lives of an entire town or region, these reference guides provide detailed documentation of the names of those living in the area, as well as much business and institutional information. These guides were often published annually and were first developed by local printers and then later, by a number of different national companies. City directories vary in their contents, but many provide a list of persons living in a town or region by last name, some by address, some by occupation, and some by all three. In addition, they often provide information on the occupations of those listed, as well as other names of persons who owned businesses in the ads. City directories, like many local history resources, provide a unique snapshot of the life of a town by documenting the names of many residents and tying those names to specific addresses and businesses. Their advertisements contain information on employees, titles, and qualifications, as well as the services and items they provided for sale. Directories also exist for some rural areas, regions, and specific types of businesses.

FORMATS AND AVAILABILITY

Many local studies collections hold city directories in a print format. The availability of these books to the public often depends on their age, condition, and

Table 8.1

Location of City Directories

Where to look for original print directories	• Libraries (public, academic, state, etc.)–check for catalog records in major holdings, such as WorldCat using the subheading "Directories" after their town or region: Titusville (Pa.) – Directories. • State libraries, and county/regional/state historical societies may maintain lists of city directories that are available in print and digital formats. • The collections of major research libraries also should be checked, using both the catalog and also by contacting the archives, in case there are uncataloged copies. • Locally, check any archival holdings, including the school district, Chamber of Commerce, historical societies, genealogy clubs, municipal archives, etc. • Check eBay.com to find copies to purchase.
Where to look for microfilmed copies of directories	• Libraries also often hold these in microfilm, and may be available through interlibrary loan. Check holdings of the Family History Library. • Commercially available: *City Directories of the United States* published by Primary Source Microfilm, a division of Gale Publishing. This is the most comprehensive collection of city directories in microform, containing "nearly 12,000" directories. It can be purchased in geographical or chronological segments.
Where to look for digitized access to directories	• Online databases should be checked regularly for updated holdings. (HeritageQuest, Ancestry, Fold3, etc.) • Online user-input indexes, such as USGenWeb maintains lists of digitized resources for each state. Try also http://www.uscitydirectories.com/. • Digital collections in the surrounding region should be checked by visiting the sites of surrounding counties, the state archive and/or historical society, genealogy clubs • cyndislist.com under the heading "Directories: City, County, Address, etc."

availability of alternate formats. It may be the case that a library will provide the directory in a different format, such as a microfilm or microfiche copy, rather than provide a fragile print copy. Many city directories have been digitized and are available at individual institutions for use through digital libraries, links to online digitized collections, and to both free and subscription databases. City directories are so widely available in digital format that local studies centers can now provide access to an increasing number of them, even in far-flung geographic areas. It is useful to monitor sites that index and link to city directories related to the region in which a library or collection is located in order to expand access.

Where should researchers look for access to city directories? In the ideal scenario, a pathfinder, web guide, or other index that provides an overview of who holds which city directories, in which formats, and for which years for your area. Since this information has not yet been compiled in many communities, a systematic search of possible leads for the accessible city directories should be undertaken. The following locations can be checked in order to compile a usable list of directories that can be provided patrons and staff alike.

DEMONSTRATED USES

The most important information one might find in city directories includes the names of persons who lived in a town or region. It also gives address information that allows for analysis of where those with the same surnames lived, and locations where individuals or families lived during the long decade between U.S. censuses, differentiation of individuals with the same names by utilizing occupational and address information, identification of women, even with their first names, information that can be hard to find in other records through the nineteenth century. This may occur only when the head of the family has died, and the wife is now a widow. There is often information that provides clues about family movement: the absence of an individual in a directory after several concurrent listings may indicate he or she died or moved to a different community. An analysis of occupation and/or residence may help establish an individual's socioeconomic status. Advertisements in directories contain information on businesses where individuals were employed, or that were owned by individuals. Also, directories give an overview of community amenities, such as government offices, churches, businesses, and other institutions during the time period it covers.

RELIABILITY

One should not assume that any directory included one hundred percent of an area's residents. Individuals might not be included for a variety of reasons. Perhaps the family was not at home when the representative from the publishing company called to collect the information. Or the family was newly arrived or moved frequently; immigrants and other restless individuals were sometimes not included. Also, people were overlooked when the representative accidentally missed knocking on some doors. There are also other problems with directory information, such as misspelling of the same surname in multiple ways, and incorrect information because of the lag time between when the information was collected and when it was published, which could have been a year or more.

TO-DO CHECKLIST

- Compare the institution's collection of local directories with what exists for your locality. Search WorldCat, paying special attention to the Library of Congress' holdings, because they are known to have a very complete collection of them.
- If funds allow, fill in gaps in the collection by either acquiring print or microfilmed copies of directories, OR identifying places where they could be accessed digitally. Identify other institutions that hold directories for your area, especially academic, and state libraries and archives.
- Examine the directories at the institution carefully, checking for changes in address numbering, what specific information about residents is included, especially women, and what additional information about the community is listed. Create a one-page guide to understanding the local directories for researchers.

NEWSPAPERS

Historic newspapers provide unique, region-specific accounts of the daily events of the residents, including birth and death notices, stories on the development of the area, politics, special events, business advertisements, etc. Many newspapers date from the nineteenth century or earlier and continue for decades, even to the current era. The preservation of newspapers is a tricky matter, since the paper on which they were printed was not intended for long-term use. It is not generally desirable, nor even feasible to put large amounts of resources into saving the newspaper as artifact. Attempts in the United States have first focused on microfilming and now digitizing the information in these papers.

Digitization is just beginning to emerge as the method of choice to preserve newspaper content, and it is offering increasingly strong access. Often patrons believe that newspapers in their original formats have great historical and artifactual value. Old town or region newspapers are frequent donations to institutions, particularly anniversary issues. These donations present preservation challenges and should be accepted only if the item is not already an issue owned by the institution (either in paper or other format). Certainly original newspapers are important in some collections, but without expensive preservation measures, they will not survive.

Newspapers vary in size and length, depending on the region and time period. They are considered a periodical because they appeared at regular intervals, usually daily, though weekly and other increments exist. Sometimes newspapers had both a morning and an evening edition. If an institution has every issue of a newspaper ever produced, that is considered a "full run." It is difficult to ascertain the exact number of issues that might have appeared for any given newspaper, especially since special issues and publications associated with the paper were common.

FORMATS AND AVAILABILITY

Because newspapers were produced and mainly read locally, it is difficult to establish a complete list of all historic newspapers that existed. Remote locales and "ghost towns" that disappeared in the rise and fall of boomtowns create additional difficulties in tracking the range of publications that may have existed. There were also possibilities for the creation of local newspapers besides the "town" paper. Military bases and posts often produced their own local newspaper as did religious denominations. A good starting point for understanding the wealth of local newspapers is at the Library of Congress site, Chronicling America, which provides a searchable union list of U.S. and colonial-era newspapers from 1690.

DEMONSTRATED USES

Newspapers can provide a huge variety of information for genealogical and historical research, especially in coordination with other document types. They announced vital events, such as births, deaths, marriages and divorces.

Table 8.2

Locating Newspapers

Where to look for original print newspapers	• State libraries and county/regional/state historical societies may maintain lists of newspapers that are available in physical and digital formats. • The collections of major research libraries also should be checked, using both the catalog and also by contacting the archives, in case there are uncataloged copies. • Locally, check any archival holdings, including the school district, Chamber of Commerce, historical societies, genealogical clubs, municipal archives, etc. • Check newspaper morgues or archives.
Where to look for microfilmed copies of newspapers	• Many newspapers have been microfilmed and may be available through interlibrary loan, or through a Family History Center. Institutions that may hold circulating copies include state libraries and archives, and presidential, academic, private, and public libraries. • Check local newspaper morgues or archives.
Where to look for digitized access to directories	• National-level digitization sites: http://chroniclingamerica.loc.gov; Internet Archive: https://archive.org/details/texts; Digital Public Library of America. • Google's Newspaper Digitization project has about 2000 titles that they added between 2008–2011: http://news.google.com/newspapers. • Subscription databases for newspapers: www.newspaperarchive.com; Proquest America's historic newspapers, and www.genealogybank.com are the largest at this point. Other online genealogical databases should be checked regularly for updated holdings. (Ancestry, etc.). • www.smalltownnewspapers.com is a gateway to current and past issues. • Larry Parker's list of free digitized newspapers: http://bit.ly/1jyysyI. • "List of Online Newspaper Archives" is international and includes free and for-pay sites. http://en.wikipedia.org/wiki/Wikipedia:List_of_online_newspaper_archives. • www.elephind.com is a search engine that only searches digitized newspapers. • Digital collections in the surrounding region should be checked by visiting the websites of surrounding counties, the state library, archives and historical societies, andgenealogical society collections.

They contained notices of probate, property sales, auctions, and even estray notices of wandering livestock. Family clues might be found in advertisements for businesses, missing people notices, passenger lists, fraternal and social club activities, and even names of people who had letters waiting at the post office.

RELIABILITY

Caveat: newspapers are often considered to be questionable in reliability. Newspaper accounts were written by reporters and were often based on interviews of eyewitnesses, so their information should not be considered a primary account in most common family history uses. Many newspapers lasted only a few years, were bought out, and resumed operation with a different owner/editor under a different name and with a different bias. Local newspapers were often published to support a specific political viewpoint, which is sometimes stated in the publication, but sometimes not explicitly stated.

Despite these issues in reliability, the information found in local newspapers is invaluable for family history research. Obituary information is among the most important for family historians. They provide clues about family members, cause of death, and the details of ancestors' lives. So, while newspapers should be used with caution and, whenever possible, their information verified by another source, they remain one of the most important resources for researching family history and should be a centerpiece of any local studies collection.

TO-DO CHECKLIST

- Inventory all historic newspapers titles for the local community and document where they are available and in what formats. Do not forget those that are held in a distant physical location like at the state library or at the Library of Congress.
- Give detailed information on how to locate these newspapers in a guide or pathfinder.
- Create a help guide for searching the digitized historic newspapers. Search the digitized versions available to check how accurate the full-text version is and what tips one might give to allow the patron faster access and fewer false hits. In some cases, there exist multiple digitized versions of the same newspaper. Is the full-text searching better on one version? Are there different editions of the same newspaper (morning versus evening, for example) in one database, but not the other?
- If the newspaper exists only in microfilm, be aware that many patrons no longer understand how to use these machines, particularly the new digital microfilm readers. Post clear directions.

YEARBOOKS

These annual publications complete with photographs, stories, and perhaps even signatures and handwritten notes, document students and teachers at schools and universities. The older editions are sought by historical researchers, but newer ones are frequently sought by the students they include. The clipping of photos from yearbooks can be a problem, as yearbooks can be difficult if not impossible to replace. Steps should be taken to safeguard them, such as documenting the names and contact information of the users, and possibly also holding an identification card, if your institution only has them available in a print format. From the standpoint of their uniqueness and limited availability, yearbooks are prime candidates for digitization.

FORMATS AND AVAILABILITY

Yearbooks traditionally were only available as print publications, but recently have begun to be digitized, both by institutions such as libraries, and by commercial websites.

DEMONSTRATED USES

Yearbooks provide a number of valuable pieces of evidence for the local or family historian, including photographs with the first and last names of students, teachers, and administrators. One may be able to document maiden names. Evidence of an ancestor's activity in sports and academic clubs can also be found.

RELIABILITY

Information can generally be assumed to be accurate because yearbooks were assembled by the people they document. However, just because an individual appeared in a yearbook, that does not guarantee that the person graduated from that particular school. Typos and misidentifications can also occur. Verification of the information, as with any other resource, is recommended.

TO-DO CHECKLIST

- Determine if any yearbooks from your area have already been digitized on websites like the Internet Archive or Ancestry.

Table 8.3

Locating Yearbooks

Where to look for original print yearbooks	• Libraries (public, academic, state, etc.): check for catalog records in WorldCat. • Check the high school alumni society or local archival holdings, such as historical and genealogical societies, and, municipal archives.http://www.worldcat.org/search?q=su%3ATitusville+%28Pa.%29+Directories.&qt=hot_subject • State libraries and county/regional/state historical societies may maintain lists of annuals that are available in physical and digital formats. • The collections of major research libraries also should be checked, using both the catalog and also by contacting the archives, in case there are uncataloged copies.
Where to look for digitized access to yearbooks	• Subscription sites, such as Classmates.com and E-Yearbook.com have recent and some older annuals. • Digital collections in the surrounding region should be checked by visiting the sites of surrounding counties, the state archive. and/or historical society. • Digital repositories such as The Internet Archive • Subscription databases should be checked regularly for updated holdings, such as Ancestry and World Vital Records. http://www.uscitydirectories.com/. • www.cyndislist.com, "Schools–Yearbooks and Annuals."

- Assess the institution's collection of local yearbooks, and compile a wish list of damaged or missing issues. Solicit donations from the community.
- Have staff members and volunteers scout local garage and estate sales for yearbooks.
- Periodically check eBay and other websites for yearbooks.

RESOURCES

Gale Directory of Publications and Broadcast Media. Farmington Hills, MI: Gale Group, 1880– , annual.

Hinckley, Kathleen W. "Skillbuilding: Analyzing City Directories." *OnBoard* 2 (May 1996): 16, http://www.bcgcertification.org/skillbuilders/skbld965.html.

Remington, Gordon L. "Directories." In *The Source: A Guidebook to American Genealogy*, edited by Loretto Dennis Szucs and Sandra Hargreaves Luebking, pp. 325–352. Provo, UT: Ancestry, 2006.

Researching City Directories—Using the Internet Archive. https://www.youtube.com/watch?feature=player_embedded&v=YiRxbOkT_f0.

Snow, Barb. "Your Guide to Using Newspapers for Genealogical Research." http://www.barbsnow.net/Newspapers.htm. This lists links to a number of resources giving information on newspaper research.

Sutton, Philip. "Direct Me NYC 1786: A History of City Directories in the United States and New York City," New York Public Library Blogs. June 8, 2012, http://www.nypl.org/blog/2012/06/08/direct-me-1786-history-city-directories-US-NYC. http://www.uscitydirectories.com/.

Szucs, Loretto Dennis, and James L. Hansen. "Newspapers." In *The Source: A Guidebook to American Genealogy*, edited by Loretto Dennis Szucs and Sandra Hargreaves Luebking, pp. 561–602. Provo, UT: Ancestry, 2006.

LOCAL HISTORIES

Local histories contain information about the past of a very specific geographic area, such as a town, township, or county. These have appeared in three separate waves. The first wave of local histories appeared in the late nineteenth or early twentieth centuries, and were mostly written and published by companies which specialized in them. They sent representatives to a given area in order to gather information and to sell orders for the books. Because people often paid extra money to have their biographical information, and sometimes portraits included, these publications are nicknamed "**mug books.**"

The second wave of local histories started to appear further into the twentieth century and was produced to commemorate an important anniversary in the community such as a centennial or sesquicentennial. They were typically produced by a committee of local citizens or a local history or genealogical organization. The bicentennial of the United States in 1976 also spurred the publication of many local histories. The third wave is occurring now. Some local groups are adding indexing to and updating older editions of local histories. Newer commercial ones are also available such as those produced by Arcadia Publishing. These have many more illustrations and photos than older versions. The lower cost of e-publications, some self-published, will spur the appearance of even more of these titles.

FORMATS AND AVAILABILITY

County histories that appeared in the nineteenth century also may appear in facsimile editions. Earlier, more fragile copies may not be available for library use, but the facsimile or digital edition contains the same information. Local historical societies may have archival, manuscript copies of memoirs or "histories" of the region that were never published, but that may be similar in the type of information provided.

Table 8.4

Locating Local Histories

Where to look for original and facsimile print histories	• Libraries (public, academic, state, etc.): check for catalog records in WorldCat. • State libraries and county/regional/state historical societies may maintain lists of local histories that are available in physical and digital formats. • The collections of major research libraries also should be checked, using both the catalog and also by contacting the archives, in case there are uncataloged copies. • Locally, check any archival holdings, including schoollibraries, the Chamber of Commerce, historical and genealogical societies, municipal archives, etc.
Where to look for digitized access to histories	• Freely-accessible digital collections, such as Internet Archive house a large number of digitized county and other histories that are in the public domain (pre-1923). • Check digital collections in the surrounding region by visiting the sites of surrounding counties, the state archive and/or historical and genealogical society websites. • Online databases should be checked regularly for updated holdings. (Heritage Quest, Ancestry, Fold 3, etc.). • The website www.genealogybooklinks.com lists digitized local histories by geographic area. • The Accessible Archives Company has a particularly broad collection in their American County Histories database.

DEMONSTRATED USES

Local histories can supply many types of facts, from information on the Native Americans who first lived in the area, to the waves of settlers. Military history of a region may be covered with specific unit and veterans named. There is information on the agriculture and industry of an area. Perhaps one of the most valuable aspects is the naming of places and how those names may have evolved and changed. Key political and religious leaders and movements are covered, as are the evolution of architectural structures.

RELIABILITY

The quality of local histories can vary quite a bit. Some were carefully composed by consulting documents from the local courthouse and other written sources; however, some publishing companies lifted general historical information directly from other sources such as almanacs and encyclopedias and then added articles on local individuals which were based on interviews with the subjects. Some of these efforts are quite sloppy, complete with spelling and factual errors, and were obviously done in haste. Because many early local histories are unsourced, it can be difficult to ascertain where the information came from. Ideas on how to evaluate local histories for possible inclusion in the collection are found in Chapter 2, "Record It: Preserving Family and Community History."

RESOURCES

Filby, P. William. *A Bibliography of American County Histories*. Baltimore, MD: Genealogical Publishing Co., 1985.

Kammen, Carol. *On Doing Local History*. Walnut Creek, CA: AltaMira Press, 2003.

Meyerink, Kory L., ed. *Printed Sources: A Guide to Published Genealogical Records*. Salt Lake City, UT: Ancestry, Inc. 1998.

More History at: http://www.accessible-archives.com/collections/american-county-histories/a-white-paper-american-county-histories/#ixzz3PmB6JZLp.

Peterson, Clarence S. *Consolidated Bibliography of County Histories in Fifty States*. Baltimore, MD: Genealogical Publishing Co., 1961.

Schultz, Janice. "County Histories and Your Family," https://familysearch.org/learningcenter/lesson/county-histories-and-your-family/36.

RELIGIOUS RECORDS

These written records generated by a religious organization are not always avail-able at local studies centers because they can be difficult to acquire, but they are a rich source of information about the community and its individuals. Many realize the value of baptismal, marriage, and burial records, but religious records often hold a variety of other information including records of membership, confirmation, communion, and other religious ceremonies, administrative minutes, newsletters, written histories, personnel information, committee reports, and photographs. In addition, foreign mission work is an important part of many denominational records, including information on activities abroad in regular serial publications.

Religious records can predate civil records in a given area and they often have greater detail, such as the exact place of origin, names of baptismal sponsors and marriage witnesses, names of parents, etc. Bear in mind that not all churches prac-ticed infant baptism, making it more difficult to find evidence of birthdates in these churches' records. Finally, records created by clergymen can be quite accurate because they probably knew their congregants far better than the government clerks who created civil records. Often, the clergymen shared the same ethnicity as their flocks, and literally spoke their language.

FORMATS AND AVAILABILITY

Genealogical purists might disagree, but it is best to begin searching for religious records in either microfilmed or digitized formats. That is because the original records, often only held by the individual congregation that generated them, are usually not easily available. Church staffs, usually small and busy, are not set up to accommodate researchers. Unless the microfilm of the originals has been poorly done and is difficult to read, it is far better to obtain the records on microfilm, and then study them at a Family History Center or library in a leisurely fashion, sparing the old, often delicate documents from wear and tear.

Luckily, some congregations are seeing the wisdom of preserving their originals and are digitizing and placing them online. For example, St. John's Lutheran Church in San Antonio, Texas has done this: http://stjohnssa.org/history/church-archives/. Others are at least creating indexes to names found in their records and placing them online, such as historic Christ Church in Philadelphia: http://www.christchurchphila.org. At the very least, there are more congregations that include a congregational history on their website, along with the names of their officiants. This information can be important because it includes the date the institution was established, when various structures were built to house it, when it changed its name or affiliation with a denomination. Sometimes this type of information is also available in local history books and in retrospective newspaper articles.

Unfortunately, religious records can be difficult to locate for a variety of reasons. Many church records have vanished or perished. Also, many Americans joined new denominations in the United States that did not become widespread, such as

Table 8.5

Locating Religious Records

Where to look for microfilmed church records	• Check the Family History Library. • Try a local, regional or state public library, archive, historical society or genealogical society. • Contact a denominational archive–some loan these to individuals.
Where to look for original church records	• Many exist in individual congregations. • These often exist in a denominational archive–either older records, records from defunct congregations, or copies of congregational records get sent there. • Look in county and local historical societies. • Also try local, regional, academic and state archives.
Where to look for digitized church records	• Few have been digitized as of yet. Look at the websites of individual congregations, their denominational archives, and FamilySearch. Also, Ancestry has a few. http://memory.loc.gov/ammem/index.html
Published church records	• See "Published Church Records" by Richard W. Dougherty in *Printed Sources*. • Use *PERSI* and other genealogical indexes to find transcribed church records in periodicals.

the Winebrennerians. Congregational records from older churches may be subsumed into other collections, or kept by other nearby congregations. Congregational records for denominations that have undergone mergers may mean the church now has a different name; for example, the Evangelical and Reformed Church and the Congregational Church merged and became the United Church of Christ, and the Methodist Church and the Evangelical United Brethren merged to become the United Methodist Church. Another difficulty is that congregational records did not exist for people in frontier or newly settled areas when they had no access to an organized congregation. They gathered informally, or were occasionally served by an itinerant preacher such as the Methodist circuit riders. Congregational records may not be available to researchers.

Do not assume that a denomination will be consistent with how they provide access to their records in different geographic areas. The Roman Catholic Church stores old records in a diocesan archive, but only a few dioceses have given permission for the Family History Library (FHL) to film these records; most have not. One exception is the records of the Chicago Archdiocese. Dozens of parishes' records are digitized on FamilySearch but are not yet indexed. Researchers in other major cities, such as New York, are not so lucky. One must ask the individual congregation to have a staff member check its records. In New Orleans, the only way to access most information now is to request a transcription of a sacramental record from the archdiocesan archives. However, the archives has begun a digitization project, and they are starting with records of people of color.

DEMONSTRATED USES

These include establishing the obvious birth, marriage, and death dates, but also church records can pinpoint when an individual arrived in a community by documenting his or her name as a founder of a congregation, someone who took communion, constructed a church building, paid tithes, as well as establish when and for where an individual left a community by documenting withdrawal or transfer of membership. The records provide clues about an individual's status in the community. Did the individual have a leadership role, or was he or she reprimanded or even expelled for a transgression?

RELIABILITY

Usually the religious officiant kept the records. They can contain errors, because they were created by very fallible human beings, although the officiants of certain denominations are known for careful recordkeeping, such as Roman Catholic priests and Lutheran ministers. For records that were produced as a natural outgrowth of church activity, such as newsletters and wedding photographs, there is a good expectation of reliability for documenting these specific events.

TO-DO CHECKLIST

- Get to know the religious organizations in the community. Visit websites, to read histories, verify names of clergymen, download photographs, and to check availability of records, but also to check indexing and sometimes, digitized records.

- Determine where the information for local religious institutions is held. Some may be local, but some may also be in a far-flung repository.

- Collaborate with a local group like the genealogy society to make a master index of local church record information, extracting names from church records in your area and the supporting information attached to the names such as baptism records, attendance/joining records, and marriages. Ideally, this would be accessible online.

- Encourage congregations to get their records microfilmed or digitized.

- Refer patrons to translation help when church records are recorded in a variety of different languages. Numerous books and online and print articles offer advice.

RESOURCES

Kirkham, E. Kay. *A Survey of American Church Records: Major and Minor Denominations before 1880–1890*, 4th ed. Logan, UT: Everton Publishing, 1978.

Latin in Parish Records, http://www.genuki.org.uk/big/LatinNotes.html.

Melton, J. Gordon. Melton's *Encyclopedia of American Religions*, 8th ed. Farmington Hills, MI: Gale, 2009.

"Religion & Churches," http://www.cyndislist.com/religion.

"Root's Web's Guide to tracing Family Trees." Religious Institutions Records," http://rwguide.rootsweb.ancestry.com/lesson17.htm.

Various online denominational directories such as: www.parishesonline.com, http://www.elca.org/tools/FindACongregation, http://www.reformjudaism.org/find-a-congregation.

Wells, Elizabeth Crabtree. "Church Records," In The Source: A Guidebook to American Genealogy, edited by Loreto Dennis Szucs and Sandra Hargreaves Luebking, 221–256. Provo UT: Ancestry, 2006.

GOVERNMENT DOCUMENTS

CENSUS RECORDS

Census records are the government's written documentation of its residents, whether or not they are citizens. It has been taken every ten years since 1790. The censuses prior to 1850 only listed the name of the head of the household, usually a male, and gave slash marks in categories that denote sex and age ranges for the members of the household. Every census from 1850 on is an every-name census. That means that every resident of a household, even the baby, is listed by name. In general, the census has become more complicated every time, with more detailed information being gathered.

The government asks many personal questions during a census enumeration. By law, because of privacy concerns, a census is sealed for 72 years from the time it is enumerated. The most current available census is the 1940 census which was released in 2012. Census records are arranged by geographical area: state, county, township, city/town, enumeration district, census ward, page number, and line number. Census information was originally recorded by hand by census takers, also known as enumerators. Census takers were paid by the government to travel throughout a region to knock on every door. Much of the original census information is in the care of the National Archives and Records Administration (NARA), but for complicated reasons, some also rests in various other types of collections, such as university libraries.

Unfortunately, not all of the U.S. Census records have survived. Probably the most distressing loss is that of the 1890 census; all but the information for about 6000 Americans was lost in a fire in Washington, DC. *Your Guide to the Federal Census* by Kathleen W. Hinckley, pages 112–114, provides a detailed list of other pieces that are missing from various censuses.

Census information has been widely microfilmed, indexed, and digitized, though not always well. The 1900–1940 census records were imperfectly microfilmed and many of the images are quite dark. Because the U.S. Congress decided to destroy the original set of census returns in order to save storage space, the microfilming cannot be completed again with better techniques and equipment. However, the tweaking of the digitized microfilmed images has somewhat succeeded in improving them.

FORMATS AND AVAILABILITY

Census records are available in a variety of formats. These include: microfilm reels which can be ordered from NARA or the FHL, censuses on CD-ROM from commercial vendors, and census information which has been transcribed and published in an article, a book, or on a website. While transcriptions can be useful finding aids, one should always visit a facsimile of the original record whenever they are available. Any transcription is prone to error.

Table 8.6

Locating U.S. Census Records

Where to look for original U.S. Census records	• They are housed at NARA, and a variety of state and university libraries and archives; usually these will only be available to researchers who demonstrate a need to consult the original.
Where to look for microfilmed U.S. Census records	• These can be found in many library and archival collections such as NARA and the FHL.
Where to look for digitized U.S. Census records	• Some years are available for free at FamilySearch, currently 1940, 1900, 1880. • 1940 is available free at http://1940census.archives.gov/ (not indexed by name). • Subscription websites such as Ancestry, Fold3, and Heritage Quest should be checked. • All census years are free at Mocavo.com. http://memory.loc.gov/ammem/index.html.

The most widely used type of census record is now digitized, which are available online through commercial sites like Ancestry, HeritageQuest, and Fold3, and also some are free at FamilySearch. One is not always looking at an original census return on microfilmed or digitized records. The government has required duplicate copies of the census reports to be produced in the past. The original was not always the copy that was sent in to the federal government and /or preserved. It can be difficult to tell the difference between original census records and the copies; however, certain pages appear to be original working copies complete with margin notes. This is significant to researchers because when censuses were recopied, there was always a possibility that errors were introduced. Also, sometimes the names were recopied with initials in lieu of first names in order to hasten the process, which meant that valuable information was lost.

Now that digitized census records are available online, do local studies centers need to retain their microfilmed and published copies of census records? Surprisingly, there are some good reasons to do so. First, if your institution is small, and the number of computers limited, then keeping the microfilmed census records allow additional patrons to view census records when the computers are all in use. Second, because there is more than one copy of census returns, the microfilmed version of the census you have may be a different version from the digitized version available on your subscription website. Hinckley's *Your Guide to the Federal Census* has a more detailed explanation. Third, the published versions of census records you may have were created when someone sat down, read through all the census returns for a given area, interpreted the handwriting, and typed it up. This interpretation of what the handwriting says may be a better one than Ancestry, or HeritageQuest, or FamilySearch used in their indexing.

DEMONSTRATED USES

The historical, cultural, and sociological uses for this information are stupendous. Not only is there obvious value in the population schedules with information recorded about family groups and individuals, but also in the Non-Population Schedules which provide statistics about communities in the Social Statistics

Schedules; deaths in the Mortality Schedules; handicaps and disabilities in the Defective, Dependent, Delinquent Schedules; as well as Veterans, Agriculture, and Manufacturing Schedules.

RELIABILITY

The accuracy of the recorded information can be very good, and it can be very bad. Think of all the obstacles the average census taker faced in completing the task; it is amazing that any of it is good information. They gathered the information in foul weather, traveling unpaved roads on foot and horseback, using pens that needed to be dipped into pots of ink. In 1790, forms were not standardized, and many census takers had poor penmanship. Many people even today do not want to cooperate because they are afraid of the government, and regardless of the era, some families do not speak English.

In addition, there can be separate problems with census indexing. Various types of indexes exist, and *none of them is perfect*. Some of the main problems with the indexing are the misreading of old handwriting, typographical errors introduced during the compilation process, the reversal of first and last names, and many others.

TO-DO CHECKLIST

- Learn what census resources are available in your area including indexing, transcriptions, and microfilmed and digitized images.
- Practice searching for an individual in three consecutive U.S. censuses. Compare the information to see if it is consistent and likely to be accurate or not.

VITAL RECORDS

Vital records are those which record the main life events: birth, marriages, and deaths. Researchers often refer to this in shorthand as BMD. They also cover divorces and adoptions. These records are generated by a government office at some level. The dates at which vital records began to be recorded, the information they contain, and which government office keeps them, varies widely from state to state, county to county and city to city. Some states did not begin recording vital records until well into the twentieth century.

Sometimes older vital records have been transferred out of the government office that created them to a library or archive. Sometimes they have been microfilmed. The Genealogical Society of Utah, has widely, but not completely, microfilmed vital records across the United States and in other countries. Some of the images are available for free on their website, FamilySearch, but sometimes only the indexed names are available. Sometimes, the images are available on subscription websites. Sometimes, a copy of the actual record is only available by sending a fee to a government office. Information professionals and researchers need to do some legwork to figure out where to find vital records for the area in which their collections are located, and also in other localities in which their patrons are researching.

Table 8.7

Locating Vital Records

Where to look for original vital records	• Locally, check the town hall, county office, or statewide office that generated them. • Most articles about U.S. states in the wiki at FamilySearch have a table that summarizes the years that vital records are available in specific localities. • Older records may be stored in government archives, historical societies, academic libraries, or state archives.
Where to look for microfilmed vital records	• Libraries, archives, and government offices of many types may hold various records. • Also check circulating collections of the FHL and some state libraries.
Where to look for digitized access to vital records	• Check websites of government offices, regional/state archives, and libraries, and especially FamilySearch. • Subscription websites such as Ancestry are constantly adding digitized records. • Online commercial record providers like VitalChek can be of use for a fee. http://memory.loc.gov/ammem/index.html.

FORMATS AND AVAILABILITY

Vital records are available in a bewildering variety of locations in different formats. In the United States, there is no standardized system of storing government documents at the state and local levels. Early New England towns recorded vital events, but many vital records in other states were recorded by a county office. To make matters even more confusing, some cities are so large that they keep their own vital records rather than depending upon the county. At some point during the twentieth century many state governments assumed the task. For example, birth certificates in many states are now available through a statewide Public Health Office. The older original records are often transferred out of the government office that created them to an archive, state library, academic library, or another repository. Often microfilmed copies of originals are placed in local studies collections. In addition to originals or microfilmed versions, it is now possible to access digitized and indexed versions online, some in free sources, like the Missouri State Archives website, and some in fee-based websites like Ancestry.com.

DEMONSTRATED USES

Vital records are among the first type of information that family history researchers turn to for obvious reasons, but they are also used by historians, sociologists, and health professionals to learn about populations at the community or state level. The exact content of what each type of vital record contains varies by locality and by time period. In general, the older a vital record, the less information it is likely to contain.

RELIABILITY

Because vital records are created by human beings, creatures prone to error, so too are vital records. They should be examined carefully in order to ascertain whether the information is correct by cross-comparing with similar information found in other sources.

TO-DO CHECKLIST

- Learn all the government repositories where vital records for the area are housed, and the conditions and methods by which researchers can request copies. For example, older marriage records may be available at the county courthouse, but newer ones are stored at a state public health office.
- Identify any institutions that have acquired microfilmed copies of area vital records such as the state library or the FHL.
- Scout out any digitized vital records at subscription and free websites.

MILITARY RECORDS

The United States government created many documents for its military. Military records generated by federal military service are held at NARA in Washington, DC and the National Personnel Records Center in St. Louis, Missouri. St. Louis has records from World War I or later, but their collection is incomplete because of a fire in 1973. The paper trail generated by a. soldier or sailor relates to the three stages of his or her service: preservice, the actual service, and postservice. The records for career military members are organized separately from those of the volunteers and draftees who served only in one specific conflict. Records are of the following types:

- Preservice records include: enlistment papers, draft registration cards, and militia rolls.
- Service records include the compiled military service file, a series of cards containing information based on several types of record groups This is a an access tool which is sometimes flawed.
- Postservice records include the federal military pension application and file, and the bounty-land warrant application file, soldiers' homes records, veterans' organizations records, and burial records.
- Pension records include four types: the disability/invalid pension, the widow's pension, the child's pension, and the mother's pension. Note: If the soldier was dishonorably discharged he and his descendants would NOT have qualified for a pension.

Records of men who fought in a state or local militia, as opposed to the federal armed forces, will not be at NARA, but held instead at the state or local level. These records, or copies of them, may be held at many different types of libraries and archives.

FORMATS AND AVAILABILITY

In the past, researchers went directly to NARA for military records, but that is slowly changing. NARA has partnered with commercial websites in order to make the records more widely available and for smaller fees. Some of these record collections are free, but some require a paid membership in the site. NARA lists these partnerships on their website: http://www.archives.gov/digitization/partnerships.html.

The best way to access information found in military records is to use an index/finding aid. Chapter 13 in *Printed Sources: A Guide to Published Genealogical Records*, "Military Sources," is a very thorough listing of indexes that exist in print form.

Table 8.8

Locating Military Records

Where to look for original military records	• In general, look for federal records at NARA and its regional locations, and look for militia records at a variety of state and university libraries and archives.
Where to look for microfilmed military records	• Some library and archival collections such as NARA and the FHL will have copies.
Where to look for digitized military records	• Some records must still be purchased directly from NARA, and are scanned onto a CD-ROM or photocopied and mailed. • Some are available for free at FamilySearch, such as WWI and WWII draft cards, as well as indexing of additional record groups. • Various other free databases exist including the War of 1812 Pension Project at Fold3, and the Civil War Soldiers and Sailors System at http://www.nps.gov/civilwar/soldiers-and-sailors-database.htm. • Subscription websites such as Ancestry, Fold3, and HeritageQuest contain indexing and some records.

Some indexes are online now, and a good inventory of these is found at: www.militaryindexes.com, a site by created by Joe Beine. Also, consult Cyndi's List under "Military Worldwide," which has subheadings.

DEMONSTRATED USES

The various types of military records contain different types and quantities of information. The record most likely to contain information about a serviceman's family is the pension file. The documentation includes proof of the serviceman's relationship to his wife and family and can include affidavits, copies of marriage and birth records, and records torn from the family's Bible. Enlistment records usually list place of birth and sometimes a physical description. The compiled military service record provides information about how and where a person served, which unit or units, the dates of enlistment and discharge, dates of muster rolls, any wounds, illnesses, and hospital stays.

RELIABILITY

It is always possible that mistakes were made in recording information during the chaos of a war, but in general, the U.S. military has done a remarkable job of capturing information about its personnel. Even when spelling mistakes were made with an individual soldier's name, sometimes "see" references are found in the compiled military service records and their indexing, attempting to correct some of these mistakes.

TO-DO CHECKLIST

• Make sure you understand which military records, and/or indexing of them, are available on any commercial websites to which your institution subscribes.

- Learn about free sources of military information available. The number of new Civil War websites that appeared for its 150th anniversary in 2012 was staggering, including the Soldiers and Sailors database of the National Park Service, http://www.nps.gov/civilwar/soldiers-and-sailors-database.htm.

- Learn where researchers can find good secondary sources such as military histories, both in your local studies center and elsewhere. These have been written by veterans groups as well as professional historians, and contain lists of soldiers in various units, locations where they fought, and dates of formation and dispersal. These are in libraries, the FHL, and also online. Example: *The War of the Rebellion: the Official Records of the Union and Confederate Armies* is online at http://ehistory.osu.edu/books/official-records.

- Consult the staffs of military libraries and of lineage societies, because they are particularly helpful with military queries.

SHIP PASSENGER LISTS

"An act of March 2, 1819 (3 Stat. 489) required the captain or master of a vessel arriving at a port in the United States or any of its territories from a foreign country to submit a list of passengers to the collector of customs, beginning January 1, 1820. The act also required that the collector submit a quarterly report or abstract, consisting of **copies of these passenger lists**, to the Secretary of State, who was required to submit such information at each session of Congress. After 1874, collectors forwarded **only statistical reports** to the Treasury Department. The lists themselves were retained by the collector of customs. Customs records were maintained primarily for statistical purposes."
                                                    "Immigration Records" at www.archives.gov

During the colonial period ships arrived at hundreds of locations where rivers met the Atlantic Ocean and the Gulf of Mexico. During the nineteenth and twentieth centuries, 101 ports were used, and additional border crossing stations were established at Canada and Mexico. A complete listing of ports is found in *Guide to Genealogical Research in the National Archives, 3rd ed.* The United States did not begin to officially keep track of who sailed to its shores until 1820, when the U.S. Congress passed a law requiring every captain to record the names of everyone who sailed on each ship, citizens and immigrants alike. Some ship passenger lists were recorded from before that time, and survive. For a discussion of such lists that have been published, consult Chapter 14 of *Printed Sources: A Guide to Published Genealogical Records*, "Immigration Sources," but there has been even more exciting scholarship published since then. For example, the most complete, authoritative source of information about the Mayflower passengers, are the databases of the Great Migration Study Project at www.americanancestors.org/index.aspx, the website of the New England Historic Genealogical Society.

Not every ship's passenger list from 1820 onwards survived, and of those that did, not all of them are indexed. Therefore, significant gaps in the historical record exist, and access to what still exists can be problematic. Some of the indexing still being used was compiled in the 1930s by the WPA. Not everyone came through Ellis

Table 8.9

Locating Passenger Lists

Where to look for original ship passenger lists	• Check NARA, and a variety of state and university libraries and archives. Usually these will only be available to researchers who demonstrate a need to consult the original.
Where to look for microfilmed ship passenger lists	• Check library and archival collections, especially NARA and the FHL. • Print indexes may still be useful to determine which ship an individual traveled on.
Where to look for digitized ship passenger lists	• FamilySearch will gradually be digitizing microfilmed lists and placing them online. • Subscription websites such as Ancestry and Findmypast.com have some lists. • http://www.libertyellisfoundation.org/ provides free indexing of ships docking at Ellis Island, but do not provide an easily readable image of the original lists. • http://www.stevemorse.org/ supplies online searching interfaces to enhance access to ship passenger lists and other record types. http://memory.loc.gov/ammem/index.html

Island, or its predecessor immigration center in New York City, Castle Garden, which operated from 1850–1890. Ellis Island did not open until January 1, 1892. Immigrant ships could have arrived at many ports, but a handful did receive a substantial portion of the immigration traffic. The "Big Five" includes the ports of New York, New Orleans, Boston, Philadelphia, and Baltimore.

FORMATS AND AVAILABILITY

Some passenger lists have been transcribed and published, microfilmed, indexed or digitized, but no one comprehensive place holds all that survive. The main collection of digitized records is at Ancestry.com. A variety of other websites provide information on immigrant ships and the people who arrived on them. The most comprehensive print index of names has been the *Passenger and Immigration Lists Index* (PILI) by P. William Filby. This multivolume set has been transformed into a database on Ancestry.com. It is necessary to read the preface of the print version and the description of the database in order to understand their scopes and provenances. In addition, there have been print indexes that focus on specific ethnic groups such as *The Germans to America* series. Again, reading the preface to discover this index's limitations is crucial.

DEMONSTRATED USES

Ship passenger lists that predate 1900 tend to have less information than ones that came later, because the preprinted forms that the government supplied changed and required more information. The early ones list name, nationality, age, profession, and the town/city lived in, which may have been different from the one where the passengers were born. Later lists included birth date, birth place, destination, and more.

RELIABILITY

The crew had a vested interest in accounting for every person aboard in order to prevent stowaways, so it is likely that a high percentage of passengers were recorded on the lists. However, the information may not have been perfectly accurate as the crew was in a hurry to record the data as the passengers filed aboard. The foreign accents and illiteracy of the passengers contributed to spelling errors.

Researchers should understand the following about passenger lists:

- Some ships stopped at several ports before arriving in the United States. For example, many Irish ships stopped at Liverpool before heading to a port on our eastern seaboard. Therefore, there may be a misleading port of departure on the top of the passenger list.

- The passengers may have spent time in another country apart from their native land before arriving at their ultimate destination. For example, many immigrants to Canada ultimately drifted down to manufacturing jobs in New England.

- Researchers should always search a minimum of a few years on either side of the alleged immigration date if they are having trouble locating an individual on a passenger list.

- The passenger list may list where the person last lived, not the birthplace.

- Alternate spellings/possible misspellings should always be considered.

- For immigrants from Latin countries, check the women under their maiden names.

- The entire passenger list should be checked to make sure other family members are not overlooked. They were not always recorded together.

- The chapter called "Searching Years Not Included in National Archives Indexes," in the book *They Came in Ships* by John P. Colletta contains valuable advice for doing an end run around indexing.

- Checking the local newspapers for an announcement of when the ship arrived, and then calculating the number of days since the ship sailed yields the length of the voyage.

- Background information on the ships can be located in old newspaper articles, books on the history of ships, and online.

RESOURCES

Ancestry.com. "10 Census Tips," http://c.mfcreative.com/email/us/guides/10_census_tips _v3.pdf?o_xid=52185&o_lid=52185&o_sch=Email.

Bockman, Jeffrey. "They Came on This Ship," originally appeared in *Everton's Genealogical Helper*, May/June 2007, p. 76, now online at https://sites.google.com/site/jeffbockman/ gatj/ships.

Census Instructions, https://www.census.gov/history/www/through_the_decades/census _instructions/.

Dollarhide, William. "The Census Day," http://www.genealogyblog.com/?p=18699.

Dollarhide, William. "Census Mistakes," http://www.genealogyblog.com/?p=18199.

Eichholz, Alice. *Red Book: American State, County, and Town Sources*, 3rd ed. Provo, UT: Ancestry, 2004. This standard reference that lists ways to access vital and other government records has been digitized and is available for free online access at: http://www.ancestry.com/wiki/index.php?title=Red_Book:_American_State,_County,_and _Town_Sources.

"Finding Passenger Lists & Immigration Records 1820–1940s: Arrivals at U.S. Ports from Europe" at http://www.germanroots.com/passengers.html. This is an important collection of links to online records and indexing.

Germans to America: Important information evaluating the print index series *Germans to America*, http://wiki-en.genealogy.net/Germans_to_America.

Guide to Genealogical Research in the National Archives of the United States, http://hdl.handle .net/2027/mdp.39015071221272.

Hinckley, Kathleen W. *Your Guide to the Federal Census For Genealogists, Researchers, and Family Historians.* Cincinnati, OH: Betterway Books, 2002.

Historical Census Browser, http://mapserver.lib.virginia.edu/. This can be used to retrieve and manipulate statistical data from the U.S. Censuses, but not to view individual returns.

Index of Questions, http://www.census.gov/history/www/through_the_decades/index_of _questions/.

Kemp, Thomas Jay. *International Vital Records Handbook.* Baltimore, MD: Genealogical Publishing Co., 2013.

Military History Centers, http://www.loc.gov/vets/bib-milihist.html.

Morse, Stephen P. "One-Step Webpages," http://www.stevemorse.org/. This is an important tool to help improve searchability.

NARA. "Military Records," http://www.archives.gov/research/military/index.html.

Passenger and Immigration Lists Index (PILI)

"Ships & Passenger Lists," www.cyndislist.com/ships/.

Soldiers and Sailors Database, a detailed analysis of this database can be found at: http://www.geneamusings.com/2012/06/civil-war-soldiers-and-sailors-database_26.html.

War of 1812 Pension Application Files, http://go.fold3.com/1812pensions/. This source of free indexing, when complete, will be a major historical reference tool.

In addition, wiki articles at FamilySearch under state and county names list sources of vital records, and USGenWeb pages for individual counties often list contact information for offices that house vital records.

VISUAL RESOURCES

MAPS AND ATLASES

One of the most important resources for local history collections are maps and atlases, because much genealogical information is organized by location. Both historic and new maps are relevant for local studies, because juxtaposing information found in them can reveal information about the development of the location.

FORMATS AND AVAILABILITY

Maps and atlases have long been collected by libraries and other institutions, but seldom circulate, which is a decided hindrance to family historians. However, in recent years many institutions have begun to digitize them. The large format of many maps means that they need to be viewed in segments on the computer screen, so it still is desirable to be able to view a large print map.

DEMONSTRATED USES

Maps are wonderful resources for identifying cemeteries, churches, schools, railroad lines, and other community landmarks. Specialty maps can document battles, agricultural and mineral production, migration patterns, settlement patterns, land ownership, and much more. Insurance maps, such as those produced by the Sanborn Company, document the building by building configuration of cities on a map that is drawn to scale. Plat maps show farm properties usually by township in a given year—the look of plat maps changed over the years as farms, and/or parcels of land changed hands. Sometimes the parcels are labelled with the owners' names. These were published only every several years, not annually. Of special interest to genealogists is the US 7.5-minute quadrangle map, which covers 49–80 square miles.

RELIABILITY

Most maps are fairly accurate because the mapmaker was striving for a true representation of the land being documented, but some were purposefully distorted in order to portray the physical place in a more favorable light. The online article "Who Made This Map and Why?" explains that knowing a little about the person who created the map "may offer hints as to the map's bias or biases" (http://historymatters.gmu.edu/mse/maps/question4.html accessed October 10, 2014).

TO-DO CHECKLIST

- Link outside websites that house your area's digitized maps and insurance maps to your institution's catalog or web page.

Table 8.10

Locating Maps and Atlases

Where to look for printed maps and atlases	• Libraries (public, academic, state, etc.): check for catalog records in major holdings, such as WorldCat using the subheading "Maps" or "Atlases" after their town or region: *Titusville (Pa.)–Maps.* • Large maps may not be in the catalog. Physically check the walls and map shelving areas of local studies collections. Ask if there are old maps available. http://www.worldcat.org/search?q=su%3ATitusville+%28Pa.%29+Directories.&qt=hot_subject • The collections of major research libraries also should be checked, using both the catalog and also by contacting the archives, in case there are uncataloged copies. • Locally, check any archival holdings including government offices, the Chamber of Commerce, historical and genealogical society collections, etc.
Where to look for digitized access to maps	• The Library of Congress has an excellent online map site, with many "bird's-eye-view" and other maps from the U.S. freely available on their digital site. • Check the David Rumsey Historical Map Collection, http://www.davidrumsey.com/ • Large academic collections such as the Perry-Castaneda Map Collection at the University of Texas contain a wide variety of maps. • Many public-domain Sanborn maps have been digitized, such as this site for Pennsylvania Sanborns: http://www.libraries.psu.edu/psul/digital/sanborn.html • ProQuest has a subscription database of Sanborns not in the public domain, but they are digitized from black and white microfilm, which is not ideal, since color coding plays a role in their use. • Check www.oldmapsonline.org. This is an index of digitized maps from a variety of online sources.

- Make sure maps are in your stated "desired" items to collect from the public. Many old maps are out there waiting to be discovered in attics. Know what other libraries, historical societies, and archives hold maps of your area, especially academic ones. They may have a duplicating service for maps not in copyright. Many map collections are listed online, but a print source that is still useful and convenient is: *Guide to U.S. Map Resources*, Map & Geography Roundtable of the ALA, 2006.

- Know where to purchase maps, both for collection development, and to assist patrons who wish their own copies: U.S. Geological Survey, International Map Trade Association, Omnimap.com, East View Geospatial.com, Rand McNally, and Jonathan Shepherd Books (for historical ones).

PHOTOGRAPHS AND POSTCARDS

Some of the most interesting resources in local studies collections are the photographs and local postcard collections, which provide a visual connection to the past. Patrons become very excited to see images of family, their hometown, or people and places of special interest to them. Local collections often have large photographic collections in need of conservation and preservation. Increasingly, local collection planning should include consideration of how to acquire and maintain digital photographs from individuals, families, and organizations.

FORMATS AND AVAILABILITY

A large number of photographic processes existed in the nineteenth century, and these are discussed in Chapter 5. Commercially-produced postcards were available throughout much of the United States from the late nineteenth century onward, often for quite small communities and their "attractions." These are a wonderful source of images for family history research.

DEMONSTRATED USES

Photographs are key pieces of visual documentation for family history research, both of people and places, and first appeared in 1839. (See Chapter 5 for a detailed discussion.) Postcards also visually document places. The dates that postcards began to be used varies according to country. In the United States, the first postcard was sent in 1873. The sizes of postcards have varied depending on the postal regulations that control their usage.

RELIABILITY

In the days before the digital manipulation of photographs, and only very limited types of photo retouching existed, it would be difficult for old photographs to lie. However, researchers should interpret them with caution. Many postcards were produced in order to promote a location or a product, and so the images were as favorable as possible. Therefore, the vast majority of postcards contain at least somewhat idealized representations.

TO-DO CHECKLIST

- Consider outside help with the nineteenth-century format photographs. Consult the American Institute for Conservation of Historical and Artistic Works (AIC) to find a professional conservator.
- Assess current housing of photos in already in your collection.
- Know what is unique and what has copies elsewhere, like at the historical society.
- Develop clear acquisitions policies for these, including releases for digitization.
- Decide what regions are "in" and which are "out."

Table 8.11

Locating Photographs and Postcards

Where to look for original photographs & postcards	• Locally, check any archival holdings, including the school district, historical societies, historical and genealogical societies, municipal archives, etc. Many of these places will not have cataloged or advertised their visual holdings. • Archive Grid, part of World Cat, can help locate other collections.
Where to look for digitized access to photographs & postcards	• Check the websites of all local historical/heritage/genealogical organizations. • Look at the websites of regional/state archives, libraries, consortia, etc. for digitized holdings. • Check national sites, such as those listed below. • Internet Archive: https://archive.org/index.php • PastPerfect Online: http://pastperfect-online.com/ • Digital Public Library of America: http://dp.la • Library of Congress American Memory: http://memory.loc.gov/ammem/index.html • www.cyndislist.com "Photographs & Memories" and "Postcards"

- Help researchers look for images of individuals in biographical sources, in archives, and on photosharing websites. See Chapter 2, "Record It" for ideas.

- Help researchers to date postmarked postcards by examining the date, when legible. Postcards without legible dates on the postmark may be roughly dated by analyzing the amount of postage. For information on postcard postage rates, see: http://www .akdart.com/postrate.html.

RESOURCES

AIC conservation wiki "Photographic Materials," https://squirrel.adobeconnect.com/ _a751959191/p3njewg3n7a/?launcher=false&fcsContent=true&pbMode=normal.

ALA Map and Geospatial Information Round Table (MAGIRT), www.ala.org/magirt/front.

Curt Teich Postcard Archives, http://www.lcfpd.org/museum/research/teich/.

Friedman, Daniel. *The Birth and Development of American Postcards: A History, Catalog, and Price Guide to U.S. Pioneer Postcards.* West Nyack, NY: Daniel D. Friedman, Classic Postcards Press, 2003.

Geographic Names Information System (GNIS) United States Geological Survey, http:// geonames.usgs.gov/index.html. This database contains documented place name variations and links to several types of digital maps.

Google street view, https://www.google.com/maps/streetview/.

JewishGen Communities Database and JewishGen Gazetteer (formerly called Shtetl Seeker), www.jewishgen.org/Communities.

Kashuba, Melinda. *Walking in the Steps of Our Ancestors: A Genealogists Guide to Using Maps and Geography.* Cincinnati, OH: Family Tree Books, 2005.

Kimmerling, A. Jon, Phillip C. Muehrcke, and Juliana O. Muehrcke. *Map Use: Reading, Analysis and Interpretation.* 7th ed. Redlands, CA: ESRI Press Academic, 2012.

Making Sense of Maps, http://historymatters.gmu.edu/mse/maps/.

McCabe, Constance, ed. *Coatings on Photographs: Materials, Techniques, and Conservation.* Published and distributed by the Photographic Materials Group of the American Institute for Conservation of Historic and Artistic Works, 2005.

Oswald, Diane L. *Fire Insurance Maps: Their History and Applications.* College Station, TX: Lacewing Press, 1997.

Penniston, Benjamin H. *The Golden Age of Postcards: Early 1900s: Identification & Values.* Paducah, KY: Collector Books, 2008.

Penny Postcards. USGenWeb Archives, http://www.usgwarchives.net/special/ppcs/ppcs .html and http://www.metropostcard.com/metropchistory.html.

Photographs: Archival Care and Management, http://saa.archivists.org/store/photographs -archival-care-and-management/337/.

Smallwood, Carol, and Williams, Elaine. *Preserving Local Writers, Genealogy, Photographs, Newspapers and Related Materials.* Lanham, MD: Scarecrow Press, 2012.

Stevens, Norman D. *Postcards in the Library: Invaluable Visual Resources.* New York, NY: Haworth Press, 1995.

U.S. Gazetteer of the Census Bureau, www.census.gov/cgi-bin/gazetteer2.

Vaule, Rosamond B. *As We Were: American Photographic Postcards, 1905–1930.* Boston, MA: David R. Godine, Publisher, 2004.

RECORDS GENERATED AFTER DEATH

BURIAL RECORDS

Burial records are created by the sexton, the person who is in charge of the burials in a cemetery. Cemeteries can be owned and maintained by an individual landowner, a church congregation, a not-for-profit cemetery association or board, a government agency, or a business. In earlier days, the written records could be sparse or nonexistent. Some cemeteries, such as family cemeteries, or ones located in the country, never kept any records at all. When that is the case, researchers are completely dependent on any surviving gravestones for evidence of interment, or the occasional mention of a burial in the local newspaper.

FORMATS AND AVAILABILITY

Some cemetery records only exist in the original format, usually in a large book or ledger, although some are in a card file format. A few cemeteries or their associations have started to put transcribed records online. One example is the Fireman's Benevolent Association, the owner of two cemeteries in New Orleans, Cypress Grove and Greenwood: www.greenwoodnola.com. Another is the Cleveland city cemeteries whose digitized and indexed records are available online: http://www.rootsweb.ancestry.com/~ohcdrt/clecems/00dexfind.html#mon. (See Chapter 7 for more information on cemetery indexing online.) Sometimes records have been microfilmed; sometimes they are not available to researchers at all, but staff may be willing to look up information. If records are held only at a cemetery office, there may be a fee for the information or you may not be allowed to see the information at all. If these records are transcribed by a historical society into books, they may only have physical copies on site and for sale, and are often pricey. These organizations often do not want to digitize these resources and lose an income stream.

DEMONSTRATED USES

Burial records may contain the following: date of death, date of burial, name of deceased, occupation, place of birth, cause of death, name of the attending physician, the plot location, and even the cost of the burial.

RELIABILITY

The information in burial records can be accurate because it was recorded very close to the actual burial, but sometimes it copies errors that were on the death certificate. One might think that any problems with cemetery records and burials could only occur in the past because laws regulate these matters now, but that is not always the case. In June 2010, allegations of mismanagement at Arlington National Cemetery were found to be true. Bodies had been placed in the wrong graves,

Table 8.12

Locating Burial Records

Where to look for microfilmed burial and cemetery records	• Check the Family History Library. • Also consult local, regional or state public libraries, archives, historical and genealogical societies.
Where to look for original cemetery records	• Try contacting the cemetery office, if it exists. • Consult a local, county, regional, or state archive. • Check at county and local historical societies.
Where to look for digitized burial and cemetery records	• Some libraries and historical societies have created online indexes of burial and/or cemetery records. • Local, regional, and state archives also may have digitized sources. • Online databasessuch as Ancestry and others may add such records. http://memory.loc.gov/ammem/index.html
Published burial and cemetery records	• Historical societies often publish books that index cemeteries.

markers were missing or misplaced, and ashes were improperly disposed of. Written records did not match actual interments in hundreds of cases. The U.S. Army hastily sent in teams of soldiers to try to inventory, photograph, and document the cemetery, and brought in new management to try to fix the problems at our most famous national cemetery.

TO-DO CHECKLIST

- Locate private/family cemetery information:
  - Maps in the library collection may mark them.
  - Local histories may give their location. Note: a single cemetery may have had multiple names in the past.

Doing a Cemetery Survey

If some local group has not already tackled this project, local studies professionals should consider gathering information about and from local cemeteries. Many cemeteries and their markers are deteriorating fast, which means that precious information could be lost daily. Projects to document cemetery information can be accomplished through cooperation between local groups such as preservation groups, local/history genealogical societies, college students (especially those in art, architecture, history, and library science), Eagle Scouts, and service organization members. Technology such as digital photography, the GPS, and apps especially designed for this purpose can all speed up the task. State preservation agencies may have published guidelines on how to conduct a cemetery survey, as well as methods for registering family plots.

"A Cemetery Survey as an Eagle Scout Project," http://www.usgwtombstones.org/eagle.html.

"Cemetery Documentation" webinar, http://ncptt.nps.gov/blog/documentation/.

Sample guidelines for a cemetery survey:

http://www.honorfairfaxcemeteries.org/downloads/FCCPA_guidelines-for-cemetery-surveys.pdf

http://www.thc.state.tx.us/public/upload/publications/sf_HP_RIP_NegCemBro_10_11(1).pdf

http://www.fgs.org/mwiki/index.php?title=A_Society_Project:_GPS_Locating_Cemeteries
_-_Making_Cemeteries_Easy_To_Find

- Locally created burial indexes may exist. Make sure you know if there are gaps in the indexing.
  - Learn the local resources available and make sure that it is recorded somewhere publically, such as the wiki on FamilySearch, the county USGenWeb archives page, on your institution's website, in a locality guide, or in all of the above.
- Make sure your local studies institution keeps a list, or can access one, of all known extant and former cemeteries in the area.
- Keep a list of all cemetery surveys, photos and transcriptions available for your area, both print and online.

GRAVE MARKERS

Not everyone's grave is marked with a stone because it was a luxury some families could ill afford. Of the stones that were used, some are so old and weathered that they are now illegible. Vandalism and poor maintenance in some cemeteries have also taken their toll on gravestones. All these factors pose challenges to researchers trying to document cemeteries or track individual burials. For the historical researcher, this is how to access the information in order of desirability:

- Visiting the cemetery and seeing, photographing, and transcribing the gravestone, and being able to see how the graves lie in relationship to each other.
- Finding a photograph of the gravestone online, or in a published book.
- Finding a transcription of the gravestone online or in a book.

To find online photos of graves, try www.findagrave.com, www.thegraveyardrabbit.com, www.graveaddiction.com, and the tombstone transcription project of www.usgenweb.org, to name a few. Some websites like these, such as findagrave.org, are user-input. These contain some errors, but are a place to start with the research. The best cases are when a photo of the tombstone is uploaded with the information, but even then, it is possible for persons to put the information under the wrong cemetery because there are two cemeteries with identical names in the same region. In other listings, the dates that were input into an individual's listing clearly do not match with the dates on the marker in the accompanying photograph. Hopefully, these websites will get more sophisticated and complete over time. A new website at www.namesinstone.com contains GPS coordinates, as does www.billiongraves.com.

Before digital photos and websites existed, people walked cemeteries armed with paper and pencil, transcribing the information found on the markers, and then publishing it in a book. For example, the Works Progress Administration (WPA) workers inventoried cemeteries during the Great Depression, and copies are housed at a variety of local and national repositories. Later, the Daughters of the American Revolution (DAR) launched a national project in the mid-twentieth century to inventory gravestones in cemeteries; many, but not all, of their chapters participated. The same type of project has been undertaken by various genealogical societies. Some of these cemetery transcriptions are posted online while others have been published in genealogy and local history periodicals or in books.

Sometimes these inventories put the names in alphabetical order, not as they are arranged in the cemetery. This is not desirable, because the arrangement of the graves often gives clues as to relationships. The best cemetery inventories should not only list the names as they are arranged in the cemetery, but should be cross-referenced with any written records, and also tie in with a map of the cemetery. Few of these transcription projects are organized in this fashion. But with some effort, the older information could be rolled into an updated project. However, the value of the information in these older transcriptions should not be overlooked, because in many cases markers that were read several decades ago, and recorded, can no longer be read today.

If one is lucky, the marker will contain the name of the person and the spouse with the date or year of birth and the date or year of death. It is common to see a person's age at death inscribed on the gravestone, expressed in years, months, and days, instead of a birth date. In this case, it is possible to calculate a birth date from the information provided. See an online birth date calculator: www.search forancestors.com/utility/birthday.html. Some markers may also list the occupation and cause of death.

A wealth of information may be found not just in the inscriptions, but also in their designs. Icons denote a person's religion or occupation, membership in social/fraternal organizations, and military service. Smaller stones sometimes decorated with symbols of innocence such as angels or lambs may be used for children. High social status and wealth are indicated by large, elaborate monuments which incorporate statuary and other artwork.

A stone marker is a document that can contain errors like any other. Because the decedent's family provided the information, it is usually correct unless the stonecutter made an error. However, mistakes do happen on gravestones, especially in the dates. Another factor is that markers do not necessarily date to the time of the decedent's death. Many markers were placed years later. Sometimes it is possible to have misread the information on an old, deteriorated marker and therefore record it incorrectly.

OBITUARIES

Obituaries and death notices are both generated after the person dies. Death notices are simple announcements that an individual has died. An obituary is more elaborate, also containing information about the person's life, surviving family members, and funeral arrangements. In some locales, obituaries did not become common until well into the nineteenth or twentieth centuries.

FORMATS AND AVAILABILITY

The obvious place to look for both is the newspaper, but they also appear in alumni directories, business and professional publications, and church bulletins. As of this writing there is a new project at FamilySearch which is going to provide an every-name index to obituaries in a large number of U.S. newspapers. This is an exciting development because obituaries can be difficult to track down, especially

Table 8.13

Locating Death Notices and Obituaries http://genealogytrails.com/penn/crawford/military/deaths.htm

Where to look for microfilmed obituaries	• Check microfilmed newspapers at local, regional and state libraries, archives, and historical societies. • Also check the Family History Library. • Look in denominational archives.
Where to look for original obituaries	• Look for clipping files in local libraries, archives, and historical societies. • Also check serial collections in major libraries.
Where to look for digitized obituaries	• Many are available in online databases of newspapers. • Also look for local library, historical society, and archival digitization projects. http://memory.loc.gov/ammem/index.html
Where to look for obituary finding aids	• Try local library and historical society indexing projects, such as clippings, card, or online files.

in small town newspapers for which no indexing exists, and which have not been digitized. Caveat: even though the names in the obituaries will be indexed, not every fact in the obituary will be indexed, and so researchers should still be encouraged to track down the full text of the obituary if possible.

Death notices and obituaries usually state when and sometimes where the death occurred. They may state the name of the surviving spouse and children and possibly other relatives, as well as the decedent's profession, residence, and membership in organizations. The woman's maiden name may be given or inferred if any of her male relatives are named. The birth date may be given or the age at death. If the name of the church where services are to be held is given, or the name of the person conducting the burial is supplied, it is possible to determine the decedent's religious affiliation. These notices can also indicate the decedent's ties to family in other communities. Either this is stated plainly when the residences of surviving relatives are listed, or subtly, by a line at the end such as "Dallas papers please copy." This is a request for the Dallas newspapers to reprint the obituary so that family members there can see it.

RELIABILITY

Some small town newspapers did not start to print death notices or obituaries until well into the twentieth century. Often the reason for this was that everybody in a small town already knew who died. When obituaries did appear, they often contained errors, sometimes many errors. Often the relatives supplying the information did not have the facts straight or purposefully omitted details such as prior marriages. It should never be assumed that every obituary contains an accurate or complete biography of an individual.

TO-DO CHECKLIST

- Keep track of any local or regional newspapers that have been digitized and where.
- Make sure that any homegrown indexes to local obituaries are made known and available to patrons.

- Transfer the information from older card indexes online, if possible. Volunteer help can be used.

FUNERAL HOME RECORDS

Separate from cemetery records are records kept by the undertaker. This profession really did not get started until late in the nineteenth century and perhaps later in rural areas. Prior to this time, families prepared the body themselves, laid it out in the parlor, had the visitation there, and buried their relatives themselves. Early undertakers often ran livery stables as well; horses were needed for both services. Undertakers usually laid out the body in a family member's home at first, but eventually built funeral parlors where greater numbers of people could be accommodated for the visitation. Funeral homes were often run by several generations of the same family, although nowadays they may be owned by a larger corporate chain. This means that the records going back many years are often still located at the business. Occasionally, old records, especially from establishments no longer in business, have been donated to a library, archive, or historical society. The LDS has microfilmed some funeral home records. The records can contain many details about the deceased such as name, age, occupation, next of kin, religion, and place of burial. The file may also contain a copy of the obituary clipped from the local newspaper, as well as graphic details of the embalming process.

If the funeral home is still in business and retains the original files, they should be available. If the funeral home has gone out of business, records may have been donated to the local historical society, the public library, or another institution. Occasionally, the records have been microfilmed by the FHL, but even a large city like Chicago has records from only five funeral homes in their collection. Usually specific information is not put online by funeral homes. One notable exception is the database compiled by the Pape Mortuary in Danville, Illinois. The proprietor, an avid genealogist, compiled information about local deaths from newspapers, cemeteries, their own records, and by asking local researchers: http://www .papemortuary.com/database.asp.

DEMONSTRATED USES

Funeral home records contain information that can lead to other information, for example, place of burial, the religious officiant, the monument company, and the name of the hospital or other place of death. Information about the funeral can help place an individual within a socio-economic context. For example, were the funeral arrangements lavish or modest?

RELIABILITY

Because the records were created by the people who were directly handling the body and orchestrating the arrangements, chances are very good that the information is accurate, although sometimes factual errors are perpetuated by copying them from the death certificate.

TO-DO CHECKLIST

- Learn about both the current and past funeral homes in the community, and trace where their records are.
- Have this contact information and preferred method of requesting information on hand for researchers.

RESOURCES

American Battle Monuments Commission, http://www.abmc.gov/. Often a soldiers' final resting place is well-documented. Try the American Battle Monument Commission if your ancestor died in battle overseas.

The Association for Gravestone Studies, https://gravestonestudies.org/.

Beine, Joe. Obituaries Research Guide–USA, www.deathindexes.com/obituaries.html. This online directory of both online death record indexing and online obituary listings is a masterful work in progress by family historian *par excellence* Joe Beine.

Carmack, Sharon DeBartolo. *Your Guide to Cemetery Research*. Cincinnati, OH: Betterway Books, 2002.

Funeral Home and Cemetery Directory, annual publication, Nomis Publications (previously published as the *National Yellow Book of Funeral Directors*).

"How to Read a Graveyard," http://dohistory.org/on_your_own/toolkit/graveyards.html.

Jarboe, Betty. *Obituaries: A Guide to Sources*. Boston, MA: Hall, 1989. This index is still of use because it lists many obscure print sources, not newspapers, in which obituaries lurk.

Keister, Douglas. *Stories in Stone: A Field Guide to Cemetery Symbolism and Iconography*. Salt Lake City, UT: Gibbs Smith, Publisher, 2004.

National Funeral Directors Association, http://nfda.org/. The website has a search directory, "Find a Funeral Home."

Powell, Dae. "Cemetery Research," http://www.shoestringgenealogy.com/article/Cemetery.htm.

The U.S. Department of Veterans Affairs has a partial online index to burials in national cemeteries: http://gravelocator.cem.va.gov/.

Yalom, Marilyn. *American Resting Place: 400 Years of History through our Cemeteries and Burial Grounds*. Boston, MA: Houghton Mifflin Harcourt, 2008.

ONLINE RESOURCES

Librarians and others who work in local cultural heritage organizations increasingly are called upon to retrieve information digitally whether it is medical, governmental, familial, etc., in nature. Such expectations tie into the movement recognized by museum and other cultural heritage professionals as "informatics," or providing access to the patron to information through technology. Regardless of what label it receives, the rapidly increasing amount of digital information available to help with family history research needs to be constantly studied in order to help researchers.

DEMONSTRATED USES

A wide variety of information is available online that can help local studies patrons, from digitized records, to maps, to background information, to indexing and how-to information. However, even though online content is proliferating, only a small fraction of the information needed to complete a family history is presently online. The rest is still stored in various government, library, and archival repositories, as well as in private locations like lonely attics and church offices. Though incomplete, online information is still considerable, and researchers may not know where to begin with the amount of information available on the sites they can access from home. They are overwhelmed and just want to ask a real person a question.

FORMATS AND AVAILABILITY

A huge variety of books have been published that discuss genealogical online research, but the information in them becomes outdated very quickly. The most important thing to know is that there are two basic kinds of genealogical websites: those that an institution or individual subscribes to and pays for, and those that are free. Of the free websites, some are created by institutions like libraries, historical societies, and government agencies, and some are created by individuals, who work either independently or in groups to make family history information available. The two best compiled websites used to locate the wide variety of helpful genealogical websites available are Cyndislist.com, organized by subject categories, and Linkpendium.com, organized by surnames and geographic locations. Both websites are free. The table below contains some of the most commonly used websites, but there are many, many more.

RELIABILITY

Not all information that is online is good information; search with skepticism and discretion. A similar type of evaluation process used with print sources should be used with online information. For instance, who compiled the website? Is it a revered institution, or an unknown individual? Is the information sourced? Has it

Table 8.14

Finding Online Resources

Some major subscription databases	Ancestry.com–main provider of genealogical resources • digitized primary and secondary documents • member-supplied information (trees) • library subscription cannot be accessed remotely by patrons • library version vs. personal subscription • some free material www.archives.com http://www.archives.com/ • lots of state-level docs www.findmypast.com • has a British bias • now the way to access PERSI www.heritagequest.com • can purchase a remote access license www.fold3.com • mainly military records and city directories plus other historical material • hosts the War of 1810 Pension Project myheritage.com • is based in Tel Aviv, Israel and offers over five billion records
Free sites	**Created by Institutions** • The LDS Church has compiled one of the largest genealogical collections in the world at their library and vault in Salt Lake City, Utah. Their website also contains a vast amount of information including: The International Genealogical Index, the Ancestral File, Pedigree Resource File, Social Security Death Index, a genealogy wiki, their library catalog, and a rapidly expanding collection of digitized sources— www.FamilySearch.org. • New England Historic Genealogical Society—www.newenglandancestors.org • Daughters of the American Revolution—www.dar.org • The Newberry Library in Chicago—www.newberry.org See their digital aids, the Atlas of Historical County Boundaries and Chicago Ancestors. • Allen County Public Library, Fort Wayne, Indiana—www.acpl.lib.in.us
Free Sites	**User-Input and Volunteer Group Sites** Various groups have published websites filled with free information, indexed and/or transcribed. • www.rootsweb.com • www.usgenweb.org • www.genealogytrails.net • www.immigrantships.net • www.genuki.net—for English research • www.genealogy.net—like a German US Genweb site
Free Sites	**Sites by individuals** • Joe Beine Death Records and Obituary Indexes • Fulton New York Postcards—this quirky website is really an archive of digitized and indexed old newspapers, engineered by Tom Tryzinski: http://fultonhistory.com/Fulton.html. • Stephen Morse One-Step Indexes

been recently updated? Does it appear to be well-researched? If the information is not sourced, it must proven with other sources. Keep in mind that no index, whether print or online, can be trusted to be 100 percent accurate.

RESOURCES

Digital Library of the Week Archive, http://www.ilovelibraries.org/article/digital-library
-week-archive.
Genealogy in Time Magazine. "Top 100 Genealogy Websites of 2014," http://www
.genealogyintime.com/articles/top-100-genealogy-websites-of-2014-page01.html.
"250+ Killer Digital Libraries and Archives," March 25, 2013, http://oedb.org/library/
features/250-plus-killer-digital-libraries-and-archives.

CONCLUSION

This chapter reviewed a wealth of resources, both analog and digital, commonly used by family history researchers, though there are countless more out there As placing information about record groups and archival collections increases, patrons will be able to incorporate more of them into their research. The increase in online resources over the past ten years provides even small institutions with limited budgets the ability to get researchers started. The next chapter will discuss how national, regional, and local digitization efforts by libraries and other consortia are bringing freely-accessible local history items to the family researcher.

Chapter 9

POOLING OUR RESOURCES:
THE DIGITAL PORTAL

This chapter explores exciting ways to access family history materials that reside in digitized local collections outside of the more commonly-encountered genealogical databases. Many new digitization projects are appearing that allow the public to view, read, and even comment on family photographs and documents that are digitized by libraries, historical societies, archives, and even family members. Information providers can aid families seeking information in digital collections, and can digitize their own collections to contribute to such portals. Increasingly, family members and cultural heritage professionals are working together to create new digitized collections that may reside in a family collection, at an institution, or both.

THE DIGITIZATION REVOLUTION

"Increasingly, users of all types expect the Web sites for archives, special collections, and historical organizations to function like the other Web sites they use. They want everything to be easy to discover, access, and share."

—Kate Theimer[1]

Imagine sitting at a computer late at night, typing in a grandmother's name, birth date, and hometown, and discovering digital copies of photographs of her childhood home, an image of her tombstone with added biographical information in a notes field, information on a set of letters she wrote to her husband that exist in a historical society, and scans of her birth, death, and marriage certificates. This is the scenario many people hope for when they sit down for the first time to do family history research at a computer, and until the Internet age, such a vision would have been unobtainable. Resources of local collections within the same town or region were separated by the physical realities of their brick and mortar housing. Some items lived in the historical society, others in the local studies collection at the library, and still others in a nearby county archive or in an academic library special collection. A multitude of informal, family archives existed in individual homes, tucked away in boxes and crates in attics and basements. People had to physically travel to the collections in order to do their research.

Enter the age of digitization. By scanning and making available online documents, family photographs, birth and death records, among others, a revolution has occurred in the world of family research over the past twenty years. From national initiatives like the Library of Congress' American Memory collection down to the private digitized collections of family photographs, the digital revolution and the Internet have challenged the way families and institutions preserve and access historical and family records.

The value and appeal of accessing digital records online can be seen in the immense growth and success of major databases focused on family history and genealogy research, such as Ancestry.com, Familysearch.org, Newspaperarchive.com, Fold3.com, and many others.[2] These sites provide a tremendous number and variety of digitized documents, but are particularly useful for their easy access to government documents, such as the recently-indexed 1940 U.S. census.[3] A large number of digitized historic books and newspapers also contribute to the value of these sites. They play a vital role in most genealogical research and their subscription rates demonstrate the enthusiasm and dedication felt by family history researchers.[4] Now, libraries, historical societies, archives, and other institutions have also joined the digitization "bandwagon" to provide online versions of their holdings.

As many local collections in libraries, historical societies, archives, and even private family collections are in the process of being digitized, it is critical for family historians to become aware of these projects and how to access them. From lofty national initiatives like the Library of Congress' American Memory collection to small collections of local historical photographs displayed on Flickr by a cultural heritage institution, information providers must help researchers discover all possible digital repositories.

How did digitization evolve in library and cultural heritage settings? Many early library digitization projects have focused on collecting photographs, historic newspapers, or especially "low hanging fruit" from a copyright perspective, publications that clearly fall into "public domain," or copyright-free status, such as postcards and books printed before 1923.[5] High school and college yearbooks, though often more problematic from the copyright perspective, are another common digitization project for libraries and university archives, as well as in companies that cater to the nostalgia of connecting with high-school classmates. Classmates.com, for example, boasts coverage of 30 million persons in over 250,000 digitized yearbooks.[6] Newspapers and city directories also have been frequently digitized by local libraries, historical societies, and archives. But discovery of these collections can be challenging without being aware of existing indexes. The following review of national, state/ regional, and local digitization projects in cultural heritage settings will aid librarians and others in directing patrons to these vital resources.

NATIONAL-LEVEL DIGITIZATION EFFORTS

Some notable digitization projects have produced more unified, and more consistent access to a wide range of digitized materials from libraries, historical societies, and archives. Information about such projects is provided through library, archival, and professional organization pipelines, but small, volunteer-based organizations may not be plugged into these information networks. It is important, therefore, for information on these sites to be a priority in educating others in the local community who may not have been exposed to the wealth of online resources available to assist in reference work. The Digital Public Library of America (DPLA) is a recent addition to a group of distinctive digital sites that embody the ideal of creating the public online space where collections of all types can reside for 24/7, free consumption for those who have access to the Internet. On the DPLA site are portions of digitized collections from U.S. cultural heritage institutions. The site is built on an open-source platform, which means that the computer coding is available to tech-savvy individuals for modification and use. DPLA's "about" pages describe a purpose to inform teachers, students, researchers, and the general public through proven, reliable resources. This portal aims to embody the notion of free access to community treasures.[7]

Working with digital "hubs" around the country, the DPLA is helping to create a national-level digital resource that will bring into their collection resources of all types that are useful for family history collections. These are materials that already exist in regional and local digital collections, but many who might be interested in the contents may be unaware of the collections' existence. As noted on their site, "Many universities, public libraries, and other public-spirited organizations have digitized materials, but these digital collections often exist in silos. The DPLA brings these different viewpoints, experiences, and collections together in a single platform and portal, providing open and coherent access to our society's digitized cultural heritage."[8] This type of collection is very useful because it helps to solve the problem of discovery. In other words, how does one locate the digitized resources that exist? DPLA is working with many partners to provide consistent access to collections and innovative apps for USING these collections, not just viewing them. As seen in the screenshot below, one may access a wide variety of collections using innovative searches, such as region or even date.

The Internet Archive also provides excellent access to digitized family materials, including publications like city directories and county histories that are searchable. Often, the contributor of an item may be geographically far removed from the locale of the item digitized. This means one might not think to check the digital collection of that far-away institution for a local county history in full-text format and the text may not have been digitized by the local library or historical society. So the digital version might not be known to the local librarians or volunteers at the historical society. By searching national digital collections, such as Internet Archive, valuable full-text publications relevant to the local setting can be found. Internet Archive, like DPLA, pulls together the collections of many institutions to provide a searchable resource of immense value for family historians and cultural heritage institutions. The Internet Archive contains a wide range of formats, such as videos, images, maps, newspapers, full-length books, and even an archive of web pages that span back to the

Figure 9.1
DPLA Home Page. http://dp.la/. Used by Permission of DPLA.

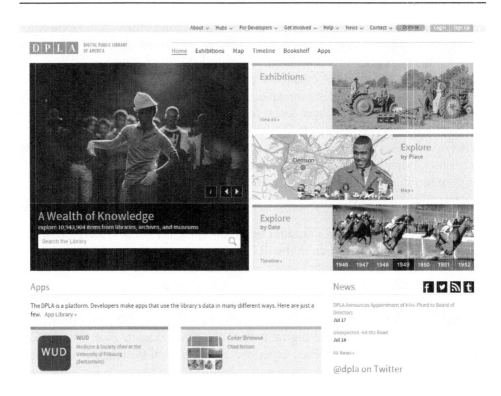

mid-1990s, called the "Way-Back Machine, which boasts documentation of over 482 billion web pages."[9]

Books and other documents on the Internet Archive are far-reaching in topic and very accessible in terms of download formats. Take, for example, a search of the Internet Archive for a history of Lewis County, Kentucky, which brings up a variety of full-text items. These include county histories written at the beginning of the twentieth century, as well as some more current writings. Such resources are invaluable for family historians and can be suggested by those working in local studies' collections in remote assistance reference when specific page references to published items are needed.

The Library of Congress presents myriad collections and support for digital projects. The National Digital Library and its leading "American Memory" section provides digital content from across the country, with vivid images and important historical texts to document the history of the nation. What began in 1990 as a program to create educational resources on CD-ROM transitioned to a digitization program of incredible importance, exceeding the goal of providing 5 million digital items available online by the year 2000.[10] To be expected are the papers of former presidents and images of military activity, such as women riveters during World War II, but the collections boast a much more diverse set of materials than those focused on national leadership and service.

Some of the more important items for family history include the historic newspaper digitization program. As a partner with the National Endowment for the

Figure 9.2
Bird's-eye View Map 1886, Bar Harbor, Maine.

Humanities (NEH) for the Chronicling America National Newspaper Digitization Program, the Library of Congress provides digital access to a wide range of historic newspaper for free.[11] In addition, the site provides information on how and where to access many other newspapers. The digital interface allows for full-text searching of those newspapers that are linked to the site, which provides a wonderful free resource for family historians and local studies collections.

Other Library of Congress digital collections that are overlooked in local studies collection sites are the wealth of local maps that have been digitized. The "bird's-eye view" maps that were so popular in the late nineteenth century are particularly useful when viewed in a digital interface. Bird's-eye view maps were intended to provide a representation of a town that represented general locations and building shapes though not to scale, and sometimes enhanced to glamorize the location. The detail was quite small and difficult to use on the physical map, but a digital copy with close-up zooming capabilities, like that on the Library of Congress site, provides excellent information for family historians. It also provides a way for local studies librarians to give information remotely to patrons who need to see the maps.

STATE AND REGIONAL COLLABORATIONS

State and regional-level digitization projects funded and supported by cultural heritage institutions also provide family materials to both individuals and institutions. The Library of Congress maintains a useful Web Guide of known regional and state-level projects, which is particularly helpful in tracking resources from states other than one's own.[12] Maine Memory Network, for example, is advertised as "Maine's Statewide Digital Museum."[13] It provides a timeline of Maine history and predominant themes to be explored. But the major purpose of the site is the aggregation of many digitized materials contributed to the site following specific guidelines. Network documentation clearly explains that contributors must be libraries, schools, or "collecting organizations," such as historical societies, churches, museums, municipalities.[14] Individuals are also listed as potential contributors, but they are directed to contact other institutions to provide their resources through that avenue. Organizations are provided with clear guidelines for digitizing and uploading their materials. These materials are then utilized in two major ways. First, Maine Memory Online showcases some items and exhibits in its written essays about Maine history. The narrative provides an overview of major themes and time periods in Maine history. Second, the Maine Memory Network section allows for a central portal and single search box for all the contributed collections.

Maine Memory goes a step further and also allows the site to host digital exhibitions. A digital exhibition, like a traditional one, would consist of selected digitized items around a theme or event. The digital exhibition feature provides an outreach and educational tool for communities. Students may work with contributing organizations to the site in order to develop digital exhibitions.[15] A number of tools assist the students and other exhibition creators in refining the images and messages for public enjoyment. Maine Memory also allows contributing organizations to create

Figure 9.3
Maine Memory Network. http://www.MaineMemory.net. Used with permission.

and use websites, thus providing for even more consistency and unification of digitized local materials. Public interaction with the items on the Maine Memory site is encouraged through the use of "albums." Users of the site may save items of interest to an online album they create, which can then be shared with others via a link back to the album site.[16]

USING DIGITIZED LIBRARIES FOR FAMILY RESEARCH

Local volunteers and others can be trained to use the already-digitized resources. Even a simple list of links to resources can assist the volunteer or librarian in providing services to patrons. In particular, many of the fully digitized books and other items available on national, regional, and local cultural heritage sites may be useful tools for family historians, and patrons should be educated about them.

For example, suppose a patron came into a library or other cultural heritage institutions and asked for help locating information on a relative, T.C. Joy, of Titusville, Pennsylvania. The patron knew that his relative had been involved in the production of iron radiators, but had little other information. Local collections should include basic biographical resources, including the local digitized historical newspaper, county histories, and obituary files. But, in this case, it would be well worth doing a general Google search for information on the individual to check for other digitized information.

Specific companies, like that of T.C. Joy in Titusville, PA, left not only a legacy of massive iron radiators (many still functioning), but a clearly-defined trail for family historians in the pages of industrial history, including a set of periodicals called *The Metal Worker* digitized from a university engineering collection. In 1895, a full obituary of T.C. Joy appeared in a scanned Google Books item, including details on his life in Titusville. The obituary discussed what he manufactured and provided information on his relatives, including the fact that he had only one son, who predeceased him.[17]

What is instructive for family historians about the T.C. Joy example? First, the information was located in a periodical that originally had been published in Chicago and New York City, not in Titusville, Pennsylvania, in the neighboring county, or even within the state. Furthermore, the publication had been collected and preserved in a collection in still another state. Only digitization of this item would make it a findable resource for the average family historian, unless an astute local historian had made copies of the obituary to be found in a local file. Therefore, one finds that the typical rule of proximity to the historical locale for initiating research really did not apply very well in this case. Second, the digitized resource provided a rich context for the obituary that far exceeds that normally found in a local newspaper. While the typical obituary of a noted manufacturer might provide more detail than that of other individuals in the nineteenth century, this one did so within the context of the person's livelihood, because it appeared in a trade periodical. Advertisements and information about others in the industry provide many other contexts and clues for the Joy family history researcher. Third, the resource, because it is fully digitized and not an index or other surrogate, provides amazingly detailed access with searchable indexes and searchable full-text information. Fourth, the resource provided images, including a sketch of Joy himself, as well as many advertisements with images of stoves and other items to help create a context for this individual's life. These pieces of information provide many clues for those researching this family or the context of this town.

Are the life and times of T.C. Joy unusual in family history research? Of course, the average person would not have been as prominent as Joy, however, many families do have relatives about whom similar amounts of information can be located for various reasons, such as contributions to their profession, their philanthropic activity, or their leadership in a community. The digitization revolution and the large amount of fully-digitized periodical, book, and primary resource material is making the discovery of information about relatives much more commonplace. The lesson here is that fully digitized information can provide amazing finds for the family historian, so checking online digital portals should be routine for the local history volunteer or librarian.

Photographic collections pose another great potential for family history research that should be explored fully by cultural heritage professionals. Local studies librarians should be aware of photo collections for the area and how to search them. In addition, if there are special access features or a list of key terms to use when conducting a search, these should be explained to the patron. Images of people digitized by libraries, historical societies, archives, families, and others often contain cataloging information that is searchable. If names are included, the search feature can assist in discovery of relatives.

Many archives are elevating their discovery features for digitized photograph collections through user-supplied information, such as tagging.[18] A tag is a word that describes some aspect of an item. The word is decided by the viewer of the information and is entered into the collection through an area designated for tags.[19] The idea of a tag is that it carries special meaning for the user. In cases of family history collections, this may mean a name, a place, an event, or even a word that has meaning only for the viewer. Tags can be entered as phrases, though tagging software tends to break the phrases into individual words for searching purposes. How would tags help family historians? They can serve as clues to the identification of persons in a photograph. Many photo software programs even allow tagging of specific faces in a photograph for better identification. These types of tools hold great promise for the family historian. User-supplied information in the form of tags or notes can allow for identification of individuals and additional information on the families to be entered into the digital site.

The Library of Congress teamed up with Flickr to allow patrons several social media applications for a digitized photo collection. One may add tags and notes to the digitized images, which are then searchable for anyone using the library.[20] The experiment was hailed a success, as the vast majority of images received user tags within a few months of the project's initiation. Other digital collections have utilized appeals to patrons to help identify the persons in digital images. The Carnegie Museum of Art's Charles "Teenie" Harris Archive, for example, used direct appeals to the community and exhibitions of photographs to help identify people in the digital archive of the Pittsburgh African-American photographer, who worked for several decades as a photographer for the *Pittsburgh Courier*.[21] Despite some local collection uses, the potential power of tagging and other social media applications for digitized photographs have not yet been realized in local history collections. As these digital resources grow, so will the user-input information on family names, events, and locations.

THE LOCAL DIGITAL PORTAL

The previous section demonstrated several reasons for local studies librarians and volunteers to be aware of major digitized collections that are created outside of the local region, but local collections are equally important. Certainly many small organizations have begun to digitize parts of their collections and part of the job of the local studies librarian is to be aware of the ongoing projects in the area. Sometimes, these projects are tied to larger ones across a state, so routing to a specific collection may be provided through another portal. It is always worth checking the page of state and county resources at USGenWeb, for example, for links to institutional web pages and also user-supplied databases and web pages.[22] But the average family historian or even historical society volunteer can soon be overwhelmed with the vast amount of information found in so many different places in a local region. Indeed, many good projects that have produced digitized newspapers, postcards, photographs, annuals, and other items, may be buried two or three screens deep on a library or archive website, while links from regional, state, and national-level indexes may be unknown to the local patron or librarian. Once accessed, these digitized collections may require individual searches of each digital collection. Additionally, a number of digitization efforts may be undertaken in a local area, with no references or links to other projects on the sites of the individual institutions. It seems that it is asking a lot of the modern, computer-rooted patron to bounce from one cultural heritage site to another trying to discover what is accessible and how.

At the local level, the creation of a common historical resource digital portal is one worth considering to assist researchers, librarians, and others in locating and using resources. At the most basic level, the portal may just give the names and locations of all the family and local history materials in the areas and links to those with web pages. Or, the portal could provide direct links to the digitized materials that exist in the area, identifying them by theme or by institution. Scottsdale, Arizona's local history pages on the public library site provide an excellent example of how a local portal can provide access to many resources in a local area. Scottsdale's site provides clear identification of its goals and missions. The landing page for the Scottsdale Heritage Connection Digital Collection indicates the site "is a community collaboration: a window to the past, celebration of the present and portal to the future."[23] A single search box to all collections is possible because various collections from across the area have been cataloged into the same library catalog. Yet individual collections are accessible on the web page through links, with large, attractive photographs to lead the viewer (instead of a list of small links).

Also notable about this site are the clear mission statement and a clear, attractive link inviting the public to submit any personal items of interest to be included in the digital collection. Instead of a form to fill out, the link provides the email address for a person. The site has this personal touch throughout, demonstrating clear organization, but also a vitality and engaged interface for local collections.

Also a common digital portal could raise visibility for family history collection. For example, if local institutions can come together to create a digital landing page, much like the locality guide discussed in earlier chapters, it could provide information on the locations hours, and services of each local cultural heritage institution. Announcements of concern to those interested in historical issues can be provided via the single site, as can pathfinders that list the resources available at individual institutions, their hours, and access methods.

Figure 9.4
Scottsdale Heritage Connection Digital Collection. Courtesy of the Scottsdale Public Library.

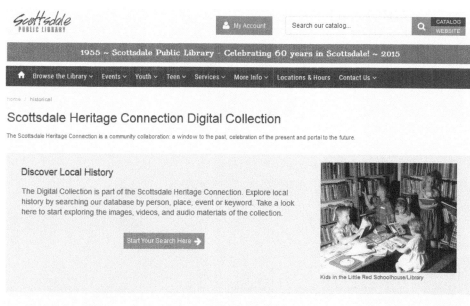

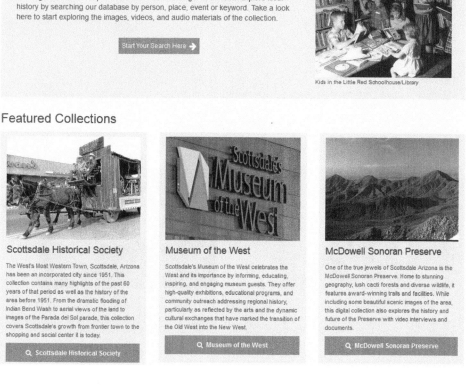

The digital portal to a community's historical resources, if well designed, can also serve to stimulate the use of onsite resources through effective programming and reference work. Though technological challenges and institutional divides may present problems for those hoping to establish strong working ties across local history communities, the rewards of collaboration in any manner possible are to increase visibility of collections, decrease redundancy in representation of collections, and, in some cases, a sharing of online work, such as genealogical reference.

Figure 9.5

Scottsdale Heritage Connection Digital Collection. Courtesy of the Scottsdale Public Library.

Walking History Book

This collection features images, interviews, and video contributed by the citizens of Scottsdale which document family histories, local events and history - both local and beyond.

Q Walking History Book

Scottsdale Digital Architecture

With this collection, explore the creative and amazing diversity of the architecture of Scottsdale's buildings. The digital content covers both the present and the past.

Q Scottsdale Architecture

Scottsdale Public Art

The mission of Scottsdale Public Art is to serve as a leader in defining art in the public realm through creative place-making, signature cultural events, exhibitions, and installations - contributing to the community's creative, cultural, and economic vitality. This collection shows images of this wonderful art along with information on the creators, locations, and histories of the pieces.

Q Scottsdale Public Art

Mission

The Scottsdale Heritage Collection collects, organizes, and makes accessible materials relating to the Scottsdale area's past, present and future; focusing on culture, geography, people, government and history. The collection engages, educates and entertains through physical and virtual resources, public programs and community partnerships.

Share Your Photos and Your Stories

Do you have any photographs, documents or other material about Scottsdale? We are always on the lookout for new historical material to add to the collection.

Email Richard Howley for more information

Get a Copy of One of Our Historical Images

Learn how to get a digital copy of one of our historical images to use in a project, hang in your home or to share with a friend.

Request high-resolution digital images from the library »

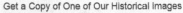

How many small town libraries and historical societies spend valuable time tracking down the answers to questions sent via email, only to realize the same person contacted every library and institution in town with the same question? Does it make sense to spend valuable volunteer and staff time in such a fashion? In an era where it may be easier to recruit volunteers for online "crowdsourcing" projects than physical work in a collection, it is advantageous to realize the interconnected nature of local history that already exists, and to create ties to other vested organizations in order to develop digital gateways to collections that may reside independently in various locations, but that can be described and perhaps provided digitally in full-text through one portal. So the concept of a local digital portal is one that requires collaborations and workflows that are tended, monitored, and updated on a regular basis. Good partnerships, or at least clear lines of responsibility, must be in place for these to work.

How do local digital portals begin? Three basic steps must occur: planning, funding, and execution. A recent article outlining the goal of a unified digital portal for local resources in Maitland, New South Wales, Australia, provides valuable insights into the importance of step-by-step planning. The Maitland group used strategic planning to develop a set of clear goals, such as the definition of a shared vision with regard to historical resources, the desire for a unified digital portal for local resources from various collections, the goals of allowing the public to contribute resources, and the clear establishment of collaborative roles within the partnerships. The city librarian reports "the positioning of the library as a community leader was achieved through a holistic vision grounded firmly in community reality. The primary purpose of preserving and providing access to the city's documentary heritage was realized through the library as driver, rather than collector."[24] The Maitland Local Studies Strategy is ongoing. The reports on their site of strategic planning and collaboration may be helpful for others entering such a project.[25]

Here are some considerations for making the one-stop information entry portal planning a success:

- Include all local interested parties in the planning process. This should include museum curators, librarians, archivists, city managers, school teachers, and future users of the site, such as family historians and genealogists.
- Create unified goals for the site. Will it be an informational site about collections with links to them? Will there be online chat/references services? If so, who will provide these services? Will the site provide unified searches of collections? Will it allow patrons to submit their digital family materials? Will there be opportunities to interact with the online materials through social media? Will the patrons be able to share on Facebook, to add a comment or tag, or to download materials?
- Create an agreement with all institutions that clearly states each participant's responsibilities.
- Create a schedule for updating the information. The actual work may be done on one site or by all, depending on how the site is created. These details should be a part of the initial agreement and revisited each year in a collaboration meeting in order to tweak the agreement and workflow.
- Plan to advertise the site by linking the page to all avenues of entry to the town, such as the Chamber of Commerce site, city government sites, regional economic and business sites, the hierarchies of each represented institution (so, the county, regional, and state levels of historical societies; library system or consortia sites, state library sites, etc.), RootsWeb, and other online indexes.

Planning for digital portals also involves the securing of funding. Many examples of unified digital portals for historic resources are grant-funded endeavors, such as the Nevada State College Digital Portal for Local & State History, which was made possible by a Library Technology Services Act (LSTA) grant from the Nevada State

Library. LSTA money originates from the Institute of Museum and Library Services, which is a federal-level agency. It is worth looking at the Institute of Museum and Library Services (IMLS) site for ideas about the many projects they have funded that encourage collection access to the public at http://www.imls .gov/. Librarians also should be aware of the Library Services and Technology Act (LSTA) grants that are made available each year by their state library. It is important to note that often LSTA grants to libraries are available to those that partner with historical societies, schools, archives, or other entities for projects. In fact, such partnerships often strengthen the applications. Other funds may be sought at the local level through private foundations. A great way to locate such opportunities is by visiting the closest office for The Foundation Center or by visiting their website, http://foundationcenter.org/.

But what about resources for very small towns with limited resources? Perhaps a small library does not have a dedicated individual to work with the local collections. Or perhaps the local studies librarian or historical society volunteers do not have any time to develop a grant application or partnerships. A variety of low-cost ideas exist in the professional organization websites for cultural heritage institutions. Online Computer Library Center's (OCLC) WebJunction provides a "computer cookbook" filled with ideas and webinars on issues related to library computers and services. WebJunction also provides resources and webinars for libraries on how to create a web presence for any library and on website design. The Association for Rural & Small Libraries (ARSL) provides an information and ideas page on resources, including information on website and technology issues, geared towards institutions with little or no technology support and funding. The American Association for State and Local History (AASLH) also provides recordings of presentations on timely digital topics.

Additionally, a local portal can be created at virtually no cost using common software, such as blogs and wikis. Blogger.com and other blog sites are fairly easy to use. They also allow for patron interaction in the format of posting responses. Simple web pages can be created for free or very low cost by using sites such as Weebly.com and Wordpress.com. The resources at www.omeka.net also provide an easy startup for a web page that is capable of containing digital images. The site requires no download, though a more developed set of tools is available if the institution has a more tech-savvy person who can use the full downloadable program at www.omeka.org. Sample sites created on Omeka show the full potential of the program with tech support.

RESOURCES

Computer Cookbooks, http://www.webjunction.org/explore-topics/computer-cookbooks .html.

Fraser, Lisa. "Partnering with Local Genealogical Societies." in Williams, E., and C. Smallwood, *Preserving Local Writers, Genealogy, Photographs, Newspapers, and Related Materials*, 159–168. Lanham, MD: Scarecrow Press, 2012.

More Recent Resources from Your Feed, http://feed.aaslh.org/more-resources?1B.

Nichols, M. "Fostering Family and Local History in Libraries: The Hawkesbury Experience." *Aplis* 25 no. 2 (2012): 66–70.

Resources, http://arsl.info/category/resources/.

Theimer, K., ed. *Outreach: Innovative Practices for Archives and Special Collections.* Lanham, MD: Rowman & Litlefield, 2014.

Theimer, K., ed. *Web 2.0 Tools and Strategies for Archives and Local History Collections.* New York, NY: Neal-Schuman Publishers, 2010.

Website Design, http://www.webjunction.org/explore-topics/website-design.html.

DIGITIZATION FOR SMALLER INSTITUTIONS: CAN WE DO IT?

What about collections that have not yet been digitized? What is local historical society volunteers or librarians would like to create online resources, but they have no idea where to begin? How would they achieve some of the digital resources shown already in this chapter? Published literature on successful library and archival digitization projects demonstrate a multistep, well-planned process as an ideal route to digitization. The planning for the creation of the Colorado digitization program, for example, required partnerships, needs assessments, and large-scale funding.[26]

What options do smaller institutions have when it comes to digitizing their collections? Those working or volunteering in small organizations may feel overwhelmed and not know where to begin with digitization projects. It is very common for those working with digitization to be approached by volunteers in small historical societies or those working in small libraries or archives with the question, "Can we do this ourselves"? It is clear that digitized local photographs, postcards, yearbooks, city directories, maps, manuscripts, and other useful items to historians and genealogists may play a vital role in raising the visibility and use of local collections. Many small libraries, historical societies, and archives may hold collections that would be of great value to their patrons, but there has never been enough of a knowledge base or time for staff and volunteers to make such a project a reality.

Different approaches can be used for different-sized institutions. For example, if librarians or volunteers at a cultural heritage institution felt that there were plentiful and useful resources for a project, but not adequate support to build a digital repository, perhaps it would be appropriate to look for any regional or state consortia or support. If a historical society has its images already digitized for use on a PastPerfect database, but now leadership in the society would like to find a way to make some of those items public on another repository, they may need to seek out guidance on file types, copyright, and cataloging from librarians. A collaboration might be in order. So, the question of can we do it comes down to several considerations: are there interested persons at the institution to undertake a project? Are there appropriate resources to digitize? Are there potential partners for the project? And, finally, are there feasible methods to put the items in a digital repository?

WHO CAN GET THIS DONE?

Digital projects for smaller repositories require a group approach and are best undertaken with strong partnerships. It is good practice to establish a committee that has the expertise, interest, and time to investigate the possibility of digitization for the institution. The details of a full-scale digitization project, from selection, to rights management, to digitizing, managing files, creation of metadata (cataloging), selection of a repository, and public launching of the collections, are vast. Even small-scale digitization projects, such as the creation of images for PastPerfect cataloging records, can be aided by a workflow that is documented in writing and can be understood and used by many, as the staffing and volunteer base of any organization naturally changes over time.

The establishment of a committee can help to develop the details of the workflow and investigate vendors, training, and consultants necessary to begin the project. The committee should have persons who will be involved with various phases of the project, though no one person likely would have the expertise or job assignment to oversee all parts of the project. Many skills will be necessary in order to initiate and bring about a full-scale digitization project, but if the steps are broken down into manageable pieces, even very small organizations will be able to achieve a collection online. The development of a strong digitization committee is an important first step that requires a good deal of thought for staffing and skill sets.

The best persons to head up the committee are those most invested in the project and with good people skills. Look for persons who are able to communicate well with a wide group of participants and who can listen to the input and advice of many. It is also vital to determine whether there are those outside of the immediate organization who would lend expertise or perhaps even create a joint project with related institutions, i.e., a historical society and a public library. Participants should have some of the following strengths:

- A clear understanding of the usefulness and relevance of the family history resources under consideration. This may be members of the local genealogical society, the volunteers at the historical society, a teacher or professor in the area, or a librarian.

- Understanding of how to do needs assessment surveys or studies. This might be a business person in the area or a manager in the library. This person would not have to have an expertise in the historical area.

- Ability to connect with the press and would be able to provide a public face or write press release copy. This person could be a member of the historical society or a friend of the library member.

- Skilled at organization for keeping the whole project on track and taking care of many phone calls, details, follow-ups, reports, and scheduling meetings. This administrative role might be a paid worker at the library or a volunteer at the historical society.

The following roles are desirable, but may not be obtainable for very small organizations:

- Computer technological expertise. If the organizations do not have a systems librarian or technology person, then look to related organizations or the community for volunteers.

- Understanding of file types and digitizing with a digital single lens reflex (SLR) camera. Look for someone in the community who has photography training.

- Experience with metadata, or cataloging for digital objects. This might be the library's cataloger (who might need to do training but is willing) or other interested persons. If there is no-one who falls into this category, then the cataloging part of the project should be outsourced. There are many companies that are able to do either scanning, the metadata, or both, at a reasonable price. Reach out to area libraries, historical societies, and archives for recommendations.

If such individuals are not locally available, check to see what resources exist at the state or regional level to assist with grassroots digitization projects. Very often, in the course of applying for LSTA or other grants, one will be directed to local authorities who are knowledgeable about restrictions, such as copyright, or about the proper equipment to acquire for the project. Additionally, considering the overworked schedules of many local studies librarians and the often thinning ranks of local historical society volunteers, a public awareness campaign using newspaper articles might bring the right people into the mix who are willing to volunteer for the duration of a specific project.

DECISION: ARE THERE APPROPRIATE RESOURCES?

Motivation for many digital projects in a library, historical society, or other cultural heritage repository begins with the resource. Perhaps someone has discovered a group of nineteenth-century documents or photographs that look like they would be highly interesting to the public. Perhaps the curator or librarian in an institution has one or two resources that are constantly in demand by patrons. Perhaps there has been a desire expressed for a project to solicit materials from families about the community's past, such as photographs. When considering the best candidates for selection, a number of practical and content-oriented issues come into play. It would be optimal for content to be the primary criteria for selection; however the project team must determine that the object is free from copyright restrictions or seek appropriate permissions to digitize from the copyright holder(s). The condition of the object may come into play, as it may be fragile and in need of conservation before or after digitization, which might make the project prohibitively expensive.

Generally, materials should meet certain criteria before being selected as potential candidates:

1. Materials should be unique to the local area, such as city directories, photographs, maps, family genealogical materials, maps, etc. AND the materials should not already be available in digitized format. Items likely to already be in digital format include city directories, county histories, published atlases, bird's-eye view maps of cities, and local newspapers. If they are already digitized, it is good practice to provide a catalog link to them and/or list the digitized versions in resource pathfinders. Below is a checklist of places to search in order to verify the resources do not already exist in digital format:

- WorldCat
- Library of Congress catalogs
- Google Books
- Internet Archive
- PastPerfect Online
- State libraries

- Major academic libraries in the area
- State, regional, and local historical societies
- Subscription databases, like Ancestry.com
- Free genealogy and historical databases online
- General web search using titles and keywords for your region

2. Materials should be high demand or high value items, either by patrons or reference staff. One way to determine whether these items are high value is to conduct a needs assessment. Assessing user expectations can provide a starting point for a digital collection, though it is not the only factor in the establishment of a strong digital collection. A needs assessment survey can be conducted among multiple constituent groups in order to determine what are the local resources most sought after for digital access. Perhaps most important in terms of new information for the facility is the opinion of the end user. A survey asking patrons to rank often-used items in the local collection that are being considered for digitization is a good way to begin the process. Other research methods, such as focus groups or interviews can be utilized as well. When combined with usage statistics and the perceptions of those who deliver reference for the local rooms on a regular basis, this information can be extremely helpful in creating a priority list for the digitization project.

Studies also can provide good evidence to potential funders that the project evolved from good planning and awareness of public need. In addition to onsite studies, formal collections assessments can be performed by outside consultants, who can prepare formal reports on the resources in a collection that are suitable candidates for digitization. A recent short article which overviewed the decision-making process for digitization suggests "putting the user at the heart of the process," by attempting to understand as much as possible the needs of the persons who will eventually be accessing the collection.[27] One should ask how the information will be accessed. What are the most important questions someone might bring to the collection? Do the selected resources fulfill these needs? If a needs assessment is beyond the skill set of those in the local setting, it might be a good idea to apply for a small grant to employ an outside organization to visit the collection(s) and write up an assessment of those items that would be appropriate for a digitization project. State library staff and district consultants would be good resource persons to ask about such an approach.

3. Materials should either be free of copyright restrictions, be candidates for copyright purchase, or be deemed at an acceptable risk level. This topic is complex. There is a reason many early collections focused on postcards and books that were printed before 1923. These are clearly in the area of "public domain," which means there are no copyright restrictions, though there is sometimes confusion in local collections about the copyright of facsimile reproduction editions of county histories. Only the publication that appeared before 1923 is clear of copyright. Nonpublished works, like diaries, typed/handwritten family histories, and snapshot photographs taken by family members fall under different rules. These are protected

for a fixed number of years from the date of death of the creator, the person who wrote the item, or took the photograph.

Two concepts prove particularly difficult when copyright is concerned. The first is ownership. If one physically owns a photograph, but did not create the photograph, ownership does not provide the right to copy it unless the creator provided a written release of copyright. The second concept is that of inheritance of copyright. Copyright goes to the heirs of the creator until such time as the original copyright protections expire. Since most small cultural heritage institutions lack expertise in this area, the best course of action for investigating copyright issues would be to examine published guides regarding copyright in order to develop a basic plan of action for attempting to obtain copyright permissions or to determine that the use of the item is within an acceptable level of institutional risk. The chart "Copyright Term and the Public Domain the United States" is updated frequently by Peter B. Hirtle and provides a short overview of the laws on copyright.[28] A full-length work, *Copyright and Cultural Institutions: Guidelines for Digitization for U.S. Libraries, Archives, and Museums* provides the local collection context for understanding these laws.[29] Copyright provisions that pertain to the archival setting should also be considered when appropriate.[30] Once a copyright plan is drawn up for the desired items to be digitized, there should be consultation with at least one copyright expert in the local region to verify that the planned course of action is advisable.

For smaller organizations, seeking council on what to digitize makes sense. Also, there are ways to focus on whole categories of information for digital portals where copyright concerns are lessened. More and more projects at the local level are focusing on copyrighted material for which there can be waivers. In other words, if libraries and archives are collecting items to digitize or born-digital items important to local families and created by them, the copyright holders can sign release forms for the project. Families are asked to bring in photographs, videos, diaries, etc. that they created. The individual who created the material signs a waiver and the library gets to keep a copy of the digitized material. This type of solicitation of family-created materials also allows families to help shape and create the historical collections of the future.

4. Materials should be evaluated for their ability to withstand the digitization process. In some cases, fragile old newspapers may disintegrate during the process. Books that need to be disbound may not be able to be reconstructed. Librarians and historical societies should consult with specialists at the state level to weigh the relative merits of the digitization process versus the cost to the original item. In some cases, preservation work will need to accompany the digitization process. In others, it may be the case that the original format will be lost in order to achieve a digital surrogate.

ARE THERE PARTNERS FOR THE PROJECT?

Smaller institutions seeking support for digital projects have a variety of options. Once they have established a committee and have determined that there is interest and that there are appropriate resources, then funding and partnerships should be investigated. This investigation should begin at the local level and continue through the region, state, and even national portals. Several questions should be asked:

- What current digitization projects are ongoing? If a neighboring town is setting out to digitize postcards from before 1923, it might make sense to join with them in creating a digital collection as a partner. If there is no awareness of nearby planning or ongoing projects, then two local groups may find themselves competing for the same pot of grant money at the state library or through a local foundation.

- What local educational partners exist at the local area that will enhance the project? Is there a high school teacher who would love to create assignments based on the digitized letters your historical society committee would like to digitize? An educational arm to the project could include content and interpretation areas of a portal for students, in addition to the primary documents? But if the committee does not ask about interest in these items, then the opportunity will go by. Check for any person who runs a history club, history event sponsors, the local history course instructor, or retired educators who still volunteer and work with historical sites in town.

- If there are larger historical museums, archives, or other entities in town that may be interested in collaborating, discussions about coordinating a project could be very fruitful.

- Examine the strategic planning documents of the town, municipality, or county. Often, there are historic preservation stipulations in them. One might find that a regional economic development nonprofit organization, for example, is able to join together as a partner in a grant application for digitization that could be used in multiple ways. Municipalities can be partners in digitization projects.

- Look for project-specific partners. For example, a project to digitize images of tombstones in a local cemetery that had not yet been indexed would best be done in collaboration with the board of that cemetery and with any other groups that have a special interest in such a project. Perhaps for cemeteries that are already indexed, collaboration with the historical society or other organization that created the index to contribute some information for the digital records could be obtained.

HOW WILL THE PROJECT BE EXECUTED?

There are several options for creating a digital presence on the web with a digitized collection. Digital collections are best housed in what is called a digital repository. This is special software created to house digital images. While it is possible to simply "attach" files, such as image files, documents files, or pdfs, to web pages, this is not the best method of maintaining digital files. A digital repository is created to hold not only a digital file, but also cataloging information about that file that is used to search for the images or information on scanned text. The software provides long-term protection to files and the ability to update them. Large-scale digital projects often employ a repository that is created onsite by technical experts to certain specifications.

Smaller organizations without the technical support to do programming can still have access to excellent digital repositories that can be built using special software. The programs may be "open source," which means one can download and install the program for free, but there is no tech support provided, other than the many user discussion and development wikis that are associated with the program. Examples are DSpace[31] and Fedora.[32] Other programs are proprietary, which means a company owns the product and sells it to the user. Tech support is generally included in the selling price. Examples of proprietary systems for digital collections include CONTENTdm,[33] DigitTool ,[34] and Luna.[35]

State libraries, historical museums, regional archives, or regional consortia may make available access to supported repository systems, such as the Maine Memory project. Another example is the Power Library PA Photos and Documents in the state of Pennsylvania that utilize CONTENTdm. The state maintains the license and provides instructions to libraries on how to become a contributing partner in the project.[36] Once images are digitized and loaded to the site, they become a part of the state-wide digital collections, but are also identified as originating from the library that contributed them. Instructions for the scanning specifications for the images, as well as the required information to catalog each item are provided for libraries. Vendors can step into the gap between the resource and the uploaded product if a library does not have tech-savvy individuals on its digital project committee. Also, LSTA grants administered by the Office of Commonwealth Libraries in Pennsylvania have supported the costs of digital projects that are hosted by Power PA. So, one option for getting the selected resources into a digital repository is checking with statewide agencies for technical support, grants, and projects.

Here are other ideas for making items available digitally:

- If there is funding for the project, work with a proprietary company, which can oversee the project and provide advice on vendors for digitizing or other aspects of the project that the team does not feel confident to handle.

- Try an open source system listed above or others that provide an interface that looks more like a web page, such as Omeka.org or Omeka.net.

- For institutions already using PastPerfect, there is an online version that allows web-access viewing of selected items from the collection.[37]

- FamilySearch provides free digitization of genealogical materials of interest, including local and county history books and compiled family history books. It also may be possible to obtain training and equipment to carry out a digitization project onsite at one's institution in collaboration with FamilySearch. Digitized materials would become a part of the FamilySearch online collection. The local institution could link to these items in their catalog or pathfinders. An institution may contact them directly to find out more about this program at books@familysearch.org.

Decision-making for Starting a Digital Project

Is there institutional or community interest?

* No—If only one or two people can be mustered, perhaps better to focus energy on ramping up the social media and blogging on the institution site with historic photos and tagging.

* Yes—Proceed to form a committee.

Are there appropriate resources to digitize?

* Yes—We have checked that the resources are

  ○ Unique, valuable resources

  ○ Heavily used or desired by patrons

  ○ Not already digitized

  ○ No longer under copyright or rights have been secured

* Not sure—Ask for outside help in assessing the collection from professional resources in the area or by paying an organization to do it.

* No—if you still want a project, then solicit appropriate resources with releases from the public and proceed.

Once the items to be digitized have been decided on, do you need funding for the project?

* Yes—look for grant opportunities

* No—proceed to project planning

During grant writing, details about the methods for digitization and delivery to the public will need to be finalized. Are there sufficiently trained persons on your committee to do the digitization or the cataloging of the items?

* No—write the grant so that it funds outsourcing of these steps.

* Yes—write the grant to include any equipment needed

Does your committee already know what digital repository or outlet is desired?

* Yes—put this information in the grant proposal or planning documents.

* No—look for options such as state-wide initiatives that are already ongoing or examine the list of open-source and proprietary systems listed above.

Once the digitization and uploading of images will occur, advertising and outreach should occur next. Also, a system of assessment should be in place. See programming ideas for help on these steps.

REIMAGINING THE ROLE OF THE PUBLIC: THE INTERSECTION OF FAMILIES AND CULTURAL HERITAGE INSTITUTIONS

It has already been noted that families may create private accounts and grouping of materials for their own use online in digital collections. But the role of the private individual is being reimagined with regard to the growth of archival, library, and historical society collections. The family archive, or "private archive," is increasingly seen as a focal point for outreach and collection development. The National Endowment for the Humanities (NEH) recently announced a program called Common Heritage that showcases support for interaction with the public. The grant applications note that:

> America's cultural heritage is preserved not only in libraries, museums, archives, and other community organizations, but also in all of our homes, family histories, and life stories...The Common Heritage program recognizes that members of the public—in partnership with libraries, museums, archives, and historical organizations—have much to contribute to the understanding of our cultural mosaic. Together, such institutions and the public can be effective partners in the appreciation and stewardship of our common heritage.[38]

The grant guidelines call for development of outreach programs to the public, where digitizing of family items would be a central activity and where copies of these items, with family permission, would be kept by the institution. Such programs are already underway across the country and even world.

Increasingly, scholars and archivists are recognizing the value and importance of saving private family history artifacts as important in capturing a collective memory and history of a people. Home movies, for example, studied as a group, can demonstrate trends in society, taste, manner, and provide evidence of social movements and change.[39] But these same family-produced artifacts provide documentation of specific families and specific events that are invaluable in a family history collection and reflect the history of specific families and of a place.[40] Once digitized, these movies can provide online research aids for family historians and scholars alike. In addition, recent "born-digital" family audiovisual materials present both challenges and vast potential for local studies collections to expand family history collections to the present. One might not think of a home movie as interesting to anyone outside a family, yet, increasingly these are the types of resources that are being thought of as collectible by traditional institutions like archives.

The public is also increasingly seen as a participant in the collections of archives, and local studies collections. Besides the tagging functions of some digital collections which were previously discussed, a wide variety of social media applications are now available on many digital sites. No longer is a museum a series of glassed, distant exhibits to be viewed passively by the patron. Instead, the patron is stepping into the scene, helping to create, design, and interpret. Crowdsourcing is a term that is heard more and more frequently in relation to digital projects, which means there is software that interested individuals can download to use in order to complete a task for a digital collection. The 1940 U.S. Census Community Project, was able to be completed in five months by using over 160,000 volunteers from their computers.[41] People of all ages and backgrounds logged onto the site, downloaded the software, and busily transcribed the digitized images of handwriting from the 1940 census. Such a feat could not have been accomplished in this short a time without a massive outlay of resources. Instead, the crowd was asked and they responded. Similar projects have allowed for the anonymous stranger, at all hours and for unknown motivations, to log on and transcribe many kinds of documents.

Families are enjoying national, regional, and local digital collections with Web.20 technologies like tagging, sharing on Facebook, and writing notes about the images. Family-produced digital sites, covered in the personal digital archiving section of Chapter 4, can create wonderful memories and can be linked to other sites. No longer is one digital area separate and distinct from others. The role of volunteers, librarians, and other information professionals in helping families to discover their past through digitized collections hinges on the enthusiastic intersection of resource with interest. By clearly directing patrons to resources with digital portals and digital collections, cultural heritage institutions are fulfilling an important role in preserving family history and local memory.

RESOURCES

Federal Agencies Digitization Guidelines Initiative, http://www.digitizationguidelines .gov/.

Koloski, Laura, Benjamin Filene, and Bill Adair. *Letting Go: Sharing Historical Authority in a User-generated World*. Philadelphia, PA: Pew Center for Arts & Heritage, 2011. *eBook Academic Collection (EBSCOhost)*, accessed June 19, 2015.

New York State Archives. *Digitizing your Historical Photographs Workbooks* 2011, http:// www.archives.nysed.gov/common/archives/files/workshops_handouts_digitizing _photos.pdf.

Ng, Kwong Bor, and Jason Kucsma. *Digitization in the Real World: Lessons Learned from Small and Medium-Sized Digitization Projects*. New York, NY: Metropolitan New York Library Council, 2010.

Recollection Wisconsin, http://recollectionwisconsin.org/organizations.

U.S. National Archives and Records Administration. *Technical Guidelines for Digitizing Archival Materials for Electronic Access: Creation of Production Master Files - Raster Images*, http://www.archives.gov/preservation/technical/guidelines.html.

CONCLUSION

The notion of a unified digital portal for family history resources has been around for a long while, but, as technology becomes more accessible to volunteers, librarians, and other cultural heritage professionals, the potential for application of these concepts even in small, rural institutions can be realized. Today there are many user-friendly, free sites, such as those provided by Omeka.net and others. Digital collaborations are possible between the information and local communities that use these free or low cost platforms, and the efforts of the volunteer and the patron are more central than ever to facilitating family history research. Through outreach, programming, and online portals, family history services can be fostered at an increasing number of cultural heritage sites in dynamic, meaningful ways.

PROGRAMMING IDEAS

1. Let's Build a Portal: Images and Tools for Building a Digital Collection

The institution uses a program to assist the public in understanding and using digital portals and collections that have Web 2.0 technology, such as tagging, RSS feeds, and sharing to Facebook. It should be a 45 minute to 1 hour event.

By the end of the session, the participants will have been able to locate an item of interest in an online collection and will have interacted with it through technology. Before the session begins, make sure each person has a laptop that is logged into a wireless network, or that each person has a computer terminal that is linked to the Internet.

- Set the tone by defining Web 2.0 and social media. Give examples from the web.
- How-to: Provide a set of links that go to relevant digital collections that also have Web 2.0 technologies on them. Or use other collections, like a library blog on history with images. Demonstrate how to search for an item and then add a tag or note. Show them how to share an item to Facebook. Or choose other applications to showcase.
- Trying it out: Circulate around the room helping patrons to try out the technologies.
- Have refreshments and discuss how these tags and shares will help others in learning about family history. Once a person shares a photo and then sees it being re-shared with family, the hook is in!

2. Fun with Images and Digitized Books

The institution uses a program that highlights historical and family images on the web. At the end, the participants will fill out a form indicating what they liked the best in terms of content and format, which will help to evaluate the need for building local digital collections. It should be a 45 minute to 1 hour event.

- Before the session begins, make sure each person has a laptop that is logged into a wireless network, or that each person has a computer terminal that is linked to the Internet.

- Preparation: Use a registration form for the event that asks for the interests of the persons attending. Ask for historical interests and family/regional connections. Put a check box for permission to discuss the person's interests in the session. Ahead of time, prepare several successful searches of local digital collections that pertain to the interests of a couple of people who are attending.

- Set the tone: Talk about how to find historical images on the web, especially those that might relate to families or life in the local area. Be sure to check the national-level collections highlighted in this chapter, as well as state/regional and local ones. Hand out a sheet that gives the names of any digitized collections relevant to the area and how to access them.

- Demonstration: Show search techniques on two or three sites. Have a prepared set of images to show for a particular family attending (get information ahead of time), so the searches do not seem random. You should be able to demonstrate some successful searches. The images should pertain to the person's interests or family history.

- Try it out and wrap-up. Let everyone have time to try out the sites.

Have refreshments and hand out a form to have the participants explain which sites/formats they liked and what they would like to see more of. This analysis could help if planning a digital project.

Additional Ideas

- Free history book night! Have patrons bring their laptops or other electronic devices and learn to download public domain historical materials directly to their devices.

- Fun with maps. Show the public how digitized bird's-eye-view, insurance, or other maps for their area can be used for their family and house research.

- Create a collage. Have children and teens take public domain images from online exhibits and collections to create a collage of the past.

NOTES

1. Kate Theimer, *Web 2.0 Strategies for Archives and Local History Collections* (New York, NY: Neal-Schuman, 2010), 3.

2. Ancestry.com, for example, saw a growth in revenue from its third year in business in 1998 of 2.6 million dollars to 23 million in 2001. J. Heifetz, "Ancestry.com Co-Founder's Lessons in Entrepreneurship," *Gallup Business Journal* (2014): 1.

3. "United States Census, 1940," Database with images, *FamilySearch*, http://FamilySearch.org, accessed 2015. Citing NARA digital publication T627. Washington, DC: National Archives and Records Administration, 2012.

4. Ancestry.com claims to be "the world's largest online resource for family history," with over 2 million subscribers, http://corporate.ancestry.com/about-ancestry/.

5. L. N. Gasaway, "Libraries, Digital Content, and Copyright," *Vanderbilt Journal of Entertainment and Technology Law* 12, no. 4 (2010): 760.

6. http://www.classmates.com/yearbooks/?dsource=pub|18932|body4|null|18384|2

7. http://dp.la/info/

8. http://dp.la/info/about/history/

9. http://archive.org/web/web.php

10. http://archive.org/web/web.php

11. http://chroniclingamerica.loc.gov/

12. http://www.loc.gov/rr/program/bib/statememory/

13. http://www.mainememory.net/

14. http://www.mainememory.net/cp/cp_howto.shtml

15. http://www.mainememory.net/share_history/share_types.shtml#exhibit

16. https://www.mainememory.net/help/help_albumfront.shtml

17. "Thadeus C. Joy," *The Metal Worker* (Sept. 7, 1895): 56, accessed Google Books, June 16, 2015.

18. For discussion of Web 2.0 technologies and archival collections, see Theimer, *Web 2.0 Tools and Strategies*.

19. http://www.webopedia.com/TERM/T/tagging.html

20. http://www.loc.gov/rr/print/flickr_report_final.pdf

21. http://teenie.cmoa.org/ArchiveStories.aspx

22. http://www.usgenweb.org/

23. http://www.scottsdalelibrary.org/historical

24. K K. Collard, "Connection our Past with our Future: A New Gateway to Maitland's History and Heritage," *Aplis* 24, no. 4 (2011): 159.

25. http://www.maitland.nsw.gov.au/Library/localstudies/Strategy

26. B. Bailey-Hainer, and R. Urban, "The Colorado digitization program: a collaboration success story," *Library Hi Tech 22*, no. 3 (2004): 254–262. doi:10.1108/07378830410560044.

27. R. Abruzzi, "Undertaking a Digitization Project?," *Online Searcher* 39, no. 2 (2015): 30.

28. http://copyright.cornell.edu/resources/publicdomain.cfm

29. P. B. Hirtle, E. Hudson, and A. T. Kenyon, *Copyright and Cultural Institutions: Guidelines for Digitization for U.S. Libraries, Archives, and Museums* (Ithaca, NY: Cornell University Library, c2009), http://hdl.handle.net/1813/14142.

30. J. Dryden, "The Role of Copyright in Selection for Digitization," *American Archivist* 77, no. 1 (2014): 64–95.

31. http://www.dspace.org//

32. http://fedora-commons.org/

33. www.contentdm.org

34. http://www.exlibrisgroup.com/category/DigiToolOverview

35. http://www.lunaimaging.com/#welcome

36. http://www.powerlibrary.org/librarians/pa-photos-and-documents/participation/#.VYQBlkZcjkc

37. http://pastperfect-online.com/

38. http://www.neh.gov/grants/preservation/common-heritage

39. See K. L. Ishizuk, *Mining the Home Movie: Excavations in Histories and Memories*, Berkeley: University of California Press, 2007, for a variety of studies on the cultural value of home movies.

40. B. Pymm, "From 8mm to iPhone: views from the crowd provide a rich source of local history." *Australian Library Journal* 62, no. 2 (2013): 140. doi:10.1080/00049670.2013.805459, 140.

41. http://www.businesswire.com/news/home/20120829005470/en/1940-U.S.-Census-Community-Project-Announces-132#.VYQKiEZcjkc

Appendix A

A SELECTED ANNOTATED LIST OF HOW-TO FAMILY HISTORY TITLES

The titles in the following lists are mostly general how-to books on family history research. No titles specifically about online genealogy research are included because they are outdated almost the moment they are published, and they can also give the false impression to researchers that all research can be completed online. Also, none of these titles were published prior to the year 2000. It is not because they cannot contain any good information if they were published before that date, but because where we search for genealogical information changes so quickly, that anything older has significant portions of outdated information. In addition to the list here, it is worth looking at the much more comprehensive work called *Guide to Reference in Genealogy and Biography* by Mary K. Mannix, Fred Burchsted and Jo Bell Whitlatch, which was published by ALA editions in 2015. It lists hundreds of titles that are organized by broad geographic areas of coverage, so it is a bit of a challenge to locate titles on specific subjects within it.

BEGINNERS

Carmack, Sharon DeBartolo. *Your Guide to Cemetery Research*. Cincinnati, OH: Betterway Books, 2002.

Why do we need an entire book about this subject? Because there is more to it than meets the eye. Scouring a cemetery for clues about the people who rest there is both an art and a science. Carmack covers the topic well, and gives many examples of how information found in cemeteries can enhance the information found in documents and in books about ancestors, and that it can even solve difficult research dilemmas. It would be wonderful if this book were updated to include information on how cemetery research is being improved by technology such as the GPS and special apps which can record the information on grave markers.

Colletta, John Philip. *They Came in Ships: Finding Your Immigrant Ancestor's Arrival Record*, 3rd ed. Salt Lake City, UT: Ancestry Publishing, 2002.
Some ship passenger lists are beginning to appear online in a digitized format in indexed databases. So this book is now worthless, right? Wrong! First, only some of the lists for the big five ports have started appearing: New York, New Orleans, Boston, Philadelphia, and Baltimore. Second, there were over 100 ports in the United States where immigrant ships could have arrived. This book does an excellent job of explaining which records NARA has microfilmed, and how to access them. It also gives clear instructions for how to search for ancestors in the unindexed records, which the majority of them are.

Croom, Emily Anne. *Unpuzzling Your Past: The Best-Selling Basic Guide to Genealogy*, 4th ed. Baltimore, MD: Genealogical Publishing Company, 2010.
Croom teaches genealogy, which is evident in her nicely conversational writing style. This book covers the basics and then some, also including information about evaluating evidence, and drawing conclusions from it. The text includes many examples of original documents, and also refers the reader to other books for further information on many topics. This is the best book for serious beginners in print.

Hinckley, Kathleen W. *Your Guide to the Federal Census: For Genealogists, Researchers, and Family Historians*. Cincinnati, OH: Betterway Books, 2002.
Because U.S. Census information is arguably the backbone of family history research, it is important to understand many details of *how*, *why*, and *when* the various censuses were enumerated. This book admirably supplies that information, as well as information about finding and analyzing the census information. However, when this book was written, digitized census records were just beginning to be available, and the 1940 census had not yet been released. An updated version is needed to cover these aspects of the topic.

Lynch, Daniel M. *Google Your Family Tree: Unlock the Hidden Power of Google*. Provo, UT: Family Links, 2008.
This is not an overview of online genealogy websites, rather a book that discusses techniques of searching for genealogical information using Google. Although Google continues to add and drop various features, the basics of searching are still the same as when this book was published. The information is presented in a very clear way, even for those who are not very computer savvy.

Melnyk, Marcia D. Yannize. *Family History 101: A Beginner's Guide to Finding Your Ancestors*. Cincinnati, OH: Family Tree Publishing, 2005.
This is a nice, short book on beginning genealogy (154 pages). It covers the basics using many research examples from the author's family history, and contains several old family photographs. For researchers who want the basics laid out in the simplest approach possible, this is their book.

Rose, Christine, and Ingalls, Kay Germain. *The Complete Idiot's Guide to Genealogy*, 3rd ed. New York, NY: Penguin Books, 2012.
Despite the obnoxious title, this is a very good beginning genealogy book that is fairly indepth to hand to new researchers. It is also written in a very casual, accessible style–no problem if the researcher has not ever set foot in a library, or in quite a long time. The text is sprinkled with perky anecdotes and practical advice. There is even a chapter about the newfangled DNA testing at the end.

INTERMEDIATE

Greenwood, Val D. *Researcher's Guide to American Genealogy*, 3rd ed. Baltimore, MD: Genealogical Publishing Company, Inc., 2000.

Some would class this with beginning genealogy books, but it is really a bit more advanced. This book is probably the best written overview of the genealogical research process and the reasoning behind it. The author is an attorney, which may explain his ability to precisely explain the *why* of the techniques. Certain sections are particularly strong: the historical information in the vital records chapter, and the information on probate, deeds, and land records is timeless and well-stated. Some information needs to be updated, such as the list of libraries in Chapter 5, and the information on the NARA branches.

Mills, Elizabeth Shown. *Evidence Explained: Citing History Sources from Artifacts to Cyberspace*, 3rd ed. Baltimore, MD: Genealogical Publishing Company, 2015.

Every institution attempting to provide family history services needs a copy of this in the reference section, and as many circulating copies as your budget will allow. Because family history researchers work with so many sources that traditional style manuals for the humanities do not cover, Mills created a guide that includes them. In it, we see how to cite everything from all types of government documents, whether they are microfilmed, transcribed, or digitized, to oral history interviews, email exchanges of information, and ephemera such as great-grandmother's Bible. The first chapter, "Fundamentals of Evidence Analysis," is required reading for any serious researcher.

Rising, Marsha Hoffman. *The Family Tree Problem Solver: Proven Methods for Scaling the Inevitable Brick Wall*. Cincinnati, OH: Family Tree Books, 2005.

Through case studies, the author explains several techniques to untangle tough research knots. Many of these are drawn from research she did as part of the Ozark Migration Project, which traced the movement of hundreds of families from Kentucky, Tennessee, and North Carolina to Missouri. Her step-by-step descriptions of complicated research processes are easy to follow and interesting. Her use of humor is a bonus.

Rose, Christine. *Courthouse Research for Family Historians: Your Guide to Genealogical Treasures*. San Jose, CA: CR Publications, 2004.

Even though many types of records typically found in courthouses have been microfilmed by the Genealogical Society of Utah, and others, it is still often useful and necessary to visit courthouses to research original records. Rose, a very experienced researcher who has visited over 500 courthouses, has put together an excellent overview of this process filled with practical advice. Included is information on everything from going through the security gate at the courthouse, to navigating the complex array of indexing systems that one encounters. A strength of the book is her coverage of estate and probate records, on which she spends three chapters.

Szucs, Loretto Dennis, and Sandra Hargreaves Luebking, eds. *The Source: A Guidebook to American Genealogy*, 3rd ed. Provo, UT: Ancestry Publishing, 2006.

This mammoth book is an attempt to cover most aspects of genealogy and family history research in a single volume. It has 880 pages of text, plus another approximately 80 pages of appendixes. The chapters are all written by known experts in the field, and they are quite thorough. The basics are well-covered, as well as several chapters devoted to specialized types of research, such as African American, Hispanic, and Native American. Two of these chapters, "Colonial English Research" and

"Colonial Spanish Borderland Research" contain quite advanced research information.

That being said, there are still holes. The discussion of photographs is fairly brief, and the coverage of maps is almost nonexistent. Because this was written several years ago, the chapter entitled "Computers and Technology" is very dated, as well as many facts scattered throughout the book, many of them having to do with where one finds a particular source. Ancestry Publishing was acquired by Turner Publishing of Nashville, Tennessee in 2010. Turner does not have any current plans to update this title, which due to the large number of writers and the ambitious scale, would be quite costly. Ancestry.com has amazingly digitized the entire book, and it is available to view for free on the Ancestry.com wiki: http://www.ancestry.com/wiki/index.php?title=The_Source:_A_Guidebook_to_American_Genealogy. It may be necessary to click on several links in order to view an entire chapter.

This is a wonderful reference source, even with the issues named above. However, this is not the best choice to hand to a new researcher because it has too much information, a lot of it quite advanced.

ADVANCED

Anderson, Robert Charles. *Elements of Genealogical Analysis.* Boston, MA: New England Historic Genealogical Society, 2014.

Anderson is the driving force behind the Great Migration Study Project, which traces all immigrants who came to the New England between 1620 and 1640. He uses the experience he garnered while doing that research as the basis for this book, which outlines his "Fundamental Rules of Genealogy," a five-step process. Those steps are problem selection, problem analysis, data collection, synthesis, and problem resolution. The author asserts that his is only one system of many, and that these methods may not be new, but that this particular arrangement is. His examples that support his system are all from Colonial New England research. Any collection supporting New England research would do well to add this title. A caveat: he defines terms commonly used in genealogical research in a way that is different from the way that they are defined by the majority of genealogists.

Jones, Thomas W. *Mastering Genealogical Proof.* Arlington, Virginia: National Genealogical Society, 2013.

Jones is the co-editor of the *NGSQ,* and an instructor at several genealogical institutes. He organizes his book around the Genealogical Proof Standard, or GPS, a method of best research practices that helps to ensure the accuracy of genealogical research. The GPS is the brainchild of the Board for Certification of Genealogists. The organization of the book is excellent. First, the GPS is defined, and essential concepts related to it are explained. Then the GPS itself is broken down into its five elements, with a chapter devoted to each. Two lengthy case studies are supplied which illustrate how the GPS is applied to real research problems. One can almost hear the author's calm, methodical voice as he walks us through this. This book is essential reading for anyone wanting to become certified in genealogy.

Morgan, George C., and Drew Smith. *Advanced Genealogy Research Techniques.* New York, NY: McGraw Hill Education, 2014.

> The authors are well-known in genealogy circles as "The Genealogy Guys," hosts of a series of podcasts. In this book, they present eight ideas for tackling the proverbial "brick wall," that every researcher hits at some point, and which seems impossible to overcome. These include examining the wall in detail, going around it, sharing the problem, using crowdsourcing, applying technology, hiring an expert, and resting to attack the wall another time. The ideas here are all presented with clear examples to support them. Some of the ideas may not really be advanced techniques, but that is not really worth quibbling about. This book helped to fill the need for more material on how to analyze genealogical information, and then revising the research plan based on those conclusions.

Appendix B

THE LOCALITY GUIDE

Many institutions produce pamphlets, handouts, pathfinders, or brochures which highlight what is in their collection, and may even contain a few instructions as to how to use some of the items in the collection. These are pretty straightforward and easy to produce. But a written guide for researchers that takes a little more effort to produce is the locality guide.[1] This is a written summary of pertinent information needed for family history research in a specific locality, or geographic location. A locality could consist of a city, a county, or even a cluster of counties, depending on how many resources need to be covered. If the geographic area is a particularly large city like New York, then the focus may be narrowed to one particular borough or neighborhood, because a comprehensive look at the entire city will result in a book-length locality guide. A locality guide puts in one place pertinent information that a good local studies information provider should be keeping track of anyway, whether it is information that is in the locality itself, or elsewhere. It should be aimed at beginning researchers, and devised with the notion that not all researchers are computer literate.

More types of sources may be included, but the following list suggests some basics:

- Background or "genealogy" of the geographic area. Include:
  - Date founded
  - Originally part of which territory, colony, state, and/or county?
  - Who owned it?
  - What are the past and current county seats?

Brief summary of historical highlights—has the area had significant settlement by particular ethnic groups? Has a war been fought there?

- Boundary changes—has the area gained/and or lost land over time? Supply specific details such as dates and a description of the areas involved. State if there have been no boundary changes.
  - Supply a link to the Atlas of Historical County Boundaries at the Newberry Library, if appropriate.
  - Supply a visual aid such as a map or diagram of the area, if possible.
- Repositories—provide a list of the main places to do research about your area. Include name of repository, contact information, and a brief description of the collection.
  - Government offices at both the local and state level that hold pertinent records.
  - Area libraries, archives, and genealogical/local history societies.
  - Academic libraries within a reasonable distance **if** they hold materials about your area.
  - The state library and/or archives if they hold materials about your area.
  - The regional NARA site that covers your area.
  - Local/regional Family History Center of the LDS Church (explain briefly what these have and how they loan microfilm).
- Extant Records—the main focus is on **vital records**, but land, census, church, etc. should also be covered.

A sentence should be given discussing any **losses of area records:** name the records and the years lost. If there are no losses, state that as well. Example: "The Chicago Fire destroyed all Cook County civil records generated from 1831–October 1871, but some deed information was preserved that was recorded at two title companies which managed to save their records."

For each type of vital record (birth, marriage, death, and divorce) cover the following:

- What years the records are available.
- Where they can be obtained. For some records, that means at the county level for one set of years, but at the state level for a different set of years.
- Other than government offices, are there copies of the records themselves elsewhere? For example, have they been filmed by the FHL, or located at a genealogical research collection, at the State library, digitized online somewhere, whether a free or subscription website?

Check: Ancestry, FamilySearch (for microfilmed, and digitized records, even if they are not indexed yet), governmental websites such as a state library/archives, to give you some ideas.

- Any indexing or other finding aids to vital records, such as published transcriptions.

Check: Same locations as for the vital records themselves, as well as the USGenWeb site, genealogy trails, the website of local repositories, and WorldCat, to name the major places. But there may be others.

Note: It may be possible to make convenient tables with the vital records information.

Religious Records

There may be too many individual congregations to list every single one that has existed in the area, but a website or article in a local history periodical may be supplied that does this. In addition, county histories may be gleaned for information on congregations that no longer exist. Help researchers by listing repositories where records from current and past local religious institutions now reside, whether that is in the local institution, or in an outside repository.

Land Records

- If the area is in a federal land state, then supply the Bureau of Land Management (BLM) URL for patent records.
- Supply the county level office for deeds, and years available, and any indexing. Has the FHL filmed them, etc.?
- What are the main plat maps and atlases for the area? Are they digitized anywhere such as FamilySearch, Google Books, Internet Archive, or Ancestry?

Census Records

List the major online places to find the U.S. Population Schedules: FamilySearch, Ancestry, HeritageQuest, Mocavo, etc., and also whatever places have it on microfilm for your locality. If your locality has missing census records, then mention what they are.

Mention if your area has any state level censuses that cover it and for what years. Some of these are on FamilySearch and Ancestry, but others are only on microfilm thus far. The book *State Census Records* by Ann Smith Lainhart can help, but it is not exhaustive.

There obviously could be more types of records in your area. Decide which would be **the most important** to include.

- Historical Information
  - List a selection of the main book titles on the history of your area. If you can find links to digitized versions of the old ones, then provide them (use the index genealogybooklinks.com).
  - List a **judicious selection of online information**—but do not just include the URLs. Also include a brief description of what is to be found at the websites. This will be helpful to track the websites when the URLs change.
- Historical Periodicals

Newspapers

- List a summary of the main titles, and **the dates** they were published. In some areas, it will be possible to list all of them.

- List the main places they can be found, both locally and elsewhere. This includes both microfilmed issues, and digitized ones. Has an institution or commercial database included any of these titles in their holdings? Think Ancestry, GenealogyBank, newspapers.com, and Gale databases for the commercial ones.
- List any major finding aids that help access newspaper content, such as the obituary index at the local library.
- List a link to the part of the union list of U.S. newspapers at the American Memory website that covers these papers.

Periodicals *about* the Area

List any local history/genealogical publication about the area, and the dates that they have been published. For example, does the genealogical society publish a newsletter? If they are widely held, refer the researcher to WorldCat to check holdings. Many rural counties are lucky to have one of these.

- Maps

It would be ideal to include both a current map, and a historical one. It may be handy to place one at the beginning of the locality guide in the section discussing boundary changes.

- Further Information

Here you could put **miscellaneous items** that give the researcher more information on doing research in the area. For example, information on ethnic groups, local historic events and sites, such as National Park Service Historic Sites, more online information, brochures, books, or articles. Has anyone written a guide to genealogical research that includes this area, even at a state level? Hint: the National Genealogical Society (NGS) publishes state guides, and the National Genealogical Society Quarterly (NGSQ) has been running articles on state research. Sometimes local agencies have websites that have good information, like the Chamber of Commerce.

There are many different ways that one could organize this. One effective way is to provide an introduction that includes information about historical background, boundary changes, and some general demographic/ethnic data about the population. Next, list all the major repositories of information, such as public and academic libraries, court houses, etc. Provide a nutshell description of their holdings along with a link to a website, if it exists. Some collections have books describing their collections; list those titles. It is helpful to have some practical information here about the collections, such as hours of operation.

Next, tackle giving information about the various record groups available. It can be effective to list that information in a table format. For example, a table listing the extant vital records for a locality, dividing them up by the format/location where they are held, helps organize a lot of information in a small amount of space. Do not forget about noncivil records.

When you list titles of histories and periodicals, make sure you clarify whether you are providing a selective list or an exhaustive list. If further sources of information are available, such as online or print union lists, then provide them. Consulting the reference book *Printed Sources* will be helpful here.

Examples of locality guides can be found online by searching under that phrase.

NOTE

1. A very basic description of how locality guides are organized appears in the book Elizabeth Shown Mills *Professional Genealogy: A Manual for Researchers, Writers, Editors, Lecturers and Librarians* (Baltimore: Genealogical Publishing Company, 2001) on pages 276–277. This appendix used the idea and expanded upon it greatly.

Appendix C

ASSOCIATIONS RELATED
TO LOCAL STUDIES

This appendix lists the names of many major, national organizations in North America related to local studies, but does not include listings for any of the numerous regional, ethnic, and other subject specialized organizations. All of the groups listed below have websites.

History

Agricultural History Society (AHS)
American Association for History and Computing (AAHC)
American Association for State and Local History (AASLH)
American Historical Association (AHA)
Association for Living History, Farm, and Agricultural Museums (ALHFAM)
Association of Personal Historians (APH)
Canadian Heritage Information Network (CHIN)
Canadian Historical Association (CHA)
Canada's National History Society
Canadian Oral History Association (COHA)
Immigration and Ethnic History Society (IEHS)
International Commission for the History of Towns (ICHT)
International Institute of Social History (IISH)
National Association for Interpretation (NAI)
National Coalition for History (NCH)
National Council for History Education (NCHE)
National Coalition of Independent Scholars
National Council on Public History (NCPH)

National History Club (NHC)
National Trust for Historic Preservation
Oral History Association (OHA)
Organization of American Historians (OAH)
Society for History Education (SHE)
Society for History in the Federal Government (SHFG)

Libraries, Archives, and Photography

American Alliance of Museums, formerly American Association of Museums (AAM)
American Antiquarian Society (AAS)
American Institute for Conservation of Historic and Artistic Works
American Library Association (ALA), specifically the affiliated Reference User Services Association (RUSA): History Section, with Genealogy and Local History subgroups
Daguerreian Society
International Federation of Library Associations and Institutions, Genealogy and Local History Section (IFLA)
International Photographic Historical Organization (InPHO)
Northeast Conservation Alliance
Photographic Historical Society of Canada (PHSC)
The Photographic Historical Society (PHS)
Society of American Archivists (SAA)

Historic Preservation

Adventures in Preservation, formerly Heritage Conservation Network
Advisory Council on Historic Preservation (ACHP)
Architectural Heritage Foundation (AHF)
Association for Gravestone Studies (AGS)
Association for Preservation Technology (APT)
Canadian Association for Conservation of Cultural Property (CAC)
Canadian Association of Professional Conservators (CAPC)
Canadian Association of Heritage Professional (CAHP)
National Alliance of Preservation Commissions (NAPC)
National Center for Preservation Technology and Training (NCPTT)
National Conference of State Historic Preservation Officers (NCSHPO)
National Council for Preservation Education (NCPE)
National Park Service (NPS) Cultural Resources
National Preservation Institute (NPI)
National Trust for Historic Preservation
Preservation Action (PA)
Preservation Volunteers (PV)
Restoration Works International (RWI)

Genealogy and Family History

Association of Professional Genealogists (APGEN)
Board for Certification of Genealogists (BCG)
Federation of Genealogical Societies (FGS)
International Society of Genetic Genealogy (ISOGG)
National Genealogical Society (NGS)

Appendix D

FORMS

Family History Reference Question Form

Patron name: _____

Phone number:_____

Email address:_____

1. Geographic location of the families you are researching:

   County_____ Township_____ Town/City_____

2. Surnames you are researching (don't forget to include your female lines):

   _____
   _____
   _____
   _____

3. Time period that your research focuses on today: _____

   _____

4. Please check which of the following you hope to locate in our collection:

   Vital records_____ Census records_____ Local histories _____
   Maps_____ Cemetery information_____ Obituaries _____
   Surname files_____ Church records_____ Other_____

   If you wish, you may attach a family group sheet or pedigree chart to this form in order to tell us more about the family you are researching today.

Sample Photo Request Letter

Dear Mr./Ms._____,

We have never met, but I am your_____[fill in relationship]. Like you, I am a direct descendant of _____ and his wife _____. A chart which shows exactly how we are related is attached to this letter.

[explains the relationship]

I am contacting you because for the past several years I have done a lot of research about our family history. I have been successful in finding out basic facts about our ancestors, and I will be happy to share that information with you.

[offers them something]

Now I am seeking old photographs of our ancestors. Do you have any old pictures of deceasedfamily members that you might be willing to share? I would like to attach them to a family tree.I would be happy to pay for you to have some photos scanned and sent to me. If you don't have any old photos yourself, then perhaps you know someone else in the family who does? [explains specifically what the writer seeks]

You might want to know a little about me. . .

[establishes the writer as a real person, not a scary stranger]

I would be very pleased to hear from you, and to discuss this project. You can contact me via email at_____, or by phone at _____.

[contact information]

Sincerely,

_____

INDEX

About the Authors

RHONDA L. CLARK, PhD, is associate professor of library science at Clarion University of Pennsylvania. Her published works include articles on local collection reference and digitization in *Annual Review of Cultural Heritage Informatics, 2012-13* and *Cases on Electronic Records and Resource Management Implementation in Diverse Environments*. Clark holds a doctorate in Russian history from the University of Minnesota and a master's degree in library and information science from the University of Pittsburgh. She can be reached at rclark@clarion.edu.

NICOLE WEDEMEYER MILLER, MA, MLS, teaches a course called "Genealogy and Library Service" at the Graduate School of Library and Information Science at the University of Illinois, Urbana-Champaign. She also teaches various family history courses and seminars at the Champaign County Historical Archives. Previously, she was a reference librarian in academic and public libraries for more than 12 years. She holds a master's degree in English literature from Northern Illinois University as well as a master's degree in library science from the University of Illinois and has published several articles in genealogy and local history journals. She can be contacted at nwmiller@illinois.edu.